Hugh Mackay was born in 1938 and educated at Sydney Grammar School, The University of Sydney and Macquarie University.

He established Mackay Research in 1971 and, since 1979, he has been publishing quarterly reports based on a continuous program of research into the changing attitudes and values of Australians. He has been awarded honorary doctorates by Macquarie and Charles Sturt Universities in recognition of his pioneering work in social research.

He is a fellow of the Australian Psychological Society, an honorary professor in the Macquarie Graduate School of Management, a consulting fellow of The St James Ethics Centre and a former deputy chairman of the Australia Council.

He writes a weekly newspaper column for *The Age*, *The Sydney Morning Herald* and *The West Australian* and is the author of three bestsellers in the field of social psychology: *Reinventing Australia* (1993), *The Good Listener* (originally published in 1994 as *Why Don't People Listen?*) and *Generations* (1997).

He has also written three novels, and is working on a fourth.

Other books by Hugh Mackay

NON-FICTION

Reinventing Australia
The Good Listener
(originally published as *Why Don't People Listen?*)
Generations

FICTION

Little Lies
House Guest
The Spin

TURNING
POINT

AUSTRALIANS
CHOOSING THEIR FUTURE

HUGH
MACKAY

MACMILLAN
Pan Macmillan Australia

Dedicated to the memory of Ian Cameron (1938–99)

And to my research associates
Elizabeth Turnock, Prue Parkhill, Margie Beaumont

First published 1999 in Macmillan by Pan Macmillan Australia Pty Limited
St Martins Tower, 31 Market Street, Sydney

National Library of Australia
cataloguing-in-publication data:

Mackay, Hugh.
Turning point: Australians choosing their future.

ISBN 0 7329 1001 3.

1. Australia—Social conditions. 2. Australia—Social life and customs.
3. Australia. I. Title.

306.0994

Typeset in 11.5/14 Times by Midland Typesetters
Printed in Australia by McPherson's Printing Group

Contents

Preface

Do you sometimes wish that you could stand still for a while, take stock, and try to make sense of the world around you? If so, then *Turning Point* might help. This is a book about Australian attitudes, based on the 94 editions of *The Mackay Report* published so far, as part of a social research project that began in 1979. The purpose of that research, and of this book, has been to diagnose and interpret the nation's mood as we approach the turn of the century.

Attitudes are the symptoms of a society's state of mind. They reveal our responses to the things that have happened to us and, occasionally, they offer a glimpse of the kind of future we are hoping for. One of the dominant themes of *Turning Point* is that Australians are now in the midst of a culture shift so radical that it amounts to the discovery of a new way of thinking about Australia.

Throughout the book, you'll come across quotations from the personal interviews and group discussions on which *The Mackay Report* is based. These are indented, in italics, to distinguish them from the main text. Occasional mentions of *Mind & Mood* research refer to a series of four Mackay Reports published under that title, in the years 1996–99. I have also made liberal use of information supplied by the indefatigable Australian Bureau of Statistics—one of our national treasures.

Many thousands of Australians have taken part in our research. I am always conscious of the great generosity of people who allow my colleagues and me into their homes, and into some of the private corners of their lives. I hope that this attempt to synthesise the things they have been telling us over the past 21 years will help to illuminate your own experience.

Hugh Mackay
August 1999

The Big Picture

Crosscurrents of Confusion ...
Undercurrents of Hope

'Booming like never before.'

That was the headline splashed across the front page of *The Sydney Morning Herald* on 7 May 1999. In a story about strong economic growth accompanied by low inflation, the journalist Tom Allard quoted the Reserve Bank: 'This combination of strong growth and exceptionally low inflation is quite unlike the experience of the preceding 30 years.' Australia, said the Reserve, looks to be reaping the benefits of 15 years of often-painful reform.

The Federal Treasurer, Peter Costello, was cock-a-hoop: 'I think we're on the eve ... of a very big lift in Australia's economic performance and a big lift in living standards. I think that the first decade of the next century could be a great decade for Australia.' He repeated that remark a few days later when he handed down the Federal Budget, in surplus to the tune of $5 billion.

The Reserve Bank admitted that it has 'an incomplete understanding of these phenomena' and some economists continued to forecast a downturn in 2000. But the economic signs, in the middle of 1999, were encouraging, to say the least.

Yet, even in the face of a battery of graphs pointing upwards, many Australians seem confused and unconvinced. In the wake of the 1999 Budget, only 15 per cent of voters thought they would be better off personally in the following 12 months; almost twice as many (29 per cent) expected to be *worse* off, and 34 per cent expected no change in their personal financial situation.[1] In a recent CSIRO survey, 52 per cent of respondents reported that life in Australia is 'getting worse', and half of those said it is 'much worse'.[2]

Hugh Mackay

Perhaps their joy over good economic news is subdued by some of the darker facts of Australian life. In the past 20 years, for example, the number of households below the poverty line has increased, and the number just above the line has increased markedly. About two million Australians are now classified by the Australian Council of Social Service as 'poor', and 800 000 children are being raised in homes where neither parent has a job. Each year, about 40 000 Australians aged 15–24 years attempt suicide. By the age of 18, about 20 per cent of children will have experienced a major depressive episode. Illicit drug use is on the rise, and it's taking a heavy toll on the health and lives of young Australians. Youth unemployment remains high—around 25 per cent nationally, and well above 50 per cent in parts of regional Australia.

But even when such cheerless realities are taken into account, and even when people assert, as they frequently do, that wealth doesn't bring happiness, Peter Costello's prediction—*the first decade of the next century could be a great decade for Australia*—resonates with us. At the turn of the century, Australians believe that our potential as a prosperous, fair and decent society has not yet been realised, and they hope that, like an awkward adolescent on the verge of adulthood, Australia might be about to discover its destiny.

And yet ... the nagging doubt. Are we really in control of our future, operating according to a clear sense of what kind of society we want? Or are we merely pawns in someone else's global chess game? Is the Prime Minister's famous 1996 wish for us—that we should become 'relaxed and comfortable'—still the blueprint? Was the dominant theme of the 1998 Federal election—tax reform—really the most inspirational policy it was possible to offer the Australian people on the eve of a new millennium?

The most glowing forecasts of economic growth, while welcome, don't amount to a vision for Australia's future. As the Old Testament's Book of Proverbs puts it: 'Where there is no vision, the people perish.' Australians have no thought of perishing just yet, but they would be reassured by the news that someone has a clearer and more coherent vision for Australia than has yet been revealed.

You might be amazed—or amused—to learn that the most common

physical disorder in the Australian population is far-sightedness. The second most common disorder is short-sightedness. One way or the other, 44 per cent of the population suffer some form of visual impairment. That isn't necessarily symbolic of anything (except the fact that we haven't yet had time to evolve to the point where our eyes can cope with the things we demand of them, like reading a phone book in a dim light at 60 years of age). But it's too good a metaphor to ignore in a nation that seems to be having so much trouble with the so-called 'vision thing'.

Some of us are obviously suffering from cultural myopia. We find it hard to focus on what's right in front of us—the radical shift in relations between the sexes, the redistribution of wealth that has created a poverty problem in the midst of our fabled land of plenty, the fundamental changes in our culture wrought by our links with Asia, new voices like 'grey power' or 'gay pride', the inexorable march towards republicanism, or even the commercialisation of sport.

But even if we think we've got a grip on the way Australia is now, most of us find it difficult to imagine what's coming next, partly because dealing with the present seems challenge enough and partly because we sense that, quite apart from the prospect of greater economic prosperity, there is a new *kind* of change taking place in our society ... a wave coming at us that might dump us if we don't catch it. We are being called on to think of Australia in a new way. We are at a turning point.

Why wouldn't our heads be spinning?

To explain our reluctance, or inability, to speculate about the shape of Australia's future, look, first, at the instability of the past 30 years. Since 1970, the rate of social, cultural, technological and economic change in Australia has been enough to upset anyone's equilibrium—and more than enough to cloud our vision of a future that has seemed ever more uncertain, ever more unpredictable. It's been a period in which many of us have lost a clear sense of who we are or where we're going.

The kaleidoscope of Australian society turned, then turned again and kept on turning. We have already been forced to think in new ways about everything from the job propects of the young to the nature of our Constitution; from our history of abuse of Aborigines to our economic and political place in the world; from our relationship with the fragile physical environment to the role and function of the family in a society where one million dependent children live with only one parent, where 60 per cent of preschool children are cared for by someone other than a parent, and where an epidemic of adolescent depression raises disturbing questions about the signals we are sending to the rising generation.

Worse, some of the signs—such as the sickening gulf between rich and poor—have challenged our beliefs about the kind of place Australia really is: belief in egalitarianism, justice or even freedom seems pale and unconvincing when set against the rising tide of poverty and, in particular, the growth of an identifiable class of 'working poor'. We have only just begun to understand that some of our most cherished ideals make no sense in a society so harshly divided on economic grounds. (To people caught in a poverty trap, 'justice' sounds more like an insult than an ideal.)

We have wrestled with the implications of long-term unemployment and the widespread sense of job insecurity. We have edged, warily but hopefully, towards accommodation of a radically new way of thinking about the roles and responsibilities of women and men—at home and at work—and we have explored new ways of managing the relationships between them.

We have found ourselves swept up in the information revolution, with consequences we can scarcely imagine. Already we are treating information as if it is the new face of materialism, a possession to be hoarded and flaunted. We are wondering whether the Internet is destined to become a surrogate community (albeit a rather flickery and impersonal one); whether the distinction between electronic money and electronic credit will finally blur into meaninglessness; whether cyberspace will seep into our lives in ways that we might come to think of as sinister rather than helpful.

And while all this is going on, we agonise about the tragic increase of suicide in our children's generation, the illicit drug trade and the cancerous creep of institutionalised gambling into our commercial and political culture. (According to a Productivity Commission report, Australians lost

$11 billion on gambling in 1997–98.) We worry about our personal safety and are troubled by the contradictory messages we're getting about crime rates. (Do they only rise when there's a State election in the air, one sceptical letter-writer to a newspaper editor wanted to know.)

As we've galloped towards the end of the 21st century, the whole world has sent us messages of upheaval, change, uncertainty: the Berlin Wall has come down, Communism has collapsed in Eastern Europe and the Soviet Union has been dismantled. While Eastern Europe fragmented, Western Europe moved closer to economic union with the launch of the Euro. The British Royal Family (still *our* Royal Family, too) was shaken to its foundations by public reaction to the death of Diana, Princess of Wales, and the American Presidency was rocked by impeachment proceedings against Bill Clinton, based on sexual misdemeanours that seemed grubby and humiliating, but hardly a threat to the nation's security. America and its allies bombed Iraq, but Saddam Hussein thrived; NATO bombed Kosovo, but Slobodan Milosevic survived; civilian militiamen in East Timor killed their fellow citizens in the conflict over independence from Indonesia, and South Africa continued to reel from the effects of its post-apartheid crime wave. France completed its nuclear testing, and India and Pakistan started theirs. Levi's jeans went out of fashion, Mercedes-Benz merged with Chrysler ... and we were hard pressed to find time for coffee with our friends.

Uncertainties, ambiguities, contradictions

It would be easy to characterise Australia as a society paralysed by its own uneasiness, gripped by insecurity, and fearful of its future—and there is some truth in that description. It's true that Australians have increasingly sought refuge in drugs designed to ease their insecurity, calm their fears and loosen the grip of anxiety on their mood. Depression is now the fifth most common disorder being treated by general practitioners (just behind bronchitis and ahead of asthma),[3] and its rapidly increasing incidence has led the Victorian Premier, Jeff Kennett, to call for the establishment of a national institute for the study of depression.

Hugh Mackay

Such a bleak picture, though accurate, is incomplete. It is actually part of a much bigger, more complex, more confusing picture. To make sense of Australia, we must explain some awkward, swirling contradictions: the clash, in particular, between our pessimism and our optimism. Yes, depression has reached epidemic proportions, but there is, simultaneously, a surge of hope, a starburst of new energy, a sense of 'buzz'—particularly in our two major cities—that sometimes overtakes us in spite of our doubts and disappointments.

We despair, as we should, about the rate of youth suicide and about the debilitating effect of young Australians' embrace of illicit drugs. Some older Australians wonder whether young people's overwhelming preference for wearing black is a sign of inherent pessimism, and whether their craze for body-piercing is a disturbing symptom of a self-destructive impulse. From there, it's easy to slip into the assumption that our young people *lack* something: guts, perhaps, or motivation, or focus, or a sense of commitment (or even a stable relationship with a caring and trustworthy adult). We fear they are giving up before they've even started.

And then we look at them from a different perspective and see promising signs: an undeniable vitality, a determination to succeed, a willingness to make sacrifices to further their education, a surge of creativity, a confidence that they can make their—and our—future work. Different bits of evidence persuade us to believe, simultaneously, that young people are on the skids and on the rise. (Both propositions are true, which is why generalisations are so dangerous.)

The news that teenagers have fewer sexual partners than was typical ten years ago, or that condom use is rising with an increase in sex education, is accompanied by reports of a rise in teenage pregnancies among less well-educated girls in the poorer outer suburbs of our major cities. When censorship battles seem to have been long won, there is a fresh round of controversy—like the one surrounding the 1999 release of Adrian Lyne's movie of Vladimir Nabokov's classic novel, *Lolita*—that makes you realise one person's civil society is another's Gomorrah. While some of us strive to define a uniquely Australian set of shared values, or even a discernible moral pattern, others declare that this is a silly goal or, at least, that it is more remote than ever.

At the very moment when some Australians want to complain about the decline of traditional religion and morality (and others wish the decline would accelerate), they are confronted by the evidence of a new boom in religious fundamentalism—especially among the young—with its associated moral strictures. And what could be more traditional than that? (See Chapter 19.)

Contradictions abound. Many of us are both proud of and embarrassed by this thing called Australia, but how do we manage to be both things at once? (And is this uncertainty a new kind of challenge for us? Have we lost some of our famous cockiness?) We mock our politicians but praise the stability of our democracy. Our famous love affair with 'the bush' is largely symbolic (country chintz in inner-city terraces; elastic-sided boots in nightclubs; four-wheel drive vehicles in suburban carparks) and is contradicted, in any case, by the steady stream of people quitting the rural scene. We claim to love our ancient physical environment, but we abuse it mercilessly and rail against the harshness of its climate and the un-Englishness of its soil.

The sociologist Michael Pusey, commenting on his Middle Australia Project, reports that nearly two-thirds of his respondents 'admit that their material standards of living have risen in the past ten years but, with their next breath, say that their quality of life is declining and that families are in trouble'.[4] My own *Mind & Mood* studies echo Pusey's findings. There is a bundle of contradictions in contemporary Australians' view of their own lives that will only be resolved by a deliberate reordering of priorities; or by ducking, like a surfer, under the next wave and pretending it wasn't a missed opportunity after all.

Another puzzle: We know that hundreds of thousands of Australian households are crippled by unemployment and underemployment. We also know that hundreds of thousands of households are crippled by overwork. So far, we haven't seemed inclined to have a sensible discussion about how we might address both problems at once. But we are approaching a turning point. The psychological distress associated with our lumpy distribution of work will drive a new wave of interest in the relationship between work and wealth, and we must soon have a national debate about its implications for the kind of society we want to become.

Hugh Mackay

People who worry about the quality of our political discourse—or the alleged mediocrity of many of the leaders of business and the professions — as a sign of Australia's weakness will point to contradictory signs of our strength: our rising standard of education, record corporate profits, undreamed-of affluence among those on the top half of the economic ladder, or even the relative comfort of the unemployed and welfare-dependent, compared with more abject poverty in other parts of the world. 'They've all got cars and TV sets, and no-one in Australia is starving: if you're going to be poor anywhere, Australia is the place to be,' declared a respondent in the 1998 *Mind & Mood* survey.

That attitude might seem cold-hearted, but it's a sentiment widely shared: many Australians defend the proposition that this is a place where even those who are worst off are still well off by world standards. (Others will decry such remarks as the self-protective prejudice of those who want to protect their own wealth against any attempt to alleviate unemployment or poverty by a more radical approach to tax reform, philanthropy, or some other means of calling on the rich to ease the burden on the poor.)

One of the greatest paradoxes of all is that while we have become a shining, perhaps unique, example to the world of how to create a successful society out of immigrants from 200 different countries, we continue to grizzle about our hybrid culture as if it is some kind of threat to our national integrity.

In spite of these confusing crosscurrents, there is a strong undercurrent of hope. For some, that hope rests on something as grandly symbolic as the prospect of Australia becoming a republic at last; for some, it's bound up with finding a way to succeed in the global marketplace; for some, it's the chance to move to a new level of acceptance of the inherent strength and richness of our hybrid character; for others, it's a matter of making local connections that will revive the sense of a functioning neighbourhood.

Waiting for something good to happen

Although Australians typically believe that Australia still has plenty of problems to overcome, there is a remarkably widespread assumption that this society is about to break through to a new level of attainment: economic, social and cultural. There's an air of expectancy, as though we know we are reaching a turning point; the next wave is the one we must catch.

Is this just an empty hope; a carryover from Donald Horne's 1960s analysis of us as a 'lucky country', content to let good fortune win the day, in spite of inadequate planning, incompetent leadership and an uncommitted populace?[5] Or is it a sign of something more positive, more energetic, more determined?

After 30 years of turbulence, it is beginning to look as if we are adapting to the changes that have caused such an upheaval in our view of Australia and the Australian way of life; *we are developing a new way of thinking about Australia*. We might, at last, be finding ways of absorbing the psychological punishment inflicted on us by an accelerating rate of change.

For some people—consistent with Horne's original diagnosis—the preferred strategy for dealing with all this is clear: disengage! One way of coping with the demands of a daunting national agenda—globalisation, Asian economic woes, deregulation, privatisation, immigration, foreign investment, Aboriginal reconciliation, youth unemployment, tax reform—is to step back; to put all that on hold. People adopting that strategy are turning their focus inward; shifting their gaze from the distant, national horizon to something closer, more local, more personal.

That's why social research in the last years of the 20th century has encountered a widespread preoccupation with issues more immediate and more manageable than those on the national agenda. If I can't control unemployment or the reconciliation process, if I can't work out whether deregulation is a good thing or a bad thing, if I can't control how the corporation that employs me is going to resolve the tension between the social conscience and the bottom line—what can I control? One answer is that I can control which video I'll rent, which school my kids will attend, where we'll go for our next holidays, whether we'll put another room in the roof, which car we'll buy, what we'll have for dinner tonight.

Another popular answer: my body. The frenzy of jogging, work-outs, crash diets and cosmetic surgery, plus the craze for body-piercing, are all symptoms of the desire to get *something* under control, even if it is only my personal appearance.

But even for people who want to duck the big questions and settle for those over which they can exert direct control, there's still a persistent hope that, on a national scale, something big, something good—or, at least, something different—might be about to happen; a palpable sense that *Australia is in some kind of transition.*

They can detect it in their own indecisiveness at election time, as if they know it's important to get this right—a conviction that is reflected in the steady rise of the swinging vote, now up around 30 per cent in most elections. They can detect it in their deepening gloom about the state of Federal politics, because the gloom is itself a sign that they want it to change; they want to be proud of their political institutions, not embarrassed about them. They could detect it in their pre-referendum confusion about the republic. (See Chapter 18.)

They can even detect it when they go shopping: customers are reporting that the shops *feel* different, and they are enjoying the difference. (Is it that Australians have rediscovered personal service? Is it the greater range of choice on offer? Is it the proliferation of coffee shops and cafes, or the more chaotic, cheerful, and less clinical ambience of the shops themselves?)

In any case, not everyone wants to disengage from the big agenda. Many Australians are as passionate as any suffragette ever was, as committed as any anti-Vietnam War protester or any human-rights activist, in their desire to change the system, to right wrongs, to stamp out injustice and to shine a light into the murk of corruption in places high and low.

Whether people are shrinking from it, confronting it or welcoming it, there is a growing sense that, after all the change and dislocation we've been living through for the past 30 years, a new *kind* of change is upon us. It's not just that our attitudes are changing towards this or that; it's that we are beginning to think in a new way. I hesitate to use the word I'm about to use, because it has become so peculiarly and exclusively associated with the idea of ethnicity, but the best way to describe the emerging view of Australia is that in its richest, broadest and most inclusive sense, we are becoming a truly *multicultural* society. (A more technical way of saying the same thing might be to say that we are a postmodern society, and we'll return to that idea in a moment.)

We are in the midst of a significant culture shift in which old and new values, old and new attitudes, are finding ways to coexist in a genuinely pluralist society where, possibly for the first time, we are understanding what diversity really means. No wonder it feels to many Australians as if they've been caught in a rip.

We are still the New World

There's a hidden imperative in Australian culture that won't be denied and now, after 30 years of confusion and uncertainty, it is reasserting itself. Australia, particularly for Europeans and their descendants, is still the New World: the place where the mistakes of the past might be corrected; where ancient hostilities might finally be forgotten; where class divisions might be broken down; where the ideal of modern civilisation might yet be realised. (This, by the way, marks one of the most significant differences between those who came here from Europe and those who came from Asia. European immigrants typically brought the dream of the New World in their emotional baggage; those from Asia saw us only as another country in the neighbourhood—one that offered special opportunities, certainly, but with none of that almost mystical sense of potential that is embedded in the idea of a New World.)

So we still believe that the faith invested in us by all those who came here by choice will ultimately be justified. That's the bedrock truth about Australia at the turn of the century: we believe that, given time, we will become what the European dream always said we would become—a kind of antipodean utopia.

We might be far from realising our potential; we might have failed to keep many of the promises we made to ourselves; we might, in some ways, be a disappointment to each other. In particular, we might have fallen for the trap of clinging to too many of the old prejudices, the old ways—the very things the New World was supposed to put away. But we are sure of one thing and, like a family secret, we scarcely need to mention

Hugh Mackay

it when we speak to each other: we know that Australia, in the end, will come good.

The tide of national confidence has not yet turned, but there are signs that it is turning. We are starting to take matters into our own hands and to speak with a new, more assertive voice. Local communities are beginning to flex their muscles in challenging the pen-strokes of bureaucratic decision makers—on local housing policies, for example, or traffic control. Community-led consultation is starting to happen on a large scale, in everything from the genetic engineering of food to the shape and character of our democracy. We are irritated by our own acquiescence. We believe that we have let too many opportunities slip through our fingers: 'too many companies sold out to foreign investors, too many inventions hawked to overseas backers, too much spending and not enough investing ... too easygoing, that's us!' Rather like a surfer sitting on a board, we've been content to rise and fall on the swell; now we are beginning to realise that waves are for catching, not watching.

From the quality of supermarket products to the state of the family, the menace of the drug trade, urban architecture or the level of political debate in our nation's parliaments, Australians are showing signs of a new willingness to become involved; to insist that things should be done differently ... and better. If we're going to be an example to the world of a just, civil and harmonious society, a society that embodies the idea of a 'new way' as more than a political slogan, then the moment is upon us.

But that's not the whole story, either. There's another way of interpreting this swirling, turning tide; another way of making sense of the crosscurrents, contradictions, uncertainties, ambiguities and paradoxes that characterise Australian attitudes at the end of the 20th century.

'Nothing is certain, nothing is simple'

Australia is becoming a truly postmodern society—a place where we are learning to incorporate uncertainty into our view of the world. The absolute is giving way to the relative; objectivity to subjectivity; function to form. In the modern world view of the 20th century, seeing was believing; in the postmodern world of the turn of the century, believing is seeing. Conviction yields to speculation; prejudice to a new open-mindedness; religious dogma to a more intuitive, inclusive spirituality. Even the concept of God receives a changed emphasis, from the materialist's 'out-there' being, to a spirit that is more intimately part of us.

If this sounds like 'anything goes', then that is precisely the criticism most often levelled at those who have embraced postmodernism as if it is a political philosophy. But this is not an 'ism' we are being called on to accept or reject: this is a fundamental culture shift that corresponds to a style shift already well established—and perhaps already passé—in the worlds of art, design, cinema and literature. It is not a uniquely Australian phenomenon: it is a new approach to the understanding of 'social reality' that has been emerging, at different rates, in most Western societies over the past 30 years.

In *Reality Isn't What It Used To Be*, Walter Truett Anderson describes the postmodern world as a place where we are all *required* to make choices about our realities.[6] Once we accept that what we take to be social realities are only ever constructions of 'reality', we realise that we have always been free to construct a view of the world to coincide with our values, our beliefs and our aspirations. It's just that most of us, having been raised within the 'constructed social reality' of a particular subculture, have not realised that we were free to explore other ways of seeing the world. In Anderson's phrase, we lived by 'the innocent belief that there are no alternatives'. Postmodernism insists that there is an infinity of alternatives, and encourages us to explore them. (See Chapter 15.)

Not everyone welcomes or admires this shift. There is a backlash against the spirit of postmodernism that will shake the foundations of many institutions, from academia to the Church. Parents will complain that their children are being taught a vague kind of 'moral reasoning' rather than distinct Christian principles; that globalism is replacing patriotism; that traditional beliefs and values are not getting the credit they deserve.

Tony Blair and Bill Clinton are classic postmodern leaders—searching for compromise (the Third Way); adapting not only their policies but also their 'principles', to meet changing circumstances; enshrining pragmatism as the highest political virtue; responding constantly to the public opinion polling that keeps them in touch with the mood swings of their constituency.

We don't have to respect or enjoy the postmodern ethic to acknowledge that it is the new order. But if we want to understand the way the world is changing, and if we want to be able to make sense of Australia in the early years of the 21st century, we will have to recognise that the cultural kaleidoscope has turned.

In the old order, differences of opinion were triggers for conflict. In the postmodern world, differences of opinion are accepted as part of the richness of our social, cultural, intellectual and religious tapestry. In the old order, adversarial politics seemed an appropriate expression of two radically different ways of looking at the world. In the postmodern world, adversarial politics looks increasingly irrelevant, archaic and unproductive (which is why esteem for politicians is at an all-time low, why new parties and personalities will constantly arise to fill in the gaps on the political spectrum, and why so many Australian voters have adopted the strategy of voting differently for the House of Representatives and the Senate).

Things are not as black-and-white as they once were. While that is confusing and disappointing to many people, others find it exciting and engrossing. Some frosty old prejudices are beginning to thaw under the influence of a new understanding of what it really means to be an Australian in *this* Australia, and in response to fresh challenges to our view of Australia's place in the world.

For instance, some people who were once dismissive of, or merely uninterested in, the plight of Aborigines now understand that the issues involved in land rights, or the so-called Stolen Generations, or true reconciliation, are more complex than they first thought. The idea of prior ownership of this continent by indigenous people comes as a shock to those who had never bothered to think about it before the High Court declared that the doctrine of *terra nullius* was nonsense, but at least it is an idea that now has currency. As a result, more Australians are thinking about it, and if the solutions to some of the issues surrounding native title no longer seem simple or straightforward, then that confusion itself could be regarded as progress—or at least as a sign that the tide might be turning. To be troubled by issues like Aboriginal health is a quantum leap from the position of being unaware of them or untouched by them. (See Chapter 11.)

People who once thought the answer to the illicit drug trade was simply to increase police activity and to impose harsher penalties on those who use drugs—as well as those who deal in them—are now wondering whether the solution is really that simple, and whether there is *any* simple solution. Controversy about the idea of controlled heroin trials has created a classic dilemma for many people: would this amount to an endorsement of drug use, or would it be an experiment worth trying? (See Chapter 3.) And people who would once have been unable to imagine themselves contemplating the legalisation of any illicit drug, even cannabis, are now finding themselves more open to that possibility.

As more families, schools and communities are touched by the tragedy of drug addiction, there are signs of people opening their minds to the idea that new approaches—and a greater variety of approaches—might be needed if the problem is to be effectively tackled. 'I used to think you could just line them up and shoot them,' said a respondent in a 1999 *Mind & Mood* survey, 'but now I'm not so sure ...'

Now I'm not so sure is becoming the theme song of contemporary Australia. While that might strike some people as a sign of weakened resolve, or abdication from a previously unambiguous position of principle, or a retreat from the moral high ground, it might simply mean that our culture—including the style of our moral judgments—is moving towards a more realistic, more genuinely inclusive assessment of life in the postmodern world.

Some of those who, from a position of comfortable prejudice, have long bleated about the state of Australian society can now be heard speaking with a gentler, more tentative voice. Even those who remain critical of aspects of our social, cultural, political or economic life will, almost without exception, still want to say that this is the best country in the world.

Here's another example of the new unsureness: the longstanding prejudice against the unemployed is finally being softened in people who find themselves having to face up to the inherent insecurity of their own jobs or the bleakness of their children's job prospects. (See Chapter 10.)

And another: while there is still widespread fear, ignorance and disapproval of homosexuality, events like Sydney's Gay and Lesbian Mardi Gras have undoubtedly brought the reality of alternative lifestyles to the attention of many people previously insulated from the idea of sexual pluralism. Greater willingness on the part of homosexuals to declare their sexual orientation to their families and friends (and even, in some celebrated cases, to the world at large) has also helped to break down the idea that homosexuals are freaks, misfits or, at worst, actually evil. Sexual identity has itself been the subject of more open debate: are we all both male and female? Are bisexuals 'normal'? Is homosexuality genetically or socially determined, or freely chosen—as in the LUG phenomenon ('lesbian until graduation') lampooned by undergraduates?

Not all of these attitudes are changing, and there are still plenty of Australians who resist the very idea of a culture shift. Inevitably, that resistance has begun to produce a backlash, a hardening of prejudice. We've seen that already in the recent tightening of the TV censorship code and in the battlelines drawn on euthanasia. There are still many Australians whose emotional security depends so utterly on the bastion of personal prejudice that any dissenting view is treated as an outrage. (Some fundamentalist Christians, for example, won't countenance alternative interpretations of Christian doctrine even by equally earnest, equally committed Christians from other points on the theological spectrum.)

But the signs of a culture shift are sufficiently widespread to suggest that something significant is brewing. There is evidence, documented throughout the chapters of this book, that, in steadily increasing numbers, we are prepared to open our minds, to see our society in a new, more realistic light (rather than as we wish it were, or as we fondly imagine it used to be), and to acknowledge that nothing is certain; nothing is simple.

The breakthrough is in recognising that we could make a virtue of living with uncertainty and ambiguity; that the title of Paul Kelly's groundbreaking book, *The End of Certainty*,[7] means what it says. This is a new *kind* of change, and there's no turning back.

The 'one-trend' fallacy

When there are signs of a turning of the cultural tide, it is easy to rush in, splash about, and come up with some dangerous oversimplifications. 'Aha,' we want to say, 'now that we understand what's happening, we can predict what will happen next.'

But this particular turning of the tide offers us no easy answers; it encourages no glib predictions, no confident assessments of what is going on. The present culture shift is a shift towards uncertainty, a shift towards diversity, a shift towards complexity. It is, in many ways, about learning to accept that we *don't* understand what's happening.

The biggest mistake we can make at a time like this is to try to pick *the* trend. What is the future of marriage? Wrong question. Marriage has many different futures, and if we were to dwell on the fact that the legal marriage rate is now at its lowest on record, and still falling, we could miss some of the nuances that have entered the vastly complex subject of partnering and parenting. (See Chapter 13.)

What is the future for retailing, a retailer might ask. Another mistake. Should we expect a renewed boom in local, suburban, 'village' shopping centres? Yes. Should we expect further development of regional shopping malls? Yes. Should we expect an explosion in the use of the Internet for shopping outside the traditional retail environment? Yes. Is the branchless bank in our future? Yes. (BankDirect has already done it in New Zealand, just as Dell Computer has created a storeless marketing strategy, worldwide.) Will computer technology allow virtual shopping, even for clothes? Yes. What about door-to-door selling, shopping by phone, mail-order catalogues, party plans? Yes, yes, yes. All will have their place in a more diverse retail world.

And here's another point: the one customer will want to shop in different ways at different times, according to stress levels, time of day,

day of the week, emotional mood, need for speed and convenience, desire for browsing, and so on. There won't be *a* trend, but many coexistent, and sometimes contradictory, trends. Crosscurrents.

Martin Hayward, director of consumer consultancy at Britain's Henley Centre, says: 'The same people want to be treated differently at different times and that's the challenge for marketers. You are not targeting the person, you are targeting the mood of that person or the ''mode''—the circumstances they find themselves in.'[8]

Howard Russell, a leading New Zealand marketing strategist, points out that 'shops will have to change throughout the day rather than according to the seasons, while tailor-made services will become the norm'. Russell notes that, in response to the need to keep up with what he calls 'the ever-mutating consumer', breweries have already tested so-called 'chameleon' bars that change their offering and their ambience during the course of the day, selling coffee in the mornings, bistro-style lunches at midday and 'turning up the music and dimming the lights in the evening'.[9]

What about housing? Bigger houses? Yes. Smaller houses? Yes. More flexible interiors? Yes. Big, formal bistro kitchens with lots of stainless steel? Yes. Is the country kitchen still in fashion? Yes. Tiny kitchens-in-a-cupboard, tucked in the corner of apartments for young singles and working couples who rarely cook? Yes. A growth in the number of renters? Yes, it's already happening: for the first time, the number of renters in the 25–35 years age group exceeds the number of home buyers. So is the dream of a traditional Aussie house-and-garden dead? No: the birth of the first child still stimulates thoughts of a more permanent nest.

Take a look at the proliferating, fragmenting magazine market. We haven't yet reached the point where there's a magazine being published just for you, perfectly reflecting your interests, values and aspirations—but the market is heading that way. (It could never happen, of course, because every reader is many things, and those things are changing too quickly for any publisher to track.)

Wherever you look—marriage, religion, patterns of work and leisure, media consumption, politics, fashion—the story is the same: there's no single story. Reviewing the 1999 Mercedes Australian Fashion Week, *The*

Sydney Morning Herald's Style and Fashion Editor, Jane de Teliga, put it like this: 'Forecasters may not agree exactly what form fashion will take in the next century but one thing they do agree about is that confusion reigns in the style world of the late '90s.'[10] Quite so: confusion reigns in the style world … and almost everywhere else, as well.

Our attitudes are changing, but they are not simply moving in a straight line from A to B. The changes—and this book—are about how we are adapting to a more flexible, more dynamic, less linear way of seeing the world.

Another crosscurrent:

materialism versus postmaterialism

There's nothing wrong with a bit of material comfort and prosperity, as long as you don't expect it, alone, to bring you happiness. If you do, you might discover what late-20th-century Westerners have been discovering in droves: that when materialism is unrestrained, when it is enshrined as a core philosophy, it rots the soul—but it might take half a lifetime to detect the smell.

The thing that seems to bring people greatest personal satisfaction is a sense of meaning and purpose in their lives, and that can be achieved across a very wide range of economic, social and cultural circumstances. In other words, you don't have to be rich to be happy and there's plenty of social research to back up that ancient bit of folk wisdom.[11] Of course, poverty can make you wretchedly miserable, but once basic needs are met, it's surprising how little difference a new swimming pool, a new car, or even a new room in the roof will make to your general level of wellbeing. Unhappy families will generally stay unhappy, even if they buy a new computer; happy families will generally stay happy, even if they don't.

Possessions can't, in most cases, bring meaning and purpose to our lives. (That's one reason why political philosophies that rate economic growth *more* highly than care of the social fabric are doomed to add to the sum of our unhappiness. When essentially materialistic policies, like

Hugh Mackay

so-called economic rationalism, are ramped up to a position of political dominance, they are likely to increase a society's human problems because they are based on the spurious assumption that economic growth is the same thing as progress.)

When you hear younger Australians talking about their outlook on life, you wonder whether, apart from all the other things that are going on, two moral universes are about to collide ... or coalesce. Their parents, the Baby Boomers, have been nurtured, raised, shaped—and *impressed*— by the forces of materialism. The rising generation, taking all that in their stride, are starting to show signs of looking for something more.

The iconoclastic Boomers, in vast numbers, turned their backs on their own parents' moral and religious frameworks. Casting around for an alternative and finding themselves in a burgeoning culture of consumerism, they grabbed it and converted it into a value system. For all their protestations of romantic and political idealism, the Boomers couldn't resist the lure of materialism: possessions became the mark of success and brands the mark of status. Citizens became consumers.

For the first time in our history, a generation had been presented with the apparently attainable prospect of material prosperity for all. The goal of egalitarianism suddenly seemed, in the Fifties and Sixties, as if it could be realised in material terms: everyone could have a car, a washing machine and a TV set; everyone could have a Hills Hoist, a Victa mower and a backyard barbecue. It looked as if everyone could be equal, happy ... and middle class.

It would be stupid to suggest that young Australians are turning their backs on possessions, but there are hints of a generational shift in attitudes to materialism. Having grown up in a society where consumerism is the boring norm—as opposed to the society in which their parents grew up, where consumerism was shiny and new—young Australians, like their counterparts around the Western world, are developing a heightened interest in so-called postmaterial values.

This is very different from saying they are only interested in 'non-material' values: the quest for postmaterialist, more inner-directed values is most likely to be embarked upon by people whose material needs—at least their basic survival needs—are already being met, so they can turn their attention to more intangible, abstract values that lie beyond the material; such things as the sense of 'belonging' (the gang is back, and *Friends* still rides high in the TV ratings), the sense of esteem (being taken seriously by yourself and others) and the importance of intellectual and aesthetic satisfaction.

One symptom of this shift is the growing emphasis on something called *lifestyle*: people in their twenties and early thirties can often be heard declaring that a job isn't worth having if it interferes with your lifestyle; children are okay as long as they don't change your lifestyle (ha!); a mortgage—or even a marriage—might be avoided on the grounds that it would inhibit the flexibility of your lifestyle. Another symptom is the relentless determination to have *fun*, and to resist the angst of their parents' lives.

Parents often interpret tension between them and their offspring as a conflict over their children's lack of commitment. In fact, this conflict is generally not between commitment and non-commitment: it arises from a commitment to different sets of goals: 'He's been studying for four years and he's due to graduate next year. Now he tells us he is going to give it all up and get a job in the local bottle shop for a while ... just for a change, just to think things over, just to see what turns up.'

Oddly enough, postmaterialism sometimes shows up as vandalism. Some of the graffiti writers are telling us—or telling each other, in a code we can't crack—that they don't respect our *things*: our property, our emphasis on possessions, our politicians' and business leaders' view of society as a mere economy.

A cavalier carelessness with their own possessions is another symptom of an incipient shift towards postmaterialism among the young. Why, their parents ask, were they so nuts about getting a pair of Nikes, or a particular T-shirt, if they were going to leave it at the beach, or lend it to someone they'd never met before and may never see again? Why do they want all this stuff so badly one minute and turn their backs on it the next?

And why do so many of them turn away from big brands altogether as they enter their teens, preferring to dress as if they are both poor and tasteless? Why is Vinnies (the second-hand clothing shops run by the

Society of St Vincent De Paul) the top teenage 'brand' in many subcultures? How did grunge ever get to be cutting edge? This, too, *might* be changing: there seems to be a swing back, in teenage fashion, towards being smart and stylish. But don't take that as read; such trends are never as distinct or unidimensional as that, and some of the signals coming from the top end of the fashion market suggest a return to the hippie look of the Seventies—Indian cheesecloth, lace-trimmed cotton petticoats, gypsy skirts and sheepskin coats. Take your pick, but assume that retro is safe. (See Chapter 14.)

The trash mentality *might* be an early warning sign (then again, it might not be: this is a time of discontinuity). It might be telling us that this generation have their sights set on different values from those that come with Brand X. (Though even the meaning of brands is changing: see Chapter 16.) Some of them might be determined to live in ways that express their conviction that greater value should be attached to the quality of their personal relationships than to the style of their clothing. They might have decided that their commitment will be to the cohesion of their social group, or to their freedom to act in less conformist and more creative ways than they believe their parents do.

They talk a great deal about 'spirituality'. Consistent with the more inner-directed character of postmaterialism, many of them seem less comfortable with the materialist's 'out-there' God than with the idea of a personal, intimate God within, and some choose to explore the limits of sensory experience through drug use rather than pursue more conventional, material goals.

Some of them are already looking at their grandparents' lives and perceiving less emphasis on material possessions, but more contentment. That makes them wonder whether they would do better to aim a little lower in material terms, but a little higher in terms of life's less tangible gratifications. (It is partly in response to this shift that, in the under-35 age group, there has been such a marked swing towards renting rather than buying homes.)

Others have retreated, for large parts of every day, into cyberspace— a place where the reality of the material world is constantly challenged by the virtual reality of the electronic flicker.

Researchers differ on the reasons for this culture shift, which seems to be common in Western, industrialised cultures. Some attribute it to rising levels of affluence that free people to pursue more high-minded goals;[12] some believe it to be the result of improved education;[13] others attach particular weight to the spreading faith in democracy, with its emphasis on free speech, one vote/one value, and the right of individual access to government.[14] Whatever the cause, the signs point to a culture shift in favour of *experience* as a personal frame of reference. For those on the leading edge of postmaterialism, 'who I am' and 'what I'm doing' (and what I'm getting out of it) are rated more highly than 'what I own'—even if I also happen to own plenty.

The rising generations of young Australians have grown up in a different kind of society from the one that formed earlier generations, so they are bound to see Australia, and their place in it, differently from the way their parents or grandparents do. The most affluent and better-educated among them are certainly *talking* postmaterialism; we have yet to see whether, in large numbers, they will live it as well—and, if they do, how the rest of us will react.

In any case, the emergence of postmaterialism in Australia is by no means confined to the young. There are plenty of older Baby Boomers (now into their forties and fifties) who are rethinking their priorities and deciding that their lives do not adequately reflect the inner-directed values in which they profess to believe. They crave greater simplicity, for example, while feeling that their lives are actually becoming more complex. They rail against their own materialism and wonder what they can do about it. (See Chapter 2.)

We don't yet know how the clash between materialism and postmaterialism will work itself out. Older Australians frequently observe all this with the rather jaundiced gaze of those who knew all along that the passionate embrace of materialism was bound to disappoint, and they are not surprised to see the symbols and trophies of a materialist culture being downgraded, if not actually trashed.

Meanwhile, postmaterialism—like postmodernism—adds another twist to our sense of uncertainty.

Looking back, looking forward

In the past 30 years, the thing that has arguably had the most enduring, transforming effect on our culture has been the women's movement. Our social institutions—marriage, the family, the neighbourhood—have been radically reshaped by the liberation of women, and the economy has been shaken to its foundations by the extent of female participation in the workforce and the implications of that not only for the relationship between supply and demand in the labour market, but also for the redistribution of household income.

Yet in spite of Germaine Greer's recent assertion that women have sacrificed femaleness by going for equality,[15] the Australian evidence suggests that many women, having achieved equality, have known how to shape it to suit their own purposes and have not always been prepared to squash and bend themselves to fit the patterns established by males. Indeed, one of the many ways in which the rising generation of Australian women are pioneering a new culture is in their determination to combine success at work with satisfying private lives. Women are redefining 'a balanced life' and many men are sitting up and taking notice. (See Chapter 23.)

Gender issues have permeated all aspects of Australian life, from the bedroom to the boardroom. But now, gender issues have themselves fragmented and multiplied. Here, too, there is a turning of the tide. Feminism doesn't mean one thing (if it ever did), and women are recognising that liberation is really about choice, not conformity to Greer's or anyone else's image of the fulfilled woman.

Feminism is no longer *a* movement, or *a* pattern; it's a swirl of ideas, a cacophony of many voices, often in furious disagreement.

So what's next?

One of the dominant themes of this book is that we are in danger of allowing our new-found acceptance of diversity and our embrace of the truly pluralistic society to rob us of a necessary sense of identity; a sense of where we came from and where we're going; a sense, above all, that we each have a safe place here—a place to call our own.

Another major threat to our psychological and cultural health is coming from the information revolution, with its promise of that greatest of all modern hoaxes, the global village.

How we deal with these two closely-related issues will determine the shape of Australian society over the next 25 years.

The nightmare scenario:

fragmentation and alienation

The gloomiest prospect for Australia—based on an extrapolation of some of the darkest trends already evident—is that we could become a society in which our cities and towns are pockmarked by no-go zones, where violence is contained rather than controlled; a society where a burgeoning culture of recreational drug use offers welcome escape from the emptiness of isolation and alienation.

In such a miserable scenario, the individual emerges, beyond question, as the social unit. Our sense of being part of a community has lost most of its force. Such a society is not only tense, competitive and ruthless; it is also a place where our traditional view of morality has undergone a radical change: we have shifted away from ideas like 'mutual obligation' and 'shared values', because those ideas can only be sustained by the experience of living with others in a recognisable community. Materialism has become the only appropriate basis for a value system.

Having lost touch with each other—by becoming obsessed with privacy and security, by cocooning ourselves in our homes and cars, and by confining most of our contacts to the pathways of electronically 'mediated' information—our moral development has been stunted. As a result, we have become a more tightly regulated society in which we accept more and more rigid rules to compensate for our lack of spontaneous social sensitivity.

In such an insecure society, new elites have emerged. The most powerful people are those who control the flow of information; those who control the illicit drug trade; the 'spin doctors' who create the political and commercial myths and images which lull the rest of us into believing that life is 'fun', that everything will somehow be all right (perhaps because a media star said it would be), and that this week's 'celebrity' is a worthy focus for our dreams of a better, more fulfilling life.

It goes without saying that, in this nightmare scenario, Australia has become a highly stratified society, with stark and unbridgeable divisions between rich and poor. The rich are feeling smug and superior, if a little nervous; the poor are angry, and increasingly prone to violent expressions of their envy of the rich.

Far from being ungovernable, such a society is easy prey for a ruthless leader who thrives on the emotional and economic insecurity of the population, and who benefits from the disintegration of the sense of a 'commonwealth'.

The dream scenario:

reconnecting with the community

Humans are herd animals, and we cut ourselves off from the herd at our psychological peril. We belong in small groups. We are social creatures. Our best defence against fragmentation and alienation lies in our natural urge to stick together.

So here's a more hopeful picture of life in the first quarter of the 21st century. (Like the nightmare scenario, it's based on some trends already apparent.)

This is a society in which we have rediscovered the importance of the community. Though the divorce rate has not fallen and many of us are avoiding marriage altogether, we have found ways of grouping ourselves into surrogate 'extended families' whose members—friends, neighbours, workmates—create networks of mutual support to help each other with child care, shopping, cooking and home maintenance.

It's a society in which we have worked out how to live like modern, urban and suburban villagers. We're eating out more, as we recognise that grazing with the herd is an important step towards reconnecting with the herd; coffee shops and cafes have become meeting places for incidental as well as planned contact. We're creating and using more communal space in the manner of a European plaza; the local park has become a kind of village green. We're watching more movies, and other forms of entertainment, at community centres, and less at home. We've reclaimed our cities by actually living in them.

We have finally decided that the community's wellbeing does not automatically flow from strong economic growth, and we have insisted that government and business strategists take 'social capital' more seriously.

This is a society in which technology thrives and is widely employed, but it's a place where we've learned how to keep the machines in their place: we're determined not to be mastered by them. We've found a way to ensure that our children don't become computer junkies or media-fed isolates. We've recognised that our most precious resource for coping with the inherently unstable and unpredictable world of the 21st century is not information, but each other.

So we're acknowledging each other more; we're tolerating our differences more easily; we're accepting that diversity doesn't have to be divisive, because we're back in touch with each other. We're more interested in understanding than influencing each other. Our shared values have re-emerged more clearly because we have understood, all over again, that the sense of morality can only evolve out of the experience of belonging to a community.

Life in the future won't ever be quite that rosy, of course. But neither need it be as bleak as the nightmare scenario, though the pressures pushing us in that direction will be hard to resist.

We must hope that in the same way as women eventually reacted, through the women's liberation movement, to the psychological distress of being relegated to second-class citizenship, so our reaction to present insecurities and discontinuities will be a move towards *reconnection*. If that is going to happen, if that is what is going to save us from the nightmare, then we shall have to pay more attention to those who are urging us to become more active in the life of our local communities. We shall have to think more creatively about postmodern renditions of village life, and about ways to ensure that our personal relationships—the things that ultimately define and sustain us—will not be swamped in the turning of the tide.

The following chapters are an A–Z of contemporary Australian life. They are only a series of snapshots, but, viewed as a montage, they offer grounds for cautious optimism.

CHAPTER ONE

Anzac Day

Yearning for a Festival that Defines Us

Turning Point: One of the surest signs of our culture shift is the quest for a uniquely Australian festival. As Australians feel more independent and more confident in themselves, they want a home-grown festival that asserts our identity. Christmas and Easter are imports, with deep meaning only for Christians, and Australia Day has an air of contrived jollification about it—too close to Christmas, too tied to Sydney—and Arthur Phillip has never been recognised as a national hero. Perhaps the day on which we become a republic will eventually become a focal point for national celebration. In the meantime, Anzac Day has reached a turning point: it is quietly changing its meaning and renewing its appeal.

What are we hoping for? A festival that does for us what Thanksgiving does for the Americans and St Patrick's Day does for the Irish. A truly national occasion that catches the rising tide of nationalism.

Before the dawn of an April morning, an autumnal mist hangs low over Sydney's Martin Place. Here, as in many other places around Australia, the 1999 Anzac Day crowd is the largest ever. People are silent, expectant.

A line of youngsters teeters on the ledge of a nearby building, hoping to improve their view. The band arrives at the Cenotaph. A description of proceedings, being broadcast on commercial radio, is relayed to the crowd via a public address system. Even with the street lights on, many people can't see past those in front of them in the crush of 10 000 people. But there is no restlessness.

Familiar hymns are sung; the words of the 'Ode to the Fallen' are read by two high school pupils: 'They shall not grow old, as we that are left grow old ...' A senior military officer speaks. A trumpeter plays the 'Last Post' and 'Reveille'. Eyes glisten. The band marches off in silence.

There seems to be some hesitation in the dispersal of the crowd, as though expressing a wish to linger. The biggest surprise is the number of young people—adolescents, young adults, some children—breaking gently away from the moment; heading, perhaps, for a train back to the suburbs, or for breakfast at McDonald's before finding a vantage point for watching the march, later in the morning.

Is their reluctance to disperse a sign of some intimate link with this occasion? A grandparent or other relative among the fallen? A family history of involvement with the services, here or elsewhere, possibly even somewhere we used to regard as alien?

Such personal links will be part of the explanation. But there is another message in the remarkable surge of interest in Anzac Day and in our growing determination to celebrate it in solemn ways. As the memories of two world wars recede and more recent wounds in our psyche begin to heal—Malaya, Korea, Vietnam—the increasing intensity of our observance of Anzac Day says something else: something about our need to rediscover ourselves, to acknowledge who we are, to find a focus, or possibly a foundation, for the new meanings we want to attach to that increasingly portentous word, 'Australian'.

Hugh Mackay

The rehabilitation of Anzac Day

Twenty-five years ago, Anzac Day was desperately out of fashion. The Vietnam War was over, but there was a lingering sense of disgrace about Australia's involvement in it. Anti-war sentiment was so strong, in fact, that even the commemoration of sacrifice in two world wars was criticised as if it entailed the glorification of war.

By the 1990s, though, Anzac Day had been rehabilitated. Far from fizzling out—as many people had predicted and some even hoped—it has been attracting increasing interest. Crowds attending services and marches have grown, and a new wave of young Australians has been drawn to the occasion.

One reason for the resurgence might be that, having a harder row to hoe than their parents did at the same age, the rising generation are more attuned to the concept of struggle. We might not be at war, but we are not at peace, either: just look, through the eyes of young Australians, at the issue of Aboriginal reconciliation, the waterfront, domestic violence, the illicit drug trade, the uncertain labour market, or even the road toll.

Young people are growing up in a less promising, less optimistic and less indulgent world than the world of their parents' adolescence. Given such uncertain prospects, young Australians might well be comforted by stories of other, earlier Australians (including their own grandparents and great-uncles and aunts) who found the resources to face overwhelming odds. They might also be intrigued by reflections on a time in our history when we were so sure of our identity that taking sides seemed easy.

But there's another reason why Anzac Day might be striking such a responsive chord at century's end. This is a unique day in our calendar: a day for thinking about timeless virtues like courage, discipline, bravery and sacrifice. It is also a day that encourages us to recount our very own stories.

Anzac Day will always be an occasion for remembering those who offered their lives in defence of our freedom. That recollection of sacrifice will always remain the foundation of the solemn celebration of the Anzac spirit. But Anzac Day's growing significance—especially for new generations of Australians who have never experienced war, or whose background is culturally remote from the British Empire—will depend on fresh interpretations of its meaning.

When the wounds of war finally begin to heal, it is time to acknowledge that the meaning of war will never be found in the spilled guts, the torn limbs, the shattered minds, the fear, or even the heroism. The terrible penalty that has to be paid in human suffering is the price of war, not its meaning.

The meaning of war isn't even located in victory, but only in the peace it brings. Anzac Day's essential question is this: what have we done with the peace that was won for us?

So it's not just a question of history, or even identity. The Anzac resurgence is as much a signpost to what's coming as an echo of what's past.

Any other contenders for our national day?

Australia Day? The Melbourne Cup?

Australians are short of festivals. Like every human society, we crave occasions that mark and define us in some way. Ritual observations are as important to societies as they are to families and individuals; our participation in such occasions is part of what actually constitutes our sense of self. They are not mere symbols; they are acts of affirmation.

Weddings, christenings, birthdays, graduations, retirements, funerals; we do our best, often with pretty meagre cultural and emotional resources, with vague rules and few conventions. We're not good at Occasions.

On a societal scale, we try to make something of Christmas, but it's lost so much of its religious significance that the vestiges of cultural heritage are all but swamped by tawdry commercial activity, and once that happens, it becomes infinitely more blessed to receive than give.

In any case, culturally speaking, Christmas is someone else's festival: we imported it from Europe. For a long time we tried to pretend it was cold in Australia on Christmas Day, so we ate the kind of dinner they eat in the depths of an English winter. As the temperature climbed towards the old century mark, we exchanged Christmas cards bearing pictures of carollers in the snow and ice-skaters on a village pond.

It wasn't that we were craving a return to Europe, or a drop in our summer temperatures; we were simply craving a festival. Recent evidence for that craving can be found in the curious trend—still gathering momentum—to stage a re-run of Christmas in the middle of winter, usually called 'yuletide' (as if that might somehow distinguish it from the midsummer Christmas). People seem to be saying that if we find anything better than Christmas for an authentic Australian festival, then let's have two of them: at least that is uniquely Australian.

Christmas and Easter will persist, of course, partly because they have intense religious significance for the minority of people, committed Christians, who use them as markers of the birth, death and resurrection of Jesus.

They will also persist because the commercial imperatives are now irresistible, and because any cultural festival—even one at the wrong time of the year, and even one whose origins have been drowned in the clang of the cash register—is better than none.

But the yearning for an Australian original won't go away. Some people are exploring ways of making it happen: the Australia Day Council has achieved some momentum, but it's hard to *invent* enthusiasm for a festival if it hasn't evolved spontaneously. In any case, the proponents of Australia Day as a national celebration are fighting an uphill battle against the fact that 26 January 1788 is still a very Sydney thing. It also comes too closely on the heels of Christmas and New Year to generate the kind of anticipation that gives a festival its crackle, and the middle of an Australian summer isn't the ideal time for feasting.

Australia Day lacks a hero with whom we can identify; someone who stands for the virtues we admire, the values we espouse, the verities we believe in. Captain James Cook strikes many Australians as heroic, as do some of the early explorers like Burke and Wills, Leichhardt, Hume, Hovell and Flinders. But Captain Arthur Phillip? For all his extraordinary achievements in getting the First Fleet to Botany Bay and thence to Port Jackson, and for all the skill, imagination and resourcefulness required to establish a penal colony a world away from Britain, Phillip has generally failed to arouse the passions of ordinary Australians. Some of his deeds (like his vengeful sorties against the Aborigines, with orders to hack off their heads and bring them back to the colony) were too dark, and his ultimate suicide too inglorious, for Phillip to be the man to personify Australia Day.

Perhaps recognising this, the Australia Day Council has tried to manufacture a fresh hero every year, in the form of the Australian of the Year. Nice idea; impressive choices—but this is no way to give a human focus to a festival. ('Happy Australia Day, dear. Now, who got the nod this year? We must remember to toast her at the barbie.')

If Australia Day is unlikely to evolve into a legitimate Aussie festival, there are several other possible contenders. Many Australians assume that when we finally disengage from the British monarchy, we might celebrate Republic Day. (Perhaps we should take care to declare ourselves a republic, or to found our own monarchy, in the middle of winter.)

And there are groups of eager promoters, dotted around the country, exploring the possible promotion of a Citizenship Day: a time to acknowledge the privileges and responsibilities of citizens; to induct 18-year-olds into citizenship; to formally welcome recently-naturalised immigrants.

Citizenship Day would certainly have the advantage of bringing together people from every tributary of Australian society. Citizenship is a nicely secular, non-partisan concept. It has no special link with any one group; it is blind to cultural, ethnic, political, religious and all other differences. It's possible to imagine such a thing, though it would be starting from scratch and, in any case, Australians are notoriously unsentimental when it comes to matters of civic pride.

So we're still looking. There's such a dearth of suitable occasions in our cultural calendar that even football grand finals are starting to develop some of the rituals and essential excitement that could, aeons from now, evolve into a spontaneous national festival. (Already, grand finals are the only time some Australians are called on to sing the National Anthem.)

The Bathurst car races, similarly, have all the ingredients of an embryonic folk festival, though it will take many generations before the event builds up enough mythology to disconnect itself from the actual cars themselves. (Peter Brock is, for Holden fans, about as close to sainthood as Mary McKillop: they already call him 'Peter Perfect', and his lustre will only increase now that he has retired. And Dick Johnson's origins as a privateer from Queensland could, given time, become the stuff of dark legend.)

The Melbourne Cup is another contender. It has the unique power to bring the entire nation to a standstill for three minutes on the first Tuesday in November and it has even had a public holiday declared in its honour in the state of Victoria. As pressure mounts to reduce the level of physical cruelty to racehorses, the future of the Melbourne Cup might be thought to be under a cloud, but that's not the way folk festivals work. If horseracing were finally to be banned—as it, like boxing, might one day be—the Melbourne Cup Carnival would undoubtedly persist in mythologised form, freed from the shackles of actual horses and actual jockeys competing in an actual race. A hundred years from now, the dressing-up in freakish fashions, the extravagant hats, the champagne and chicken eaten from the open boots of Rolls Royces, the furious race-calling, the jockeys' silks, the whips, the pageantry ... all this will have evolved into the stylised rituals of a carnival whose origins will gradually blur.

Festivals need two things to work: a symbolic hero—or a symbolic group of heroic figures—and a powerful sense of relevance to the lives of ordinary people. Phar Lap, Rain Lover and Might and Power have done it for the Melbourne Cup (along with the adrenalin-rush of punting, of course). The Pilgrim Fathers do it for Thanksgiving in the USA. Jesus certainly does it for Christmas.

The beginning and end of the life cycle are natural points of connection, which is why spring has been, through history, a favourite time for festivals—Eostre, the dawn goddess, being the precursor of Easter (though here in the Antipodes, we have to make do with autumn).

Sacrifice, too, is a powerful theme. The idea that anyone would be prepared to die to ensure the freedom of the rest of us is such an astonishing and inspiring concept that even when it is linked to the horror or futility of war, it becomes noble.

Which is where Anzac Day comes in.

The new meaning of Anzac Day

The signs suggest that Anzac Day is well on the way to becoming an authentic, original, legitimate, uniquely Australian national festival (unique even in the characteristic inclusion of another nation, New Zealand, in its name). It is no longer, as people once thought, anything to do with the glorification of war. It is about sacrifice and hope. More than any other day in our calendar, it calls on us to answer some curly questions. Who are we, these people for whom so many others gave up their lives? What are we making of this way of life for which people were once prepared to die? Are we building the kind of nation that justifies the sacrifice of so many, not only those who died, but those who thought our ideals were worth fighting for?

That's the emerging focus of Anzac Day. That's why it has captured the attention of the rising generation of young Australians. Anzac Day is about self-examination, about the celebration of what has been achieved, and about contemplation of our future.

For a nation supposed to be so committed to having fun, Anzac Day is an enigma. For all the revelry of military reunions, it's an essentially solemn day. We seem to be creating a festival that combines solemnity with celebration, as if to say that we are not so heedlessly hedonistic after all. Don't sell us short, Anzac Day declares; don't think that beer and football and thrashing the Poms at cricket are the only things we care about; don't fall for all that 'she'll-be-right' garbage. Those are the symbols—the outward and visible signs—of something that runs deep in our culture; something that casual observers can easily miss when they criticise us for our vulgarity or superficiality or bombast.

The truth is that for all our insecurities, all our uncertainties and all our anxieties, we are an example to the world of a 'have-a-go' society. We cheer for the underdog because we've been there, most of us, through our own cultural or family heritage: convicts, rejects, refugees, emigres from cultures where, for one reason or another, we or our forebears didn't fit comfortably enough to stay. If we had a say in the matter, we came here because Australia offered something—some prospect of prosperity, perhaps, or even a promise of serenity—that seemed attractive because it was superior in some way to our existing circumstances. And if it was our parents or our grandparents who made that decision, we are still caught up in its dynamic implications.

Inevitably, we sometimes lapse into the so-called 'cultural cringe'— and why not? Our cultural roots haven't yet gone deep enough to sustain the idea that we are in full flower. We are bound to wonder, from time to time, whether the Old World still does it better, and we're also bound to acknowledge that, in some ways, it does. We sometimes strut with silly arrogance when we win more than our fair share of victories on the international sporting field, particularly against England. And why not? For a nation built on such humble foundations, victory over those who spawned us is bound to be sweet.

We're a country that knows about struggling against the odds and learning to cope with the vagaries of the weather, of international economics, of colonial patronage.

Various commentators have remarked on the powerful symbolism of the Melbourne Cup as our premier horserace: a handicap event in which some of the most popular winners have been rank outsiders, battlers, who symbolise the idea that this is a place where you can come from nowhere and succeed ...

... as many people have. Jim Spigelman arrived here with his immigrant parents, a three-year-old boy from Poland. He first came to public attention as a student participating in the Freedom Ride of 1965, exposing racial discrimination against Aborigines. After a distinguished career as bureaucrat and lawyer, including three years as Principal Private Secretary to Prime Minister Gough Whitlam, he became Chief Justice of New South Wales at the age of 52. Pat O'Shane, born to an Irish father and an Aboriginal mother in unpromising circumstances, became a magistrate, the Chancellor of the University of New England and an Officer in the Order of Australia. Jason Yat-Sen Li, the Australian-born son of Chinese immigrants from Hong Kong in the Fifties, was elected an independent delegate to the 1998 Constitutional Convention and is credited with having played a crucial role in drafting and brokering majority support for the model of republican government put to the people in the referendum of November 1999.

The Anzac legend sprang from the realisation that heroic figures could emerge even from the carnage and hopelessness of Gallipoli. Anzac Day is all about the triumph of the spirit; it is not about victory in battle. Anzac Day is about making something out of very little. Anzac Day, more than any other festival that has so far emerged in the Australian almanac, captures the essence of how Australia began, and how we have built on a shaky start to make something worthwhile of ourselves.

If the diggers could see us now ...

So what would all those Anzac diggers think, if they could see the kind of Australia we have created out of the legacy of their sacrifice?

They would be astonished to find so many representatives of our former enemies, in various wars, living harmoniously in our midst.

They would marvel at our vibrant, cosmopolitan culture and its mockery of the racial, religious and ethnic tensions that persist in many other parts of the world.

They would love our optimism and our unshakeable belief that Australia is the best country in the world.

They would be relieved to see that the culture of the 'fair go' has survived, even if it has taken a bit of a battering in the last decade of the century.

But they would be troubled—as we all are—by the signs that our egalitarian ideal is evaporating under the pressure of new economic divisions in our society.

They would weep over our cynicism.

They would be incredulous at the news that 40 000 young Australians try to commit suicide each year.

And they would urge us, almost certainly, to shake off our cocoon of self-absorption and engage with the big issues that face us at century's end: violence, poverty, the globalisation of capital and labour markets, the information revolution, unemployment, the future of the family, the state of politics, the republic, the fragility of our physical environment. Don't give in to apathy, they would say; fight for what you believe in.

Hugh Mackay

Anzac Day might well turn out to be the festival we are looking for; the one that acknowledges the importance of our past as a resource for evaluating the present and creating the future. Anzac Day says, with a voice that grows louder every year, that we expect something good to happen; that we are still capable of becoming the kind of society that would justify the sacrifice of those who thought we were worth fighting for.

Viewed from that perspective, Anzac Day is bound to flourish. But if we are to seize it as an opportunity for self-examination, it won't always be a comfortable occasion for us. We might have to confront some awkward truths about ourselves and about the gap between the values we judge to be worth defending—justice, tolerance, a fair go for all—and the darker realities of our present situation.

CHAPTER TWO

Baby Boomers

Catch-up Time

Turning Point: The children of the Cold War are surprised to find themselves in middle age and, for many of them, it's a midlife crisis. They are the instant gratification generation who thought they were here for a good time, but not for a long time. Now they are carrying record levels of debt, their private lives are often painfully complicated and the prospect of an unfunded retirement is looming. It no longer seems so easy to 'do your own thing'. Boomers are beginning to re-examine their lives and their values: will those who can afford it unleash a new splurge of self-indulgent spending in their fifties? Or will they start to plan, and save, for the future in ways they have previously been reluctant to do?

What are we hoping for? A manageable solution to the problem of what to do when the Boomers' elastic adolescence finally snaps.

When the 20th century ends at midnight on 31 December 2000, the 4.3 million Baby Boomers—the largest generation Australia has ever produced—will be aged between 39 and 54.

Particularly for the early Boomers, those in their late forties and early fifties, the realisation that they've made it into the 21st century and, more poignantly, that they are undeniably 'middle-aged', will come as something of a shock. This, after all, was the Cold War generation whose catchcry was: 'We're not here for a long time; we're here for a good time.' Faced with the ever-lurking possibility of nuclear annihilation, the Boomers' impatience to grab their birthright was understandable.

But now they know they're here for a long time as well. The bomb didn't go off. The threatened nuclear holocaust hasn't happened, and seems less likely to happen now than at any time in their lives. The nuclear stockpile has actually been reduced. The global struggle between the forces of capitalism and communism has given way to an endless series of local, territorial skirmishes between ethnic, rather than ideological, enemies.

Civilisation, broadly speaking, has survived. The future that was never going to weigh them down with boring mortgages, quarter-acre blocks and all the other paraphernalia they associated with their parents' more conservative generation has, indeed, weighed them down. And not only with the relatively straightforward and predictable responsibilities associated with marriage and parenthood. The Boomers have found themselves on the cutting edge of social change and the experience has been unexpectedly demanding: sometimes exhilarating, sometimes painful.

They are the first generation of Australians to have coped, on a large scale, with the trauma of divorce and the complexity of divided families. 'Custody and access' have become part of their, and their children's, vocabulary. Boomer women are the first generation of women who have tried to live out the messages of feminism in their daily lives; the first to have experienced the particular stresses of being wife, mother, house-keeper and paid worker all at once; the first to have taken the initiative in most divorce proceedings.

They are the first generation since the Great Depression to have seen living standards eroded for a vast chunk of Australian society and to have experienced retrenchment on a large scale. They are possibly the first generation of Australian parents to have a hunch that their children will, in the long run, be worse off than they are. They are the generation who have been quietly and painfully coming to terms with the fact that egalitarianism, at least in an economic sense, may no longer be a realistic ideal since Australia has been splitting so starkly into haves and have-nots. (See Chapter 5.)

Above all, they have had to come to terms with the fact that the promises of the Sixties will not be kept; the rosy predictions of prosperity for all will not come true. The economic escalator has not continued to rise at the same rate as it did then, and although they have, in fact, reshaped our social, cultural and economic landscape, they have paid a high price for doing so. They wanted to be iconoclasts, and they were; many of them are now feeling the strain.

So, yes, they're here for a long time; but, no, it hasn't been the unrelieved good time they might have thought was their due as young Australians of the postwar boom.

Now, in their middle years, the Baby Boomers are adapting, as they must, to the realisation that not only are they still here, but they're likely to be here for a while longer—all the way into retirement, in fact.

So the generation that has always prided itself on being 'younger' in mind and body than their parents were at every stage of the life cycle; the generation that has wanted to 'stay close to the kids' (partly to protect their children from the ravages of an increasingly hostile and pressured society, partly to prove their prowess as parents, but partly, no doubt, to prove the youthfulness of their own outlook)—this is the generation that is now having to revise its self-image. Their apparently indestructible 'elastic adolescence', stretching all the way into middle age, may not be about to snap, but it is beginning to look pretty thin.

Perhaps they won't give up their blue denim jeans, and perhaps they won't abandon their Beatles and Elvis records, but the Boomers are 'getting on', and they know it. Even if they are not necessarily having a generational midlife crisis, they are, in growing numbers, starting to think about the ways in which they could more closely align their values and aspirations with the emerging prospects for the second half of their lives.

Some of them will decide it's time to settle to the serious business of planning and saving for retirement. Others, with every prospect of earning good money well into their sixties, will embark on a fresh round of spending, especially on recreational and 'experiential' pursuits, and on items like sports cars or cosmetic surgery that might sustain the adolescent fantasy for a little longer: 'middlescents', some researchers have dubbed them.

Whichever way it goes—and this being Australia at the turn of the century, it will probably go every which way—any new wave of Boomer fashion will catch us all in its turbulence. The sheer size of their generation means that any resetting of Boomers' priorities, or any rethinking of Boomers' values, will have an impact on everything from health farms to the investment market.

The search for a religious substitute

The postwar baby-boom generation were peculiarly vulnerable to the blandishments of materialism. They grew up at a time when the promise of prosperity was central to the Australian culture; when the prospect of endless economic growth seemed attainable; when a healthy labour market and burgeoning middle-class suburbs became the symbols of a society which had driven out the devils of the Great Depression.

As the Boomers came to adulthood, the flowering of a heady consumerism coincided with a sharp decline in the practice of religion and in support for its associated moral codes. In the short term, Boomers committed themselves to a variety of alternative gratifications, almost as if they were creating substitutes for the religious observance of their parents' generation: sex, food, travel and 'personal growth' were all approached with religious fervour and invested with a kind of religious significance. Some tentative approaches were also made towards Eastern mysticism—though yoga generally turned out to be more appealing than fasting.

Now, in their middle years, many of those Boomers are discovering for themselves that materialism, even in its subtler disguises, leaves a black hole where they were hoping 'the meaning of life' might have appeared. Boomers are experiencing that classic midlife question—*Is this all there is?*—with the particular poignancy of a generation who thought this sort of stuff would never bother them. Having rejected, on a large scale, the spiritual framework of conventional religion and having typically opted for a morality based on the quest for personal freedom and fulfilment, they are peculiarly discomfited by the intimations of mortality.

In response, there's no sign that they are going back to church in large numbers, or seriously reconsidering mainstream Christianity. But that old Sixties pull of Eastern mysticism is still there. Buddhism has become positively chic as a focus of Boomer interest; if not as a fully committed religious pursuit then, at least, as a framework for meditation and other forms of stress reduction. Boomers routinely complain that stress has become the hallmark of their generation, that getting their stress under control would be the first crucial step towards regaining control of their lives, and that stress is their greatest health hazard.

For a generation famous for its combination of impatience and enthusiasm, it's a short step from meditation to medication. So the appeal of herbal and other alternative, especially Eastern, remedies has become an important new expression of the Boomers' yearning for peace and contentment *and* their desire to get their health under control. For a generation of action-orientated materialists who demand instant gratification, the popping of 'natural' pills seems like the perfect solution. Herbal healing nicely ties mysticism and health together. As one Boomer put it, in a 1992 study of the self-medication market: 'The thing about all these alternative forms of medicine is that you really have to believe in it, and that might be what does the trick.'

Ginkgo biloba, ginseng, echinacea—these are the new code words exchanged by the faithful. They signify an almost religious belief in the efficacy of 'natural' remedies that transcends the need for rational proof to which conventional medicine is subjected.

At the same time, Boomers are not about to abandon their hard-won scepticism entirely: they might be willing to light scented candles and explore the joys of everything from iridology to foot massage, but when it comes to serious illness, it's off to the doctor for the strongest possible antibiotic: 'I would think of a naturopath as keeping you healthy, whereas

I would think of a doctor as bailing you out when your little ship is sinking.'[1]

Hey! Remember those old 'family values'?

As part of the process of re-evaluating their journey through their middle years, many Boomers are also having another look at some of the values they associate with their parents' generation, values they were eager to jettison with the iconoclastic zeal that was characteristic of the Sixties.

This is partly because Boomers have shocked themselves by their own rate of marriage breakdown and family dislocation. They didn't expect to find themselves raising someone else's children, or raising their own second crop at an age when their friends are no longer thinking about night feeds, babysitters or school holiday arrangements.

Even if their marriages have run smoothly, they are disturbed by the level of drug abuse and the number of suicide attempts in their children's generation. Such ugly developments cannot be ignored, and many Boomers are being driven to accept that their own attempts at parenting have not always been as successful as they might have wished.

So there's a good deal of re-examination going on; a willingness, in particular, to reconsider some of those so-called 'family values' that were once rejected as old-fashioned: loyalty, discipline and mutual obligation. There is a new earnestness about the idea of personal responsibility. Boomers are particularly anxious to find ways of gaining a greater sense of control over their lives, and they acknowledge that this will involve some inner exploration.

But there is still a tendency to think that money can buy the solution: one of the reasons for affluent Boomers' growing enthusiasm for private schooling for their teenage children, for example, is that independent— especially church-based—schools are thought to emphasise such values. Boomer parents are prepared to pay high fees for a private school's help in 'catching up' with the moral education of their young (sometimes admitting that they are too busy or too tired to administer the consistent style of discipline they would wish to impose on their children).

That example of a gap between the ideal and the real is echoed in frequent Boomer talk about an aching disappointment at not having been able to adequately express, in the way they lead their lives, the values they say they believe in. The simplicity they crave seems to elude them. They want to slow down, but feel as if life is constantly getting faster: 'Why are we always in such a hurry?' Even their stated desire to teach their children to be less materialistic is often contradicted by the example of their own materialism.

Such talk might turn out to be nothing more than talk. But Baby Boomers are clearly giving serious consideration to their priorities and to exploring ways of realising their aspirations. Many Boomer fathers, for example, are becoming more active parents, sometimes because their wives have asked for more active parenting help to relieve their own heavy workload, but sometimes because the fathers themselves have realised what they've been missing.

Many Boomer mothers, similarly, are reassessing the practicalities of combining a full-time paid job with the responsibilities of being a mother: again, this is sometimes a spontaneous process, but it is sometimes in response to criticism from their own mothers and, indeed, their own daughters. (See Chapter 23.) There is by no means a stampede of working mothers out of the workforce, but there does appear to be a new willingness to explore alternative ways of combining motherhood with a career. (See Chapter 10.)

In all this re-evaluation, *time* is of the essence! Parents speak of their desire to 'enjoy the children while we have them'. Spouses speak of the need to take 'time out' to work on the repair and maintenance of their relationships. The problem of stress is generally interpreted as being really a problem of time.

Boomers regard themselves as having been idealistic teenagers and young adults, and they are keen to recapture some of their idealism before it's too late. The celebration of 'family values' is a particular focus of that desire.

'Will we start saving for retirement, or lash out and have fun?'

The greatest imponderable about the Boomers' journey through their fifties and on into retirement concerns their attitude to saving and spending. Phil Ruthven of the IBIS economic and demographic forecasting organisation has repeatedly described the baby-boom generation as our worst-ever savers, while being the wealthiest generation Australia has seen since the 1880s. They earn more and spend more than any other age-based demographic group this century, Ruthven says.[2]

But if they are such notoriously poor savers—and if there is no following generation, as large and affluent as they were, to fund their retirement through tax-based pensions—how will they cope when the time comes to withdraw from the workforce?

Will they rely on a share of the wealth coming to them and their siblings from their parents' estates (since their parents' generation have been assiduous home-owners)? Will they start setting aside money, via superannuation and other investment vehicles, to try and make up for lost time? Or will they breeze through their fifties with blithe disregard for the financial consequences of still more zealous spending?

Some of them, certainly, have recognised that they are appallingly ill-prepared for the retirement that is rushing towards them. Although the introduction of compulsory superannuation lulled them for a while, they have only to start doing their sums to realise that decisive action is called for if they are to arrive at retirement looking as if they always expected to get there.

A 1999 survey commissioned by Mastercard International found that 17 per cent of Australians had no retirement savings at all, and a further 24 per cent said that in addition to superannuation, they put aside $150 or less, each month, towards their retirement. Yet the same survey showed that people's estimates of the money they would need to fund their retirement called for far greater provision than this.[3]

Phil Ruthven asserts that for a person retiring in 2010 to sustain a retirement income of, say, $50 000, assets of over one million dollars (including a debt-free home) would be required.[4] Financial planner Kevin Bailey was quoted in the *Sunday Age* as saying that if a person retiring in 2010 wished to purchase an annuity that would yield an annual income of $41 500, this would involve an outlay of $487 000.[5]

Faced with figures such as these, some Baby Boomers are undoubtedly sitting up and taking notice: they have moved into *catch-up* mode and are exploring every possible avenue for enhancing their saving and investment arrangements. Superannuation and other funds management opportunities, investment properties, forays into the share market ... some Boomers are now as impatient to save as they once were to spend.

Some, but not all. Experts in the financial services market are waiting for the rush of Boomer investments ... and waiting, and waiting. They are now wondering whether the Boomers' famous reluctance to plan and save is as powerful as ever, and that their pre-retirement years will be characterised by as much spending—and borrowing—as before.

Phil Ruthven says that the rule of thumb for previous generations was to save about 15 per cent of annual income, but the Boomers have defied history by saving, on average, just 6 per cent of their annual income. As they age, their pattern of spending might change—with more emphasis on such things as guided adventure tours that express their fading faith in the joys of simply buying more stuff—but the level of spending shows no sign of letting up.

Writing in the *Bulletin*, Mark Abernethy noted that:

'Boomers still comprise one-fifth of the Australian market for denim jeans and, amazingly, they are the country's most numerous holders of motorcycle licences. For a generation that was supposed to be slowing down and handing over to the next mob, they are pulling on leathers and helmets at a time when their parents were reaching for cardies and slippers'.[6]

The same article reported a startling forecast from the University of Canberra's National Centre for Social and Economic Modelling: that the Baby Boomers will actually increase their spending on recreational goods and services as they get older to the point where they will actually outspend couples with children. The Centre's director, Professor Anne Harding, says that the phenomenon of empty-nest retirees spending as much on recreation as young families is an economic milestone in the making.

So what's new? Boomers have created an endless series of economic, social and cultural milestones. That has been the story of their lives.

If, when they finally run out of steam, they create the predicted crisis in healthcare funding, they will presumably expect someone else to pick up the tab—and they will be lobbying hard to ensure that government spending patterns change to match their changing needs. (Professor Harding predicts that universities will be one area where Boomers will be quite happy to see services cut back, since they will have no further use for them.)

The Boomers are the product of an extraordinary period in Australia's history: those unprecedented and probably unrepeatable years of the Fifties and Sixties. The marriage boom and the baby boom were themselves potent symbols of the optimism generated by the economic boom that followed the end of World War II. The children of that boom certainly learned how to spend: their tendency to keep doing it when all the evidence says they should start saving is just the latest sign that those formative years really *were* formative.

It's true that 'catch-up' means 'start saving' for some of them, but for most, apparently, it means 'we're here for a long time *and* a good time, after all ... so let's make up for lost time'. On the other hand, we should take nothing for granted: these are the Baby Boomers, after all, and they've surprised us before.

CHAPTER THREE

Control

Should We Lock Everyone Up
and Be Done With It?

Turning Point: This has been one of the most turbulent 25-year periods in our history. We're anxious, edgy and insecure, and looking for a way to regain our peace of mind. If we're not escaping into mind-altering drugs (legal or otherwise), we're increasingly concerned about finding ways to get our lives—or our pain, or our children—back under control. 'Getting back to basics' sounds like an attractive strategy but how basic, exactly, do we wish to get? The drugs laws, and their implementation, may be a crucial test of our ability to face unpalatable realities.

What are we hoping for? An antidote for our insecurity; a sense that order is being restored. (Some hope this will come about by 'getting tough'; others seek less draconian strategies.)

'I couldn't live without my Palmolive Antibacterial,' said a woman taking part in a 1998 social research project.

You might imagine that when it comes to things you feel you couldn't live without, a handwashing detergent would not rate as highly as, say, your partner, your religious faith, or your regular round of golf. But there it was: she said she couldn't live without her Palmolive Antibacterial.

She could, of course. But hyperbole has its place, and people do tend to use rather colourful language when they talk about their favourite brands, so we know what she meant. But that is still a pretty extreme statement and, like most extreme statements, it tells us something significant, even if the message isn't quite what the words themselves seem to be saying. The rush to embrace antibacterial products is just another sign of the fact that we are alert, almost to the point of neurosis, to anything that might offer a cure for our feelings of edginess, anxiety and insecurity.

It's almost as if the anxiety were there first ... and then we started looking for something to pin it on.

In this case, the 'something' was the prospect of killing germs. The woman went on to say that she had read a news report about a study that showed the average domestic kitchen was a haven for bacteria of every imaginable kind. Forget the hazards of going to hospital: to hear this lady tell it, golden staph, or worse, was stalking her swampy sink, ready to pounce on her innocent children.

So she reached for her Palmolive Antibacterial with a sense of relief and gratitude. There was nothing, presumably, she felt she could do about the killing in Kosovo or the fragility of the Japanese economy, but germs in her own kitchen were definitely something she ought to be able to control.

Control. That's become the holy grail of the late Nineties simply because so many of us feel that life has raced beyond our control.

In a 1997 journalistic *tour de force*, 'Deconstructing the Decade', Dierdre Macken put it like this:

Control. Most of the time it was in someone else's hands and we were out of it. But we sought it everywhere. In social constraints, in pain relief, in our quest to know all about our bodies, from the genome to the epidermis ... Often it was only our belly button we truly controlled.

So we pierced it. Along with noses, lips, eyebrows, nipples and—gulp—elsewhere. Body piercing: the ultimate sign of control. If you could no longer define yourself by your job, home, garden or suburb, you defined yourself with your body. Pierce it, paint it, tuck it up, suck it out and sculpt it.[1]

Macken also noted the 'undercurrent of fear that makes us see muggers in every lane, bludgers in every social welfare queue, depression in every setback and lies, damned lies, in every political statement'.

So we welcome everything from surveillance cameras on our city streets to the proliferation of security guards in shopping centres—and the addition of ingredients in our dishwashing liquids that are lethal to bugs. (Wasn't hygiene itself supposed to keep germs at bay? Have we been wasting our time washing with ordinary soaps and detergents? Should we immerse ourselves regularly in Dettol?)

It's easy to giggle at such insecurity. I was once caricatured in The Sydney Institute's *Quarterly* as a person whose social analysis is so shallow that he offers 'insecurity' as an explanation for everything. Not guilty, Your Honour, but it's rather hard to ignore its role in our present malaise. It's true that insecurity sometimes manifests itself in weird ways. I once saw some unpublished research that suggested about 25 per cent of Australians believed their phones had been tapped at some stage. What had they been saying, I wondered, that caused them to imagine they might attract the attention of the police or ASIO?

You could argue that Australians, at the turn of the century, should be feeling reasonably relaxed and comfortable—the very state John Howard had in mind for us when he was campaigning to become Prime Minister in 1996. After all, we are not at war, most of the economic signs are looking rosy, and as long as you live in one of the 70 per cent of households perched safely above the poverty line, you might be getting on reasonably well. If you're at the top of the economic heap, you probably can't believe the level of prosperity you're now enjoying. Even if you're at the bottom, you might be able to afford to buy the occasional bottle of Coca-Cola (still our top-selling grocery item, by the way).

But when you realise that we are setting new records for the consumption of tranquillisers and anti-depressants, and that more Australians commit suicide than die on our roads, you might want to accept the possibility that something is amiss. The ravages of relentless change, cultural and economic, are taking their toll. (If you believe the evolutionary psychologists, those changes have been destabilising us for the past 200 years, not just the last 20 or 30. We simply haven't yet had time to adapt properly to life in a post-industrial revolution society.)

Learning to live with uncertainty

Uncertainty is, in fact, a perfectly sensible response to an unstable world. If our experience is teaching us to view society in a new way—less rigid, less black-and-white—then, as part of that process, we shall have to start thinking of our feelings of uncertainty in a new way. Instead of resisting them as inappropriate or unwelcome, we may have to try to incorporate them into our view of what life is really like. (When did life ever offer these mythical black-and-white certainties, anyway?)

The problem seems to be that in our present circumstances, uncertainty has become an integral part of *everything*: where once people could rely, at least, on the stability of their marriages, or the predictability of their employment, or the comfort of an unchallenged religious faith as a bulwark against the ravages of disease, war or any of the other contingencies of life, the new order seems to offer none of that security. This is a world in which we can't take anything for granted. Even the theologians are in wild disagreement about some of the tenets of the Christian faith, like the resurrection of Jesus, and the days of security of tenure in any job are virtually over. It really is the Age of Uncertainty, the Age of Unknowing.

The question is, how should we handle it? How should we absorb it into our world view? How should we build it into our expectations of the future? How should we prepare for this next wave of uncertainty?

Perhaps there's a prior question: how do we, in practice, handle it? Looking around, it seems that some of our strategies turn out to add to our insecurity, rather than allaying it. Witness the mobile phone craze.

Ring me! Tell me where you are! Ask me where I am! Stay in touch! 'Relieve my existential angst by endless dialogue,' we seem to be saying, but, by staying plugged in, we create the additional stress of being on continuous call (and—horrors!—exposing ourselves to the possibility that no-one actually called).

Here's another popular, but disturbingly ambiguous, cry: 'Back to basics!' That sounds like a clear call to restore some fading values, or to re-habilitate some neglected aspects of the Australian way of life. The trouble is that it can mean anything from putting more effort into the teaching of literacy, to encouraging young people to embrace the ideal of premarital chastity, and one person's 'basics' is another person's repression. Nevertheless, the back-to-basics movement has borne fruit in fields as disparate as economic rationalism and religious fundamentalism.

But our favourite strategy is simply to blame our edginess on the alleged 'breakdown of society': this has become such a commonplace diagnosis that it is rarely questioned. (See Chapter 21.) The rising divorce rate, excessive permissiveness in the raising of children, rampant materialism, less emphasis on the value of the traditional family unit, or even the appearance of graffiti on a suburban shopfront can be cited either as a cause or an effect of the breakdown of society. (Society is changing, certainly, but there's no evidence, yet, that we've actually destroyed its fabric. Nor is there any evidence that society has 'broken down' to anything like the extent it did in the 1890s, for instance.)

Once you adopt the 'breakdown' position, it's a short step to feeling that, among all the issues that concern us most, law-and-order is the big one.

The 1999 state election campaign in New South Wales was a graphic example of politicians' willingness to exploit voters' vulnerability on this very point. In spite of declarations by the leaders of both major parties that they wouldn't become involved in a bidding war, the prospect of tapping into the fears of an already nervous electorate was an irresistible temptation. The recruitment and disposition of new police became a major point of campaign debate (and the capacity of police training establishments to handle this promised influx of cops became a matter of controversy).

Hugh Mackay

On the Coalition's side, law-and-order proposals grew increasingly shrill as the prospect of electoral victory dimmed: one thing that finally soured many voters was the prospect of juvenile offenders having to wear distinctive clothing (fluorescent jackets, branded with the words 'Community Services') as they went about the business of removing graffiti from public buildings. Television commercials and public statements in support of this proposal suggested that young vandals might be suitably humiliated and that, if they were made to feel more responsible for their actions, this would stop them 'spiralling into a life of crime'.

Federally, John Howard has been intent on following up his popular 1996 gun-law legislation—the initiative that has drawn more praise than any other of his Prime Ministership—with a similarly tough stance on drugs, especially the heroin trade. While the New South Wales Director of Public Prosecutions, Nicholas Cowdery QC, was advocating the licensing of dealers and much tighter regulation of the illicit drug trade (treating addicts, for instance, as a medical rather than a criminal problem, and supplying certain drugs via prescription rather than on the street), the PM was squaring his shoulders and signalling an iron-fisted—some experts in the field thought ham-fisted—approach that appealed, especially, to frightened parents. It also reinforced the public perception that all our anxieties about drug-related crime are justified.

In an address to NSW Young Lawyers in February 1999, Cowdery gave an intelligent assessment of the true law-and-order situation, ranging over the subject of crime rates, the philosophy of zero-tolerance policing, the proposal for mandatory sentences, the futility of capital punishment as a deterrent, among others. His conclusions were clear, careful, but, unfortunately for him, out of tune with the prevailing mood of a worried public and a conservative political climate.

Cowdery's position was unambiguous, and it was based on rock solid research by Dr Don Weatherburn, the director of the NSW Bureau of Crime Statistics and Research (though the Australian Institute of Criminology, working from different data, has a somewhat less reassuring view). This is what Nicholas Cowdery said: 'Crime rates are not up, courts are not too lenient and tougher penalties will not reduce crime.'

But try telling all that to the people who are installing electronic security systems in their modest homes in quiet suburban streets, as if their lives, literally, depended on it. Try telling it to people who are putting bars over all their windows and who are afraid to go out alone at night. And try telling it to politicians who know that, whatever the facts of the case, a nervous electorate is bound to approve of tougher measures of every kind, *whether they can be shown to work or not.*

In May 1999, the Sydney radio broadcaster and newspaper columnist Mike Carlton reported receiving the largest pile of mail he had ever received on any subject. It arrived in response to a column he had written in *The Sydney Morning Herald* in which he berated a New South Wales judge for having aborted the trial of Leslie Camilleri because a comment made by a state politician was thought by the judge to have prejudiced Camilleri's chance of a fair trial. While Camilleri was free in the community awaiting the reconvening of his trial, he raped and master-minded the murder of two teenage girls. The sheer volume of Carlton's mail—overwhelmingly supportive of his criticism of the judge—was another telling sign of the community's edginess. This is a community that, alarmed by its own level of insecurity, wants things back under control, even if it means tightening the screws on some of our previously cherished freedoms and abandoning some of the most hallowed legal conventions (like the one under which the judge in question aborted Camilleri's trial).

This is actually quite a hard time to be a responsible and moderate leader in any field—the law, religion, business ... and especially politics. (See Chapter 12.) An insecure community is not only more volatile than usual, but it also puts pressure on leaders to act tough and to sound as if they have solutions to all our problems, even if no solutions exist or the possibilities are nuanced by complexity and contradiction. In this kind of climate, there's no room for subtlety, and any sign of 'weakness'—like a willingness to consider all sides of an issue—is political death.

So let's get things back under control! Zero tolerance! (Hey, that sounds great, but what does it mean?) Tougher sentences! More prisons! More cops on the beat! More guns! More handcuffs! Curfews for teen-agers! Confiscate the licences of drivers over 70! (Why stop there? Confiscate their cars!) Bring back the lash, the stocks, the gallows!

There ... aren't you feeling better already? Just one more thing: maybe we should issue the police with antibacterial spray as well.

How far do we really want to go?

(Are illicit drugs the test case?)

Nowhere has the talk of zero tolerance been louder than in relation to the grimy area of drug abuse and the illicit drug trade. When people not directly involved in the tragedy of drug abuse try to make sense of it, and try to reach a reasonable conclusion about the best way to solve a problem we all want to solve (except, of course, the dealers), they find themselves confronted by a cacophony of competing and often contradictory voices.

Parents and other relatives of addicts, counsellors, medical experts in the fields of addiction and rehabilitation, lawyers, police ... the range of experts is impressive, and the fury of their disagreement with each other is bewildering.

On the one hand are those who advocate harm minimisation: safe injecting rooms to help protect addicts against the risk of overdose, needle exchange programs to discourage needle-sharing, controlled methadone administration to 'unhook' addicts from their illegal heroin supply, and trials of legally prescribed heroin. That group includes some parents of addicts, doctors, and frontline drug workers who believe that if addicts can be monitored, supported, and kept alive through the most dangerous phase of their addiction, they will eventually become candidates for constructive rehabilitation.

One of the most outspoken advocates of the harm-minimisation approach is Dr Alex Wodak of St Vincent's Hospital in Sydney, the man credited with having alerted the community to the need for a needle-exchange program to combat the spread of AIDS (a program which has contributed to Australia's remarkably low rate of HIV among drug users).

But there is a strong coalition of people utterly opposed to the proposition that addicts should be supported en route to rehabilitation. In an article in *The Sydney Morning Herald*, Deborah Snow identified organisations with names like Drug Watch Australia and Keep Our Kids Alive as being prominent in this coalition, along with rock music legend Normie Rowe, and Angela Wood, whose daughter, Anna, died in 1995 after taking a single ecstasy tablet in circumstances that attracted national publicity.

Describing their common ground as being their support for the Prime Minister's 'zero-tolerance' approach, Deborah Snow wrote:

> They want money spent on community and school education, on treatment, on cracking down hard on drugs supply. Their catchcry is 'prevention', not tolerance. Politically, they tend towards conservatism. For them, safe injecting rooms are anathema, sending the wrong signals to their children and marking the first step along a road they believe will lead to legalisation.'[2]

In the same article, Snow quoted 'an exasperated health professional' as saying that people who have suffered as parents of drug victims are 'experts on suffering', but that doesn't make them experts on drug use.

Tony Trimingham, the father of a heroin addict who died at 23, has been a leading voice on the harm-minimisation side of this remarkably bitter conflict. Deborah Snow quotes Trimingham: 'Just because we favour safe injecting rooms and heroin trials doesn't mean we are not also in favour of education, rehabilitation, and prevention.' That view is echoed by Craig Patterson of the Royal Australasian College of Physicians: 'We've got to look at what works and what doesn't. We should be looking at things like heroin trials as a research issue, not a moral issue.'

Unfortunately, such apparently reasonable statements don't appear to cut much ice at a time when so many people are troubled by their generalised sense of uncertainty and, correspondingly, their yearning for a greater sense of control. When the experts can't agree, many lay people will respond to their own feelings of anguish about such matters by simply going with the hardliners. 'Zero tolerance' sounds like an appealing strategy, especially when it is supported by so many political leaders, from both sides of politics.

But not everyone is convinced that this is the moment to get tough.

Hugh Mackay

The drug trade has been one of the significant catalysts for a new open-mindedness among people who are beginning to think that, in the drug scene as elsewhere, 'nothing is simple any more'. Even for people with no personal links to the drug problem, such violent disagreements among the experts are themselves a warning sign: if the people close to the problem aren't coming up with consistent answers—here, and around the world—then the rest of us would be wise to suspend judgment.

In any case, as 22-year-old non-user, Bryony Jackson, said in an interview for *Time* magazine: 'To deal with this we have to look at why people want to escape society, why they want to be numb.'[3]

Why would we want to create

our very own Al Capone?

What are we to make of these earnest proposals for a zero-tolerance approach to the illicit drug trade? Are we really so eager to forget history that we can't recall the lessons of the infamous Prohibition era in America?

The drug in question then was alcohol. Today, alcohol is almost universally regarded as being so dangerous as to require careful regulation of its manufacture, distribution and purchase. It is recognised as being, among a number of other more pleasant things, a potentially lethal and socially destructive drug, responsible for deaths and injuries on the roads, in workplaces, at the beach and at home.

If you doubt the potency of alcohol, just ask wives battered by drunken husbands, or children neglected by drunken mothers, or parents shocked into despair by the effect of alcohol abuse on their adolescent offspring. It's such a dangerous drug that we wouldn't dream—would we?—of driving its manufacture and distribution underground where it would be controlled by racketeers, preying on those who wish to enjoy its positive effects.

We wouldn't be prepared to tolerate a situation—would we?—where Australia actively promoted crime and corruption in the cause of getting tough on alcohol. We wouldn't want to institute policies whose implementation was bound to swell the coffers of drug czars ... would we?

In the same vein, we haven't wanted to abandon gambling to the control of criminals, so we've legalised and regulated that, too.

There's a pattern here. In our society, we generally take a regulatory approach to inherently dangerous practices—like driving cars and owning guns—and dangerous substances—like Prozac and morphine. We protect ourselves by controlling people's exposure to these things, and we know that prohibition would only unleash the evil influence of illicit operators.

In the case of alcohol and tobacco, we actively discourage young people from consumption; we warn everyone about the health hazards involved; we restrict the advertising of such products; we offer counselling and other forms of treatment for those who, in spite of the care we've taken, have found themselves in the grip of a harmful addiction.

So why do we approach the problem of heroin—or cocaine, or even marijuana—any differently?

Does anyone, from the Prime Minister down, seriously believe that the so-called war on drugs can be won by prohibition, by policing, or even by public education? Drug education is obviously an urgent priority, but sex education doesn't prevent venereal disease or unwanted pregnancies, and anti-tobacco propaganda hasn't prevented the rate of teenage smoking from increasing through the Nineties, especially among girls. Education is necessary, but not sufficient (just as rehabilitation is necessary, but not sufficient; even safe injecting rooms are necessary, but not sufficient).

Does anyone believe that, in the long term, people will simply turn their backs on these exciting mind-altering substances (and others yet unheard of), when the inescapable lesson of human history is that some people, willingly and knowingly, will always wish to use them?

The reasons why people decide to experiment with drugs of any kind are as diverse as you can imagine. The list might include bravado, curiosity, peer-group pressure, the desire to attract attention, the wish to escape into a hazy world of unreality that's more tolerable than an ugly or hopeless reality, the belief that some drug-induced states stimulate heightened perception or enhanced creativity. Or it might just seem cool.

You can argue that it's irrational, absurd, dangerous and debilitating, to say nothing of potentially lethal. And it is all of those things. But what will saying any of that achieve? At least in the beginning, people take drugs because they want to. Later, they might become habitual users because they enjoy the effects or because they are helplessly addicted.

So which would you prefer: a policy that actively promotes corruption and sleazy profiteering from an illegal drug trade, or one that brings the whole process under legal and medical control? Would you prefer a policy that places young Australians at physical and financial risk, or one that combines education, counselling and rehabilitation with fully regulated and monitored manufacture, distribution and consumption?

It seems almost inevitable that, one day, we'll have government-licensed drug clinics dispensing the stuff. Like most Australians, I don't like that idea any more than I like legalised prostitution, but I prefer it to a policy that is virtually guaranteed to create our very own Al Capone.

No-one likes to predict that illicit drug use will increase in Australia, yet that seems to be the inescapable implication of present trends. Already, 46 per cent of Australians over the age of 14 have used illicit drugs, the overwhelming majority of those having used cannabis. (The rate of cannabis usage among males aged 20–29 is 44 per cent, and usage is said to be skyrocketing among teenage girls.) About two per cent of the over-14 population have used heroin.[4] Back in 1967, the Reverend Ted Noffs of Sydney's Wayside Chapel was warning us that there were drug users in 60 per cent of Australian schools, so this is hardly a sudden issue.[5]

If we can't prevent this unwanted wave from dumping us—and killing too many of our young people—then we shall have to work out a way of harnessing it, riding it safely, or controlling it in some other way.

The American example from the Prohibition era—and, indeed, from its more recent attempts to control the illicit drug trade—doesn't seem all that attractive.

We are approaching a critical turning point. The NSW Drugs Summit, held at Parliament House in May 1999, decided that safe injecting rooms should be established, on a trial basis, in spite of previous strenuous objections to such a room having been established by the Uniting Church's Wayside Chapel at King's Cross. A more tolerant attitude towards cannabis use was also recommended. At the conclusion of the Summit, the New South Wales Premier, Bob Carr, offered this remarkably compassionate assessment of the drug problem: 'Life is an inherently disappointing experience for most human beings. Some people can't cope with that.' He went on to declare his support for a harm-minimisation position based on policies that will 'ease people through a period of maximum risk'.

Sooner or later, we will be forced to heed the advice of Nicholas Cowdery and others who are advocating full legalisation and full control of the drug trade. Kids will still die, addicts will still suffer, mistakes will still be made. But at least the power of that menacing wave will have been brought under control.

When that happens, it will be an important step towards recognising that, whether the problem is drugs or anything else, 'control' doesn't always mean prohibition. The only morally defensible position in a pluralistic, postmodern world is the position where we agree to respond to people's need for help, even when we strongly disapprove of the activities that got them into trouble in the first place.

CHAPTER FOUR

Diversity

Hands Up, All Those 'Typical' Australians

Turning Point: Our quest for a clearer sense of national identity might be premature and misguided. If you had to settle for one word to describe contemporary Australia, it would have to be 'diverse', but when was that not true? The nature of our diversity may have changed—less religious, more generational, for example; less overtly class-based, more ethnic—but this has always been a hybrid culture and the idea of a once-homogeneous Australia, based on the ethos of the bush, is largely a myth. If we are to ride the wave of increasing diversity, we'll have to accept that we are a relatively young, still-evolving culture: our true identity is yet to emerge. For the time being, talk of the 'mainstream' misses the point. (We're still not entirely comfortable with the theory of multiculturalism, though.)

What are we hoping for? A cosmopolitan society in which we can celebrate our diversity as part of our emerging Australian identity; in which ethnic groups continue to enrich our culture without involving us in ancient and bitter hatreds. A heterogeneous society where people from every ethnic and cultural background regard themselves primarily as 'Australian'.

Whether we like it or not, we're a tribal lot—and that's because we're human. From the moment we step into the school playground, our nature is to align ourselves with some people and distance ourselves from others; to form cliques; to define our personal identity in terms of our affinity with in-groups and our antipathy or indifference towards out-groups.

For all our perfectly sincere proclamations of support for the notion of diversity, our commitment to tolerance, and our endorsement of that awkwardly-named creature, 'multiculturalism', we continue to nurture our secret prejudices. Absolute impartiality towards every kind and condition of person, though vaunted as an ideal, seems to be reserved for saints.

'Your feet are dirtier than mine,' runs the joke about two Aussies standing barefoot at a bar. 'So they should be,' comes the reply, 'I'm older than you.' We laugh at Irish jokes, Polish jokes, even anti-Australian jokes, not usually because of virulent or unkind racism but because we recognise in such jokes the truth about our tribal natures.

The humour of racist jokes taps into our embarrassment about our ready acceptance of ethnic stereotypes. Scots are mean. Jews are devious. Germans are relentlessly thorough. Swiss are coldly efficient. French are romantic. Italians are impulsive. Americans are brash. Australians are easy-going to the point of sloth. Poms whinge. There's a shorthand prejudice for every ethnic group on earth.

But not only ethnic groups. String players exchange tasteless jokes about brass players (especially tuba players: 'What's the difference between a pizza and a tuba player?' 'A pizza can feed a family of four'). Football forwards tell jokes about backs; batsmen about bowlers; economists about accountants (and vice versa: 'What's an economist?' 'Someone who didn't have the personality to become an auditor').

People who can't afford Porsches make jokes about their drivers, and everyone makes jokes about old Volvos. Catholics make jokes about Protestants, Protestants about each other's denominations, and everyone makes jokes about the Pope.

We can't seem to avoid making the assumption that people who are socially, culturally, sexually, politically, aesthetically, intellectually, theologically or ethnically different from us are … not inferior, of course (we're too sophisticated to fall for that one), but somehow *other*. We know they will never understand the nuances, the codes, the secret signs that bind us to those with whom we feel a sense of tribal connection, and we rather enjoy that sense of otherness.

When it comes to cultural and ethnic differences, we tend to refer to those others as 'them', with a satisfying implication that they are not 'us'. We praise, very faintly, their distinctive 'contribution' or if we're really stuck for something nice to say about them, we simply acknowledge their right to exist—to live as they wish, to say what they like, to dress as they please—because one of the virtues of *our* tribe is that we're generous enough to recognise that this is a pluralistic society.

Above all, we love to identify people as belonging to 'minorities', because that gives substance to the huge and disabling myth, beckoning us like a mirage, that we ourselves are, by contrast, part of something strong and safe called the 'mainstream'; or we're 'true-blue'; or if our strength is not in numbers but in our sense of power or superiority, we might be pleased to regard our tribe as 'the establishment' or 'the A list'.

How homogeneous was our famous

'British stock'?

Back in 1936, there was a public outcry when it was revealed in the Federal parliament that the number of Australian residents coming from British stock had fallen below the previously sacrosanct minimum of 98 per cent. In his new history of Australia, *Claiming a Continent*, David Day reports that, 'To the anger of MPs and the shock of the press, the figure had dropped to just 97 per cent'.[1]

We have a long history of being obsessed with the idea of creating and preserving a mainstream culture, with implications of homogeneity. But it has always been a ridiculous goal, and the claim that we ever achieved it is equally ridiculous.

One of the most enduring fantasies about Australia's history is that when European settlers arrived here in 1778, they imported *a* culture which came into conflict with *the* Aboriginal culture already established here. But it was never that simple, never that neat.

For a start, about 250 recognisably separate Aboriginal nations co-existed here before any Europeans arrived. And among the new settlers, the cultural differences between, say, an Irish Catholic, an English Benthamite, a Scottish Calvanist and a libertine from anywhere were at least as significant as those between a convict and a soldier, or, indeed, a private soldier and an officer.

It's true that those original settlers, and most of our forebears, came from British stock, but can you imagine anywhere with a greater array of subcultures than the United Kingdom? The dialects of England, alone, mean that some regional groups can barely understand each other, and the cultural chasm between a Cornish fisherman and a London banker can scarcely be bridged. The ancient rivalry between the Celts and the English has found its latest expression in the new Scottish and Welsh parliaments, and the cultural gap between Scotland's two greatest cities, Edinburgh and Glasgow, makes Sydney and Melbourne look like best friends. ('Edinburgh folk think we're so dirty,' runs the old Glaswegian joke, 'they complain you cannae pee in the sink for dishes.') Whether they like to use the word or not, the UK has always been about as multicultural as you can get—in terms of class, culture *and* ethnicity—even before the influx of West Indians and Pakistanis in the Seventies.

Since the establishment of our various colonies (and let's not lump them together: imagine how culturally different Adelaide must have been from the convict settlements), we have continually added new chips to the mosaic of our cultural identity. We invented a funny kind of landed aristocracy who, on the British model, were encouraged to take themselves seriously for two or three generations. We created a vast and prosperous middle class, symbolising our faith in egalitarianism, and then, by our failure to anticipate the impact of economic restructuring, we let an inequitable redistribution of work fracture it.

Meanwhile, we kept persuading more and more people to come here

Hugh Mackay

and help us build this essentially hybrid thing called 'Australia'. And come they did, from about 200 different nations at last count.

We're still bothered by the m-word

To suggest that multiculturalism is somehow strange and new is to overlook an entire history. Certainly, our official policy towards immigrants was, until the 1970s, assimilation: that's why we coined the term 'New Australian'. But that didn't stop the Chinese or the Italians or the Greeks or the Yugoslavs from looking and sounding different from the 'Anglos' for a while. It didn't stop them from dreaming of home, or from wanting their children to understand their ethnic origins (just as the children of British parents or grandparents were taught theirs).

Neither, by the way, has the more recent official policy of multi-culturalism prevented many immigrants from eagerly encouraging their children to integrate themselves into Australian society while still acknowledging their proud ethnic heritage.

How the children themselves handle it varies from case to case. Some can't wait to blend into the local culture; some lead double lives—fiercely Greek at home, for instance, and 'wog-baiting Aussie' with their friends; others amaze their parents by taking on an assertively ethnic persona:

I have tried to bring my daughter up as if she is an Australian. She knows I came from Yugoslavia, but I have tried to put all that behind me. I'm not having much luck with her: she is telling everyone she is a Serb.

My daughter seems intent on being Italian. I say to her, 'you not Italian ... you Australian'. But she's determined to be Italian. If she knew what she had left behind, she would not be so keen ...

I tried to make myself Australian, and I tried to make my children Australian. I never taught them anything but English, and now they can't talk to their grandmother on the phone. I dressed like an

Australian, I ate like an Australian, I even went to an Anglican church instead of Orthodox. But in one way I will never be Australian. When I see people in the street, I say hello to them. Australians don't do that.

Although Australians are overwhelmingly in favour of the multicultural ideal—Newspoll research showed that more than 70 per cent of us supported multiculturalism even at the height of Pauline Hanson's popularity—it is true that there are still many misgivings about it.

It's a dreadful word, of course. It sounds dreary and contrived, as if you might have to fill out a form to qualify. It's a word that makes many Australians uneasy because it suggests something potentially divisive has been done to us—a 'policy'—rather than something we might have achieved, through cultural evolution, all by ourselves.

Say 'multiculturalism', and some Australians will think of the potential for certain suburbs in major cities to become ethnic enclaves or even 'ghettos'. Others will express resentment about the reluctance of some immigrants to learn to speak English. The threat to our sense of national identity, or our 'shared values', will trouble others. Some, even including people with no religious convictions of their own, will mutter about the strange religious beliefs and practices of Muslims. Some will complain about shop signs appearing in foreign languages without the English equivalent. And the ultimate threat: 'being made to feel like a minority in our own country', as though the host community might be suffering some kind of reverse discrimination in its desire to be hospitable and accommodating to newcomers. 'We have to fit in with them; they don't have to fit in with us,' said one respondent in a 1995 study of attitudes to multiculturalism—clearly a person who had never experienced the trauma of trying to adapt to life in a new country.

The following exchange between two participants in the 1995 study sums up the dilemma that many Australians experience:

Probably the worst thing about multiculturalism is that Australia doesn't have its own identity. There are too many cultures here, so it's a bit of everything ... But how can we be anything but multicultural when we live in a relatively young country? Nothing's really Australian because two or three generations ago, someone had to come from overseas. You're only Australian because you live here: your background is from overseas.[2]

But say 'cosmopolitan' instead of 'multicultural' and watch the mood change! We like the ring of that: it emphasises the strengths, rather than the threats, that ethnic diversity brings. The question of assimilation virtually evaporates when Australians talk about the richness of their ethnic diversity. Yes, many of them still focus more on the food than the people, but the idea has taken root that Australia is an example to the world of how to build a harmonious society out of a diverse array of immigrants from everywhere.

The primacy of the British tradition is taken for granted: in our language, our legal system, our parliaments. And in spite of the misgivings of some members of the host community, immigrants themselves typically talk of their desire to be part of Australia—not separate from it—and their intention that their children should become unambiguously 'Australian'. That doesn't deny their ethnic heritage, nor their wish to perpetuate their own cultural traditions as well.

As the Prime Minister, John Howard, put it in a speech to launch his new National Multicultural Advisory Board:

We respect and understand the fact that if you were born in another country, you retain a special place in your heart for that country, and there is nothing, in my view, that diminishes the wholeness of the Australian nation in that being fully recognised.[3]

Ethnicity is only part of the story of our diversity

The word 'diversity' has become almost exclusively linked to ethnicity. Perhaps that's inevitable: we recognise, without really thinking about it, that if you grow up in a different culture, your attitudes, values and outlook on life are bound to be different. (You can hardly ignore our ethnic diversity if you live in a city like Sydney, where 25 per cent of the population speak a language other than English at home, 30 per cent of the population were born overseas, and one of the most common names in the phone book is Nguyen, right up there with Jones.)

But, given the breathtaking social changes of the 20th century, what about the cultural gaps between different generations of Australians who were born right here? Imagine the attitudes and values formed by a childhood spent in the Great Depression, compared with those formed by the experience of growing up during the postwar years of economic boom, or the turbulence of the present Age of Discontinuity. Which of those is 'mainstream'? Which is the 'true' Australian experience?

And what about the increasing diversity of life choices and lifestyles? In strictly statistical terms, you could talk about 'average' families and 'typical' households; you could define majority behaviour as mainstream. But what would that mean? More importantly, what diversity would it conceal?

Take the changing pattern of marriage and divorce. We could say, right now, that most Australians marry once and stay married, and that would be literally true ... but only just. As we surge towards the third millennium, that majority is shrinking and will soon be overwhelmed by the combination of those who will choose either never to marry, or to marry two or more times. (See Chapter 13.)

Or we could say that mainstream children—what a curiously flat concept that sounds—live with both their parents and that, too, would be statistically true. But the one million children who live with only one parent represent such a huge minority that it is simply silly to exclude them from any description of what is typical.

Similarly, it's true that most Australian babies are born to married parents, but almost 30 per cent are not, and that proportion is rising.

We're a middle-class society: how's that for a safe generalisation? Not bad, when you consider that the vast majority of us *think* of ourselves as middle class. But what will we say about the 30 per cent of Australian households with a combined household income of less than $20 000 per annum? Or the 32 per cent of adults who are now primarily dependent on welfare payments for their income?

Class is a more complex matter than income, of course, but what seeds of class diversity—old-fashioned class distinction—are being sown by the present inequitable distribution of household income through the inequitable distribution of wages and salaries? One reason for that inequity is that our patterns of work are rapidly becoming more diverse. Twenty-five per cent of the workforce have part-time work, and well over a million Australians either have no work at all or much less than they want. Meanwhile, full-time workers are so stretched that their overtime alone, mostly unpaid, is estimated to absorb about another half-million full-time jobs. (See Chapter 5.)

So, which is the 'typical' worker?

When the *Australian*'s social affairs writer, Michelle Gunn, analysed the ABS's latest series of social atlases, tracing the demographic patterns within and between our major cities, she came to this conclusion:

> On either side of the Great Divide, Australia's cities are becoming more diverse, and the myth of a nation of equality is being challenged ... suburbs [are] becoming increasingly divided along ethnic, socio-demographic and generational lines ... the 1996 maps show great concentrations of affluence and of poverty and disadvantage.[4]

Gunn quoted Professor Bob Stimson of the University of Queensland:

> You have much higher concentration of low incomes in the outer regions now. There is just no way that someone who is an unskilled person, making beds in a hotel or working as a doorman, could afford to purchase a house anywhere else.

In other words, economic diversity is reshaping the character of our cities and towns, more starkly than ever. There are already six or seven different 'Sydneys', and they are increasingly alienated from each other.

If you're still grasping for evidence of homogeneity, try convincing yourself that we're a Christian country. It's true that 69 per cent of us describe ourselves as 'Christian' on a census form, though fewer than 20 per cent attend church regularly. The fastest growing religion in Australia is actually Buddhism, and we now have more than twice as many Muslims as Jews.

Thanks for nothing, Banjo

Our belief in a distinctive, homogeneous set of Australian characteristics—an essential Australianness—is sustained by the rural myth. This is the idea, popularised by the stories of Henry Lawson and the poems of Banjo Patterson, that the 'real' Australian has always been found in the bush, the outback, where values are more clear-cut and more enduring, where there is a discernible 'Australian way of life', and where the chaos and fragmentation of city life has largely been averted.

We've never, in fact, been the predominantly rural society that the myth assumes. And if it were once true that rural Australians had a more stable and distinctive ethos than urban Australians—more prepared to help their neighbours; willing to share useful new information—even that is becoming less true. Divorce, suicide, drugs—to say nothing of poverty and the forced sale of family businesses—take their toll more heavily in the country than the city. (Even the idea that life is healthier in the bush seems to be challenged by the higher-than-average incidence of heart disease and respiratory disorders in many parts of regional Australia.)

It's possible to see the rural myth as essentially harmless and rather romantic but, in fact, for a society which is as urbanised as ours, our determination to cling to the rural myth weakens us in two important ways.

First, we don't adapt—emotionally—to the way life really is in the city: by clinging to the rural myth, we increase our sense of restlessness and dissatisfaction with the reality of urban living and we don't cope with it as well as we might if we embraced it more realistically as a legitimately Australian way of life.

Second, we find it difficult to face the bleak truth about rural Australia and its problems. We prefer the myth of the bush pioneer: the flinty, resourceful, sardonic, laconic stockman who can cope with anything. The more we embrace the romance of the outback, the more we are blinded to the harsh realities of life in the bush, and to the special needs of rural communities.

But as long as the myth persists, it fuels the mistaken idea that there is a 'typical' Australian to be found west of the Great Dividing Range. In his runaway bestseller, *Among the Barbarians*, Paul Sheehan reinforces the idea that 'the people of the bush [are] closest to the ethos on which Australian culture and mythology was built ...'[5] He is right about the mythology, but not about the culture: our culture has always been more urban, and more diverse, than the rural myth admits.

A personal reflection: diversity, even in the suburbs of the Forties

There we sat in our primary school classroom, circa 1948, in the days when Australia was supposed to be so much more culturally homogeneous than it is today.

If you'd looked at our sexually segregated socialising at lunchtime, carefully keeping to the correct side of an imaginary line drawn down the middle of the playground (perhaps *that's* where we learned to keep the sexes apart at parties), or inspected our handwriting, or watched us marching into school to the beat of the school band, you might have been tempted to think we were little conformists, part of that great Australian 'mainstream' eulogised by those now in the grip of a fevered nostalgia.

But when we visited each other's homes, we couldn't help noticing how different other people's lives were from our own. We were friends at school, but strangers to each other's private lives. Some families' meals began with the saying of grace; others were punctuated by the dark cursing of a father trying to quell, with drink, the demons in his war-torn mind.

All of us were products of the same middle-class suburbia, possibly even the same street, yet our glimpses into the intimacies of each other's families evoked a surprising sense of difference: different smells, different food, different manners, different stations on the radio, different parenting styles; endless differences in the nuances of conversation, the jokes, the language.

And different beliefs. What gulf could be greater than the one that used to be fixed between Catholics and Protestants? (The recently retired Dean of Melbourne, Bishop James Grant, remarked that one of the great changes in his lifetime has been the reduction in the amount of energy squandered on sectarian conflicts.) People who rejected notions like papal infallibility and the real presence of Christ in the eucharist thought that those who embraced them were very weird, or possibly evil; and vice versa, of course.

Tensions today between ethnic subgroups, or between new waves of immigrants and their host communities, could not exceed the tension, prejudice and conflict in the Thirties and Forties between Roman Catholic and Protestant, or, at its most extreme, between Catholic and Mason. It affected attitudes from the workplace to the sporting field. Some major companies were well known for their anti-Catholic employment policies, and when Don Bradman was accused of anti-Catholic prejudice against some of his fellow Test cricket players, people readily understood and accepted the potential for such problems, even if they were not, in fact, present in the Bradman case.

My father, a child of Melbourne's Fitzroy, used to tell tales of Protestant boys pelting the roofs of Catholic families with stones. It really seemed that those from the other side of that particular divide were unapproachably, unimaginably different. (My father, and many of his friends, claimed to be able to pick 'em: 'She had the map of Ireland all over her face,' he would say scathingly, though two of his closest friends were Catholic.)

In those days, the cultural line between bosses and workers was starkly drawn; 'white-collar' and 'blue-collar' were labels that had deeply symbolic as well as literal meaning; the serious commitment to egalitarianism was yet to emerge.

Once upon a time, you'd never see a shearer come into the same restaurant where the boss and his wife were having dinner. Now

*you wouldn't give it a second thought ... except to think that he's
probably making more money than the boss.*

*My parents had servants. That's what they called them: servants.
These days, you have to treat the ironing lady like your best friend,
or she won't bother coming.*

So there we all sat in our 1948 classroom, in the days when Australia
was ... what? Less ethnically diverse than it is today, certainly; possibly
less tolerant. But less culturally diverse? I doubt it.

This hybrid is us

The truth is that the elusive 'mainstream'—the mythical, single, true-blue,
Australian style—has never been anything other than a collection of
cultural tributaries, each with something distinctive to contribute to the
whole. We have been, from the beginning, a hybrid culture.

Today, wherever you look, the answer is diversity ... in everything
from shopping habits and media consumption to parenting styles, sexual
mores, voting patterns, fashion and, yes, ethnicity. Whether we choose to
describe our social heterogeneity as 'divisive' rather than diverse is up to us.
'Divisive' is probably a fairer word when the issue is the growing disparity
between wealth and poverty; it's less fair when you're talking about the
fact that we have come here from every point of the compass, or that
contemporary Australians are choosing to live in ways that are
increasingly different from each other.

In such a fragmented and kaleidoscopic context, we shouldn't be
embarrassed about our natural tendency to form close-knit tribal groups—
Net-surfers, Continuing Presbyterians, Collingwood supporters, single
parents' shopping co-ops. Our sense of identity, threatened by a fracturing
of the natural connections of traditional village life, needs all the help it
can get.

But if we keep looking over our shoulders, hankering after some
mythical homogeneity, we will be swamped by the wave of increasing

diversity. Our mental health, and the health of our society, demands that we master the art of being two things at once: proudly cosmopolitan as well as comfortably parochial. That's what citizens of the modern world have always needed to be.

Hugh Mackay

CHAPTER FIVE

Egalitarianism

Still Dreaming of Equal Opportunity

Turning Point: Is the egalitarian dream fading? Ask almost any Australian what we most like about Australia and the answer will usually have something to do with our commitment to the ideal of an egalitarian society. Sometimes we say we're a 'middle-class' society or even a 'classless' society ... and perhaps we came close, around the middle of this century. Yet one of the great disappointments of the past 25 years has been the widening gap between rich and poor, exacerbated by the rural crisis, and the resulting inequality of access to education, health and other services we think of as fundamental to life in a decent, just and fair society.

What are we hoping for? A society that resists the pressure to give up on egalitarianism; that refuses to institutionalise socio-economic class; that rates need ahead of entitlement.

Myths can be a great source of comfort. They can inspire us, educate us and offer us moral guidance. They can motivate and uplift us—like some religious myths, or those mythical tales of courage or compassion or heroism that come to us from the ancient Greeks. Some stories, rooted in fact, have become legends in the endless retelling, as their moral purpose was refined. Such myths are often beneficial and, at the very least, harmless.

But some myths are dangerous: they can weaken us by blinding us to the way things really are. We can take refuge in myth; anaesthetise ourselves; insulate ourselves from reality.

Take that myth that delights us whenever we recite it, because it reminds us of a romantic ideal about our society. It's a myth that acts like a mantra, reassuring us that all is well—or, at least, might soon be well. Yet it is a myth that has the power to blind us to some startling changes taking place in our society.

This is the myth of *egalitarian Australia*; the myth that Australia is a place characterised by justice, equality, fairness and tolerance.

The egalitarian myth is closely related to, but different from, the myth of the 'classless society'. No-one really believes that Australia is a classless society: my own research suggests that not many Australians expect that will ever be true (and some don't even want it to be true). Although we often characterise ourselves as a middle-class society—and most Australians would describe themselves as belonging to the middle class—a more accurate interpretation of Australians' attitudes towards class is that we are all located on a kind of *class continuum*, in which there are no easily identifiable points of division but where each of us can draw comfort from the rather fluid, flexible nature of this continuum— and where people in need of reassurance can safely assume there are others below them on this rather vaguely-defined ladder. (When all else fails, you can point to the Aborigines: most white Australians would still position Aborigines, as a group, as being off the bottom of the scale—or on some other scale entirely—when it comes to social class.)

It is true that a big, comfortable, prosperous middle class has been an important symbol of egalitarian Australia, but egalitarianism itself is a different thing. It refers to political equality, legal equality, social equality

Hugh Mackay

as to rights and welfare . . . but, above all, it refers to *equality of opportunity*.

That's a very different thing from equality of outcome, of course. Egalitarianism does not imply a culture of mediocrity; a culture of the average; a culture in which all of us pass through a kind of social and educational meat-grinder that processes us into a homogeneous mass.

No, egalitarianism doesn't imply any resistance to diversity, nor to exceptional success, achievement and excellence. It doesn't even imply any objection to 'tall poppies', as long as they don't swagger and betray an arrogant self-consciousness. Egalitarianism is not inconsistent with the notion of elites of various kinds, ranging from the sporting to the intellectual. (In fact, Australian culture has always encouraged sporting elites, in particular, within the context of the egalitarian ideal.)

So the true egalitarian's emphasis is on equality of opportunity, not of outcome. Even those Australians who have a vaguely-formed social hierarchy in their minds aren't necessarily anti-egalitarian; knowing that there are other places in the hierarchy can be seen as defining opportunities to move—up or down—according to your ambition, your ability, your changing circumstances, or even your desire for a quiet life.

Nevertheless, it is true that for most of the past 50 years we have regarded a dominant middle class as a reassuring sign that our society is within reach of becoming truly egalitarian.

It is no accident that the egalitarian dream really took hold of our imagination at a time when the Australian middle class was blossoming. The great economic growth and development of the Fifties and Sixties, the postwar boom in manufacturing (and consumer marketing), construction, housing and mining, created a mood of optimism which fuelled, in turn, the marriage boom and the baby boom.

This was a period of zero unemployment; a time when the income earned by one breadwinner could keep a middle-class family in relative comfort (or, in some cases, undreamed-of prosperity); a time when it looked as though the economy was on an endless roll.

In other words, the dream of egalitarianism came into full flower when it looked as if we could *all* be prosperous. Now, 30 years later, the scene has changed. The rosy expectations of the Fifties and Sixties have darkened into the bleaker realities of the Nineties. Things are tighter, tougher and less certain. The dream of egalitarianism is turning sour, especially for those who are being denied equal access to Australia's employment, education and health-care opportunities. It is also turning sour for some of those at the top of the economic heap who are beginning to realise that thoroughgoing egalitarianism might involve some sacrifice. (When, in 1998, the Howard Government announced proposals for income tax cuts that were more generous to high-income earners than low, a participant in one of my *Mind & Mood* research projects responded like this: 'It's about time someone did us a favour. The low-income people always get the benefits.')

Nevertheless, we keep *saying* that we are an egalitarian society in the hope that we will all be prosperous again soon.

But will we?

We'd better drop 'the middle class' as our symbol of egalitarianism

Research published in 1998 by Monash University revealed that 32 per cent of Australian adults are now *primarily* dependent on welfare payments for their income. The same study reported that 41 per cent of children under the age of 15 live in households which are at least partly dependent on welfare.

The top 30 per cent of households control about 60 per cent of household income; the bottom 30 per cent control less than 10 per cent of household income. According to Hans Baekgaard of Access Economics, the concentration of wealth at the top of the income ladder is proceeding apace. Baekgaard has found that the share of the nation's wealth held by the richest 10 per cent of Australians has increased from 43.5 per cent to more than 48 per cent in the five years from 1993 to 1998. More startlingly, the richest *one per cent* of Australians now own *15 per cent* of the nation's wealth.[1]

Even the recent news that 40 per cent of Australians directly own shares—mostly Telstra and AMP—only serves to remind us that, according to Trevor Sykes, four per cent of Australians own 55 per cent of all shares.

The increasingly obvious divisions between rich and poor call into question our comforting view of a broad middle class as the symbol of our egalitarianism. But there is emotional as well as economic evidence: there is a widespread sense of resentment, disappointment and alienation in our community that gives the lie to our fond dream of egalitarianism. (See Chapter 17.) A major source of that sense of disappointment is our growing awareness that success—material, social, educational, medical, vocational—is not equally available to all.

The most obvious, most pervasive sign of this emerging sense of inequality can be found in the way our society is distributing the available work among those seeking it.

Somewhere between one and two million Australians are either unemployed or seriously underemployed, and approximately 800 000 dependent children currently live in households where no wages are earned. At the same time, the overtime being worked by the full-time workforce amounts to the equivalent of about 500 000 full-time jobs. In other words, full-time workers are doing their own work and they are absorbing an additional half-million full-time jobs into their overtime—often in the name of 'enhanced productivity'.

One interpretation of that data is that there simply isn't enough work to go around. If that is so, is it because of a temporary hiccup in our economic progress? Or is it a sign of permanent structural change? Was the talk of a 'jobless economic recovery' after the 1991–92 recession more serious than we thought?

Suppose there is not enough work to satisfy the demand of all the people who want work, and suppose that situation will persist for the foreseeable future. Should we be disturbed or excited by the discovery that there are more willing workers than jobs? Should we feel that this is a shadow across our society, or should we welcome it as a sign of the kind of future we have always dreamed of: the Golden Age of Leisure when no-one would have to work too hard and when extensive leisure and recreation would be available to all? Should we see long-term unemployment as a signpost, or a threshold, to a kind of New Renaissance?

It's not as if the current state of unemployment is a sudden and dramatic bolt from the economic blue: for at least 20 years, we have been aware of three factors which would more or less guarantee our inability to return to the halcyon days of full employment, Fifties-style:

There has been a steady increase in female participation in the workforce over the past 30 years, as a result of the impact of the women's movement. The participation rate for women, at 54 per cent, is at its highest level ever. (Occasionally, you still hear men saying, 'If only all those women would stay home and look after their children, we wouldn't have an unemployment problem.' Strangely enough, you rarely hear them saying, 'If only more men would stay home and look after their children, we wouldn't have an unemployment problem', though the male participation rate is, in fact, falling.)

The information revolution, based on electronic technology, is carrying on the work of the Industrial Revolution, but at an even more breathtaking rate. It is doing what technology has always promised to do, steadily replacing people with machines that can do the work more reliably, more efficiently and more cheaply. It also drives a gradual redeployment of labour.

The process of microeconomic reform—espoused on all sides of politics—is, in essence, an anti-employment strategy, at least in the short term. It involves trying to get the existing work done by a smaller number of people or, alternatively, getting the same number of people to do more work than ever. (But who in their right mind would say they were against microeconomic reform: it would be like saying you were against one-day cricket.)

Understanding the direction in which those three factors have been pushing us, we *could* have arrived, by now, at the threshold of the Golden

Age of Leisure. But try asking a 19-year-old who has applied unsuccessfully for 200 jobs whether this feels like the dawning of the Golden Age of Leisure and see how far you get. Ask a 52-year-old middle-ranking executive who has just been retrenched whether this feels like the dawning of the Golden Age of Leisure. In both cases, you'll find yourself on the receiving end of a diatribe from someone who has been made to feel like a casualty of a nasty economic accident.

Young Australians are bearing a disproportionate weight of the burden of unemployment: about 40 per cent of all unemployed Australians are under the age of 25. The Dusseldorp Skills Forum's *Deepening Divide* report found that 15 per cent of teenagers are at risk of not making the step from education to stable work, and that the proportion of teenagers in this predicament has doubled in the past decade.[2]

Lumpy distribution of work means a lumpy distribution of wealth

It's not just work which we have been distributing in this lopsided way. The primary source of household income in Australia is wages and salaries, which means that an increasingly inequitable distribution of work will inevitably lead to an increasingly inequitable distribution of household income.

Australian Bureau of Statistics figures tell us that about 50 per cent of households have an average annual income (after tax) of less than $50 000. But the *polarisation* of household incomes is graphically revealed by estimates prepared by Ibis Information Systems. In 1997–98, Ibis estimated that the top 20 per cent of households had an average annual income of $142 000, and the next 20 per cent had an average annual income of $78 900. The bottom 20 per cent, by contrast, had an average annual income of $12 625.

With rapid growth at the top and bottom of the household income scale, it is obvious that middle-income households have been shrinking at an extraordinary rate over the past 25 years.

As always, the story is complicated; it is not just an economic story. At a time of dramatic social, cultural, economic and technological change, every factor you might think is significant turns out to be part of a fragile, vibrating web of interconnected factors. For example, the growth in both wealthy and poor households is, to some extent, linked to the changing roles and responsibilities of women—their enhanced earning power and their greater sense of independence.

One, but only one, of the factors contributing to the proliferation of high-income households has been the steady increase in the number of two-income households. A growing number of wives have taken full- or part-time paid jobs, not only to swell the family coffers, making private schools for the children or overseas holidays possible, but also, at least partly, as a symbol of their liberation. (The symbolism doesn't always work out as planned: as Chapter 23 points out, many working mothers are asking, 'Is this liberation, or just another form of enslavement?')

Paradoxically, the new-found independence of working mothers has been one factor—but only one—driving the increase in the number of low-income households as well. One-parent families are on the increase and most of those sole parents are women who have chosen independence over an unhappy or unsatisfactory partnership. Approximately one million dependent children now live with one parent, and in some of the poorer outlying suburbs of our major cities, almost 50 per cent of households are one-parent families.

So the single parent *and* the working mother—two symbols of women's liberation—have, ironically, contributed to growth at both ends of the economic spectrum in a way that directly threatens the economic dimension of the egalitarian ideal. Some women are now sharing in the life of affluent two-income households while others, equally committed to a more independent view of female roles and responsibilities, are fighting for economic survival at the bottom of the heap. They may have seized their independence and escaped from unhappy circumstances, but they have unwittingly contributed to our massive redistribution of household income.

Another factor driving this unequal distribution of wealth is the rise in part-time work. Part-time jobs are the only segment of the contemporary labour market showing strong growth, which is another way of saying that demand for work exceeds supply. Some people, of course, love their part-time jobs and have tried very hard to negotiate a part-time arrangement, often with a reluctant employer. Even those who have been forced unwillingly into part-time work sometimes report that life can be simpler, saner and more satisfying when you're not slogging away at a 40-, 50- or 60-hour job each week. Many others, though, are settling for part-time jobs because nothing more substantial is on offer, and they would dearly love to get their hands on more work. (The rise of part-time work might well be a signpost to the future: it could be one of the factors which will finally drive us to rethink the 'gold standard' of the five-day working week.)

Don't mention the e-word in the bush

But there are even broader national issues here. There are questions to be asked that force us to acknowledge that, in Australia at the end of the 20th century, basic human rights are being denied to large chunks of the Australian population. What does that say about our commitment to egalitarianism?

The 1999 report on young Australians in rural areas by the Human Rights Commissioner, Chris Sidoti, highlighted the plight of people living in rural towns and villages where the withdrawal of even one service, or the closure of even one business, can start a process that one woman in the Commissioner's research described as the 'dying town syndrome'.

A bank might close its branch in a particular town, for example. Five or six jobs might be lost, meaning that five or six families will leave that town in search of work elsewhere. Some of those remaining will travel to a neighbouring town to do their banking, and do some other shopping while they are there. Back in their own town, the local retailers suffer a corresponding loss of custom.

A mine might be closed down, or a railway workshop moved to a larger centre. The loss of all those employees and their families will not only affect the businesses in the community but might also mean that there are no longer enough children to support all the teachers at the local school.

Parents might have to face the agonising decision of whether to keep their children at home in a town where they won't be able to complete their secondary education, or send them to a boarding school elsewhere, at vast expense. For many parents, that is no choice at all.

And so the spiral twists downward, sucking many of the young people in those towns into depression and despair.

The problem is not just unemployment. In such 'dying towns', medical and other social services are typically well below the standard available in bigger population centres. Even in the outlying suburbs of our major metropolitan areas, the poor standard of available care has led one prominent medical specialist to refer to hospitals in some of those areas as being of third-world standard. Even allowing for some exaggeration, this is a human rights issue: are we prepared to accept that the poorer members of our society and those who live in remote areas will, by reason of their income and geographical location, have restricted access to the best available medical care?

Experts say that there are people in rural areas suffering, and even dying, from illnesses that could be treated if the appropriate medical services were available in those areas. Is this equality of opportunity?

Can money buy 'equality'?

The inescapable consequence of all of these interconnected social and economic factors is that we have a big new wealth class whose wealth buys them all kinds of associated benefits (like top health care and access to the best educational facilities) and an equally big welfare-dependent underclass whose poverty traps them in disadvantaged and deprived circumstances.

If we are like every other society on earth, then we have probably already sown the seeds of an ugly new class system as distressingly predictable as the socioeconomic tiers that have been institutionalised so many times throughout history. We have probably already begun to create

Hugh Mackay

a situation where the rich will feel protective of the benefits their wealth brings them, and the poor will feel increasingly angry and resentful of their exclusion not only from the wealth they see all around them, but from basic services to which they should have a right. The 'poverty trap' is as real here as it is in any other society, and it is a trap which makes our claim to be an egalitarian society sound rather hollow.

So one question we shall have to ask ourselves is this: are we prepared to institutionalise class in a way that we would previously have thought of as unacceptable and unAustralian? Are we prepared to 'let the market decide' and to allow our lumpy distribution of work and our inequitable distribution of social services, especially medical and educational services to outer-suburban and rural areas, to lead, inexorably, to the creation of divisions between the haves and have-nots which will be increasingly difficult to straddle?

If we decide to let that happen—or even if we let it happen by not deciding to attack the problem in a serious and compassionate way—we will start to notice some other, less obvious implications that will flow from our view of ourselves as a less egalitarian society—implications that, on the surface, might seem to have nothing to do with wealth. Some of the following examples might seem relatively trivial, but they are nevertheless symbolic of the things that happen when a society weakens its commitment to equality of opportunity.

Once you start to think of Australia as a socially stratified society— once you let yourself drift away from the egalitarian ideal—you can find yourself accepting, or even demanding, all kinds of status distinctions that you would previously have resisted. At the local swimming pool, for instance, you will come to accept that although this is a public pool, open to everyone, the so-called 'lap-nazis' are automatically entitled to dominate 'their' section of the pool because of their claim to have a superior commitment to serious fitness.

You can see the same thing with joggers on a public footpath who swear and gesticulate at other users of the path who have failed to give the joggers absolute right of way. 'I'm a jogger,' you can almost hear them saying, 'and that gives me superior rights to the use of this space.'

Mobile phone users often behave in public places, like theatres and restaurants, as if the mere ownership of a mobile phone confers special status on them, entitling them, apparently, to ignore the conventions of established etiquette.

This is a two-way trap. You can get caught in it by thinking that egalitarianism is already dead, so what the heck! Or you can get caught in it by thinking that egalitarianism is such an inherent and immutable feature of our society, there's no need to work at it at all. If we start taking egalitarianism for granted, it's a short step to the belief that I can please myself, and so can everyone else.

The trouble is that not everyone *can* please themselves. And nowhere is that more evident than in the labour market. When people don't have equal access to work, when some are shut out of the labour market either by explicit rejection or by discouragement, some of the costs to those individuals will be even higher than the economic cost. Unemployment is, unambiguously, a health hazard, both physically and emotionally. In a society conditioned to think of 'work' in traditional ways, the *loss* of work involves a loss of the sense of identity, a loss of the regular gratifications available to people with steady work, a loss of self-respect, and a loss of the social network of workmates which, for most of us, provides an important emotional support system.

When a person loses all that, their needs can be far greater than the need of mere money. So if we can't offer equality of access to work for all who want it, what then?

Will it be enough to treat them like casualties of a new kind of industrial revolution, fobbing them off with glib references to IT, globalisation, downsizing, privatisation, corporatisation and restructuring? Will we simply expect them to accept that the eternal tension between the social conscience and the bottom line will inevitably be resolved, every time, in favour of the bottom line?

Will it be enough to mail them a dole cheque and leave it at that, possibly making them feel ashamed of themselves in the process?

Or will we find a way, outside the labour market, of meeting their emotional and psychological needs *as well as* their financial needs? If we really understood the therapeutic nature of work, wouldn't we be more actively exploring ways of providing 'work replacement therapy'?

The spirit of egalitarianism: responding to need because it's there

We must remember that *need* has nothing to do with what we or anyone else think people might *deserve*. In an egalitarian society, we have only to establish that a need exists to have defined an entitlement. In an egalitarian society, we must take each other's needs on trust. To quote the distinguished British writer and broadcaster Michael Ignatieff:

> If the powerful do not trust the reasons of the poor, these reasons will never be reason enough.[3]

It is easy to find reasons to deny charity, compassion or even comprehension to those whose needs are different from ours, especially when those needs threaten, by their very existence, our cosy view of ourselves as a society that is stable, secure, healthy, prosperous ... and egalitarian. It is too easy to be part of a two-income household—hogging the jobs *and* the overtime—and simultaneously to complain disparagingly and dismissively about dole bludgers.

'Dignity' and 'respect' are not words we normally associate with the unemployed, or with our attitudes to them. Yet if we aspire to be an egalitarian society in the post-industrial age, we shall have to bridge the chasm of prejudice between the employed and the unemployed.

Perhaps we will even need new language for discussing those states, as we once had to create a new vocabulary to shock ourselves into facing issues of gender inequity and inequality. Perhaps words like *employed*, *unemployed*, *part-time/full-time work*—even words like *taxation* and *welfare*—will have to give way to new words which help us to understand that work may be acquiring new meanings in this new era, and that the distribution of society's wealth must take account of the needs of all of us, wherever we live and however much work we can obtain.

Those whom we now call unemployed or underemployed might actually be sending us a message from our future. Perhaps we should be regarding their situation as a signpost to the time (now being predicted by a growing band of economists and social analysts, like Hans-Peter Martin and Harald Schumann in their international bestseller *The Global Trap*)[4] when only a small minority of the potential labour force will be needed to do the available work. Will that, finally, see the dawning of the long-awaited Golden Age of Leisure? Will creativity flourish? Will we find ways of providing fulfilment to people, inside and outside the traditional workplace? Or will it be a nightmare of inequality and social unrest leading, ultimately, to an insurrection against the aristocracy of wealth?

What is certain is that we urgently need to recapture the spirit of egalitarianism and apply it to no less a task than finding a new way of thinking about the place of work and the meaning of work. We must find more creative ways of distributing the available work, but we must also find a more compassionate way of dealing with those who, through no fault of their own, can't find any paid work to do.

Being human is what defines our nature and our needs, and it is what binds us to each other in communities. If we fail to respond to anyone's need for work (or for gratifications equivalent to those which work provides), then we run the risk of diminishing that person's sense of their own humanity. If we were to allow that to happen, we couldn't even call ourselves civilised, let alone egalitarian.

Hugh Mackay

CHAPTER SIX

Food

Healthy Eating: Much More Than the Food

Turning Point: A paradoxical revolution is taking place in food, with the development of medicinally beneficial food coexisting with an increase in the amount of processed and take-away food in the nation's diet. Faced with disagreement among the experts, the mysteries of genetically modified food, an ever-changing set of dietary warnings, and an ever-expanding range of choices, our dietary behaviour is becoming as postmodern as everything else: diverse, fragmented, contradictory, quirky and experimental. People are inclined to think there is more to 'healthy eating' than the food: the mood, the pace and the company all contribute.

What are we hoping for? A clear and unambiguous set of dietary guidelines, with an emphasis on realistic balance, rather than absolute prohibitions. But we're also hoping for a saner life, in which there will be less talk of food as 'medicine' or even 'fuel', and we will rediscover the simple pleasure of eating.

The latest thing is a margarine that actually lowers your cholesterol level. In Finland, where the population smokes its head off and heart disease is the number-one killer, it has been credited with dramatic results. (In Australia, it costs about twice as much as normal margarines, which is unfortunate, since coronary heart disease is more prevalent among low-income earners than among those who can afford expensive food.)

And there's bread on the market that contains fish oil. (Don't leave it lying around for too long, though: ageing fishy bread is not a nice smell.) We'll be hearing more of such innovations: food is back in the scientific spotlight, all set for another round of dietary hype in which the object seems to be to get food items to do more than just look good, taste nice and be nourishing as well. The new challenge is 'targeted' food that is created and modified to offer highly specific health benefits, rather like medication.

Genetically modified food is all the go, and it won't be long before it evolves from perfectly shaped and coloured tomatoes, every time, into foods that have been engineered to do more for us than they were ever capable of doing in their natural state.

How would you like a carrot that really does improve your night vision, because it is genetically programmed to do so? Or a muesli that precisely times your bowel motions to suit your schedule? Or an apple with fluoride in its juice that actually prevents dental caries, or even an apple that, eaten once a day, keeps the doctor away? (All the old myths could come true, given enough research and development.)

Antibiotic bananas? Analgesic ice cream? Anti-depressant orange juice? Peanut butter that's a banned substance for athletes, because it's *too* good for you? Vegemite with Valium? We don't have any of these things yet as far as I know, though many parents have discovered that ice cream does seem to have miraculous pain-killing properties in young children.

Targeted foods could add a new dimension to the idea of a balanced diet. In addition to watching our intake of protein, carbohydrate, fats and sugars, and on top of our attention to vitamins, minerals, anti-oxidants and folates, we'll have to start taking a whole new range of possibilities into account: cholesterol-cutters, free radical-chasers, sleep-inducers, growth-promotants, blood-enrichers, mood-elevators, brain-food ...

Food as medicine. It's not a new idea: 'Eat up your broccoli' has been the cry of many parents who have tried to influence their children to think of their diet as the fuel that builds their bodies, as well as keeping them alive. 'Eat what you like, your genes will take care of you' is not nearly so popular a theme, though some medical researchers go close to suggesting it. But 'eat up your stimulants, dear', certainly has a novel ring to it.

In an article in the St James Ethics Centre's journal, *City Ethics*, Gawen Rudder, a Sydney-based marketing strategist, reported on the consumer's growing list of worries about food. He quoted figures from a 1999 study by the Dangar Research Group, involving 800 telephone interviews, that showed 65 per cent of people 'really worry' about the amount of chemicals in food, 53 per cent wonder what is done to fresh fruit and vegetables so they can be bought out-of-season, and 40 per cent express concern about gene engineering. Overall, the study found that, one way or another, 88 per cent of people are worried about the integrity of food (up from 58 per cent in 1992). Reflecting on this rising level of concern, Rudder wrote:

> Why would we not worry about herbicides and pesticides when we know that something ending in 'cide' is likely to kill? And ... ponder the twin meanings of 'pure'. On the one hand, pure can mean something that is natural, simple, a product of sun, rain, soil and organic growth, unaltered by man. On the other hand, pure can mean something almost the exact opposite: scientifically clean, safe, super-refined, hygienic, chemically quantifiable and free of germs and microbes.
>
> The odd thing is that we can actually hold both these views simultaneously ... a demonstration that many of us are happy to put our trust in God and science at the same time.
>
> And so it is with food. Was it not our dream of finding a tomato that tasted the way tomatoes used to taste that encouraged the geneticist to bring out his biolistic gene gun and shoot selective DNA into the plant cell to create the perfect tomato ... 'and will you have carcinogen protection with that?' Because while the seed is being manipulated it's not too difficult to throw in some cancer preventative nutrients like lycopene or quercetin.[1]

So now we can be more specific: 'Eat up your quercetin, dear, we don't want to get cancer, do we? Here, have another GM tomato.' (That's GM as in 'gene modified', not General Motors ... though goodness knows what new products the General has in mind in this postmodern world.)

Rudder also referred to a gene-splicing operation conducted in Cologne last year, in which a potato was modified so that, if it caught a particular fungal disease, it would commit suicide. ('No mention of what might happen if we got one of those dead spuds at the supermarket,' Rudder muses.)

'Give me spots on my apples, but leave me the birds and the bees'

(Joni Mitchell, prophetically, in 1971)

Prominent Australian nutritionist Rosemary Stanton has weighed in with the observation that 'there is more than enough food in the world, and much deliberate wastage. The poor ... will be worse off if they have to pay royalties every time they use GM seeds.' Stanton regards the move towards genetic modification of foods as a move away from Australia's top-selling image of clean green food: 'If Australia avoided all GM crops, our farmers could sell everything they grow to Japan and European countries that wanted food guaranteed to be GM-free, as happened this year with Australian non-GM canola.' Stanton speaks for many concerned consumers when she says this:

> Rational consumers ask why we need GM foods. They note the paucity of safety studies, the potential ecological problems (which could cost future farmers dearly) and wonder why we should let multinational companies use emotive arguments to control our farming industry.[2]

The GM food debate has scarcely begun. The first Australian Consensus Conference, held in March 1999, was devoted to gene-modified food. It strongly recommended that labelling should be introduced to allow consumers to make a free and informed choice about whether they will buy GM or GM-free food. (Early British experience has suggested that, given the choice, British consumers tend to prefer the GM version, though Gawen Rudder notes that 'GM-free' might become as common, and as potentially misleading, as 'fat free' in food packaging and advertising.)

American futurists are confident that genetic engineering will be America's second biggest industry by 2020. Yet Rudder identifies a counter-trend: a growing interest in 'real food', organic food, simple food . . . food that has not been tampered with.

When you start listening to Australian consumers talking about their eating habits and food choices, contradictions abound and the 'one-trend' approach is clearly fallacious. Here, as much as anywhere, you realise that Australian society is, indeed, in transition. While 48 per cent of people claim to have a weekly 'traditional roast', 88 per cent say they have 'ethnic food' at least once a week. According to the Dangar survey, 70 per cent of Australian homes have a wok. Yet, as more and more people claim to be cutting down on fat and eating lighter and healthier food, especially pasta and salads, the nation's obesity levels continue to rise. We are apparently placing more value on eating with the family at home *and* we're eating out more. Take your pick.

Most risibly, 75 per cent of Australian males currently claim to enjoy cooking, compared with only 60 per cent of females.[3] (Clearly, the blokes like the *idea* of cooking, but prefer to leave it at that.)

In the current climate, one thing you can rely on is that in food, as in cars and fashion, retro will never be far from the top of the list of favourites. The appeal of so-called comfort food (chops, casseroles, soup, mashed potato, ice cream) is undiminished as Australians seek relief from their uncertainties and insecurities. As in childhood, so in adulthood: there is a special kind of solace to be extracted from the pantry and the fridge. While we know our diet is changing in ways hard to imagine even ten years ago, and while the new is exciting, nothing is quite as reassuring as food that reminds you of the way things were.

Don't confuse me with the facts

There is a soft rattle being heard in dining rooms across the nation. It's the sound of saltcellars being pressed, once again, into service by an army of salt-starved diners who've heard the latest news.

According to a study reported in *The Lancet* in 1998, the less salt people eat, the higher their risk of untimely death.

Dr Michael Alderman, leader of the research team at the Albert Einstein School of Medicine and president of the American Society of Hypertension, didn't go so far as to suggest that the sky's the limit, but he did say that a modest increase in dietary salt was associated with a reduction in mortality.

Local news reports of this study contained the ominous rider that 'Australian experts have serious reservations about the findings', and no wonder: the study contradicts dietary advice given to an entire generation of Australians. But that won't deter some of them from embracing Dr Alderman's findings with relief. 'Fie!' they will say to the worrywarts who urge caution.

Salt was going to kill us all ... remember that? Now we know it's good for us, in moderation, like most things, I guess.

Who can blame the consumer for feeling a little confused? The academic researcher's distinction between statistical correlation and proven causation is often murky and, in any case, if people are supposed to be impressed by research that scares them into giving things up, why wouldn't they be equally impressed by studies that seem to encourage them to resume their old habits?

It is now seen as one of the ironies of the 'diet-mad' Eighties that the plethora of dietary advice, while obviously well-intentioned, might actually have contributed to rising stress levels in the community. Looking back, many people now believe they became confused by messages that seemed to be at odds with each other. They were swept along by the onrush of the 'latest news' about diet; their responses to these messages sometimes led to adjustments to their diet which, on reflection, makes them wonder if they were doing more harm than good.

Hugh Mackay

Not that the confusion has subsided: hardly a day goes by without a media report of yet more research into the effects of this or that food. Red meat has gone in and out of favour—fat is bad, iron is good—though *some* fat is good, and too much iron is bad. (Probably.) Just when you thought monosodium glutamate (MSG) was consigned forever to the dustbin out the back of Chinese takeaways, the World Health Organisation places it on its list of 'safest foods' and we learn that it's a natural product that also occurs in parmesan cheese.[4]

Remember when sugar was tagged 'the white death'? No sooner had we learned to live with less sweetness in our lives than, hey presto, sugar had become 'a natural part of life' and we were hearing about the hazards of too little sugar in the blood.

I virtually gave up sugar until I saw a girl faint at a wedding, and a doctor called for a bar of chocolate to get her sugar level up.

(Now, it seems, we are about to be hit with a new wave of American anti-sugar research. 'Moderation!' someone is bound to cry, eventually.)

And how have we managed to sustain dinner-party conversation since we stopped comparing our cholesterol levels? (One answer: we talk about the medicinal value of red wine.) We know cholesterol is still bad, but we have become confused by the different types, by the suggestion that too little could be as dangerous as too much, and by our suspicion that medication might deal with the problem more easily than a drastic overhaul of our way of life.

Let's face it, we went overboard about bran. It was a bit like Fly-Buys ... you had to have so much of it to do any good, you ended up thinking it was all too hard.

Not surprisingly, one of the themes now emerging from the cacophony of dietary advice is that it's hard to generalise. One dietary factor might be lethal for you, but safe—and possibly beneficial—for me. The Lawrence Berkeley National Laboratory in California, for instance, has reported that low-fat diets might be useless or even potentially damaging for two-thirds of the population. Their research suggests that response to a low-fat diet depends on a person's genes.

Even tobacco smoking may be a more vexed question than it appears. A perfectly respectable study by the late British psychologist Hans Eysenck found that heart and lung disease were strongly associated with smoking *among certain personality types, but not others.*

According to Eysenck, if you are the type of person whose psychological make-up predisposes you to cancer or heart disease, you should steer clear of the dreaded weed. But—and here's the part that vexes the anti-smoking lobby—he also found that if you don't have any of the vulnerable types of personality and temperament, you could smoke like a chimney all your life with little risk to your health, which explains why some heavy smokers do manage to live to a ripe old age.

The trick, of course, is to establish whether or not you're the kind of person for whom smoking would be dangerous, which is why Eysenck recommended that personality testing should be an integral part of any medical examination related to smoking.[5] (Still, no-one is suggesting that tobacco is actually good for you, so it seems sensible to avoid it unless you enjoy smoking so much that you are prepared to take the consequences—or to trust the personality test.)

The most bizarre bit of recent research is the study reported by *Time* magazine which found that, in the USA, Christians are more likely to be overweight than other groups, but that—wait for it—their obesity has no effect on their wellbeing.

That might relate, in a curious way, to yet another medical report out of London, via *The Times*, in which a certain Dr Geoff Lowe has discovered that carefree people who enjoy life are less likely to become ill than worriers. No surprises there. In particular, Dr Lowe says that people who don't carry a burden of guilt are less liable to heart disease.

In the same vein, research reported by the *New Scientist* indicates that 'people who suffer from severe depression are up to four times as likely to suffer from heart disease triggered by obstructed blood flow as people who are not depressed—even allowing for classical risk factors such as smoking and high cholesterol levels. In fact, depression is a greater risk factor than smoking.'[6]

Perhaps our folk wisdom has been right all along. Perhaps health is not the pathway to contentment; perhaps contentment is the pathway to health.

It's not just what you eat, but how you eat

Through the Nineties, in response to their own doubts about the consistency of advice they are receiving, and in the face of an increasingly tantalising array of food choices, Australians have wished they could be more relaxed about food. They have a hunch that there's something fundamentally crazy, something unhealthy, about being too uptight about an activity that is meant to be a source of pleasure as well as nourishment.

Here's a picture that strikes many people as absurd: a harassed executive, hunched over his desk, is stuffing bean sprouts into his mouth, washed down with carrot juice, while firing off a series of e-mails, one-handed.

Healthy? No way. The apparently healthy food is cancelled out, in our minds, by a situation so stressful and unhealthy as to render the food useless as anything but basic fuel. This is not 'healthy eating' as Australians would like to understand that term.

Here's another, more ambiguous picture: a family is sitting around a table at McDonald's, talking and laughing while munching their hamburgers.

Healthy? Hmm. Harder to say, because we know the food mightn't be as nutritious as we'd like (too much fat, for a start), but we like the look of the scene; we think a bit of laughter and good company might be important ingredients in 'healthy eating' ... possibly *as important* as the food. So fast food is sometimes praised, especially by working mothers, for creating the possibility of slow eating.

I don't think McDonald's does them any harm occasionally—and we wouldn't go there more than once a week. The thing is, the kids like it, it lets me off cooking, and we have a nice time. I think that's healthy.

Sometimes we just order in a pizza. It's more relaxed. I just toss a salad, and I think that's healthy enough. When people are relaxed and having a good time, I call that healthy eating.

European families, especially Greeks and Italians, are credited with not only having introduced new food items into the Australian diet, but also with showing Australians how to enjoy eating, and how to turn mealtimes into a social occasion. Some Australians are following suit; others recall a similar approach in earlier generations of their own families.

I try to make sure the whole family are together for one meal each week ... it might be brunch on Sunday, or a Friday night. I don't care when it is, but I think it's important to sit around the table together and catch up on each other's news. That's part of a healthy family life.

I'm sure one reason why my grandparents lived to such a ripe old age was that they knew how to eat. They made it a ritual. They took a break and sat down and ate their meals properly. The food wasn't great—too heavy, too fatty, too salty—but it was a lovely occasion for the whole family ...

The more I think about it, the more I think that how you eat counts as much as what you eat. If you're relaxed, and in the right company, you can enjoy a meal so much more.

Alcohol is a potent symbol of the tension between nutrition and pleasure: it is the classic example, for many Australians, of how to judge the integrity of a diet by reference to two popular touchstones: *balance* and *moderation*. Widely acknowledged as an inherently unhealthy substance, and clearly damaging when used immoderately, alcohol enhances the pleasure of eating when it relaxes the diners and heightens their enjoyment of the whole occasion. (Recent news about the beneficial effects of red wine has also provided 'scientific' reassurance to those who need it:

there's no dietary advice as welcome as the advice that encourages you to do what you want to do.)

With or without alcohol, the backyard barbecue is widely regarded as the healthiest of all mealtimes. Whether charred sausages would qualify as healthy food is scarcely the point: 'healthy' salads have become standard barbecue fare, partly, perhaps, to compensate for any burnt offerings (though, in fairness, it should be acknowledged that many Australian men have developed quite sophisticated barbecue skills. Perhaps that 70 per cent of men who claim to love cooking are thinking of the barbecue.)

The *al fresco* setting, and the presence of family and friends, create precisely the kind of atmosphere that Australians have in mind when they think of the pleasure of eating. And it's the pleasure of eating that is, increasingly, the focus of their attention. Here, as in so many aspects of contemporary Australian life, the challenge is both to *simplify* and to *slow down*. Barbecues come close to achieving both goals (though they have been known, occasionally, to fall short of the ideal, in circumstances where balance and moderation are both abandoned, resulting in verbal if not physical violence, strained relations all round, and an aftermath of stressful recriminations).

It would be premature to assume that family meals, inside or out, have become universally joyful and relaxed affairs, with the TV turned off and stimulating interaction the order of the day. In many households, mealtimes—especially breakfast—are still described as 'a shambles' too often for comfort. But we're getting better at enjoying ourselves with food.

Similarly, let's not get carried away with the idea that Australians are no longer vulnerable to health fads. But we are at a turning point, not only in relation to the food we eat (and whether it is going to be gene modified, irradiated, organically grown or just 'normal'), but also in our desire to integrate the specific question of *healthy food* into the much larger question of *healthy eating*. When it comes to food, 'back to basics' doesn't mean a return to bread and dripping; it means a return to the idea that eating should be a simple pleasure, unsullied by the prospect of having to pass an exam on the latest information from the frontier of genetic engineering.

In his *City Ethics* article, Gawen Rudder quoted French food philosopher Brillat-Savarin whose 1825 treatise, *La Physiologie du Gout*, included this bold assertion: 'Tell me what you eat and I will tell you who you are.' A social analyst on the threshold of the 21st century would want to go further: 'Tell me what you eat, how you eat it, when and where you eat it and with whom, and I will tell you who you are.' Food is still a significant indicator of a person's—and a society's—taste, style and attitude to life, but *how you eat* is even more revealing.

CHAPTER SEVEN

Grey Power

'Will You Still Need Me, Will You Still Feed Me, When I'm Sixty-four?'

(The Beatles, 1967)

Turning Point: Will the coming wave of Baby Boomers entering retirement change our society's attitudes towards old age? And which attitudes need to change? To hear older Australians talking about retirement, you would think there's not much to complain about, but they themselves believe things are becoming more precarious for pensioners and those on fixed incomes. They also fear for their personal safety.

What are we hoping for? Older people are hoping for more respect and recognition. We are all hoping for security and serenity in old age ... and for the resources to support the Boomers when the time comes.

The first decade of the 21st century will see a trickle of Baby Boomers heading into retirement. By 2015, it will be a flood. Their sheer numbers will stimulate demand in all the markets providing goods and services to the elderly. From retirement villages and nursing homes to leisure and recreational facilities, the Boomers will be expecting the same level of attention they attracted when, at earlier points in their life cycle, they virtually created the teenage market and then expanded the markets for education, fashion, housing, travel and cars.

If anyone is going to ensure that seniors are taken seriously in this society, it will be the Baby Boomers. Their entry into retirement might mark the moment when Australian society begins to venerate old age. Then again, it mightn't: if the Boomers' spending patterns continue as they are now, younger generations might come to see them as an unacceptable drain on the public purse—a massive pain in the fiscal neck, rather than a precious resource of wisdom and experience. Those generations will, of course, be the taxpayers when the Boomers, in huge numbers, start looking for support from the social security and health-care systems.

Peter G Peterson, chairman of the Institute for International Economics, believes that the greying of the population might well be one of the major global hazards of the 21st century.[1] The combination of greater longevity and lower birthrates could trigger a crisis, Peterson argues, that engulfs the world economy. If that happens, Australia's Baby Boomers will certainly have made their contribution: indeed, Australia's birth and death rates fit Peterson's 'hazard' scenario to a tee.

So far, it looks as if Australian Boomers are hoping that in spite of all the warnings to the contrary, our social security system will be as generous to them as it has been to their parents. (Or perhaps they're hoping it's their parents who will turn out to have been generous, when it comes time to read the will.) Some of them are buying a few shares, it's true, and their compulsory superannuation contributions will offer them something, but there's no sign, yet, of much serious commitment to retirement planning. As Chapter 2 suggested, the strongest signal coming from the baby-boom generation is that they are getting set for another spending splurge in their fifties.

Hugh Mackay

Meanwhile, what of those already in retirement? What advice might they have for the Boomers, or have they long since abandoned any thought of giving advice?

In *Generations*, I reported their description of themselves as the 'lucky' generation: they believe they have had a much better life than their parents had, and they are now coming to the conclusion that they probably had a better time, overall, than either their children or grandchildren are likely to have. Their great blessing, as they see it, is that they inherited the strong and enduring values of their parents' generation (values hammered out on the anvil of the Great Depression), and they put those values to work in lives of relative prosperity and material comfort, certainly compared with anything their parents had experienced.[2]

They acknowledge that their children—the Baby Boomers—grew up in such an optimistic and 'easy' atmosphere that those values were rather overwhelmed by the messages of a burgeoning consumer society. So the next generation did not have such a solid foundation of values to rely on when they reached their middle years and found themselves caught up in a confusing but relentless process of social and economic change.

And now they see their children's children, today's teens and young adults, facing an even more uncertain future, without having inherited a stable value system, and without the compensation of assured employment.

We worked hard but we have something to show for it.

I've always had a theory, based on my own lifetime, that I was born into the peak time and place in history. I missed the war. I got a good education. Employment was easy to get. I was able to afford to buy a house ... I feel I live like a king in the world—in a nice little three-bedroom cottage with a garden.

Life was much tougher for my father than it has been for me. I was brought up in the Depression. My father virtually supported three families because neither of his brothers could get a job. And he took a 10 per cent pay cut to keep his job.

Older Australians find it harder than younger generations to anticipate the future with enthusiasm. While some of them believe in the benefits likely to come from riding 'the next wave', others see a bleaker prospect. They particularly fear the impact of the illicit drug trade on the culture of young people, and they despair over the dangerous chasm opening up between rich and poor. A recurring theme is 'I wouldn't like to be growing up in today's world'.

So what are their messages to the rest of us?

'A bit of hardship never hurt anyone, but ...'

Here's a surprise: the very generation who had a depression and a world war under their belts before they reached adulthood, believe that today's young Australians are facing a tougher world than the one they faced.

And here's another: although they believe that their own hardships were the making of them, they don't have much faith in the idea that today's brand of hardship is character forming in quite the same way.

The solution to those puzzles seems to lie in their perception of a difference between hardship then and hardship now: hardship based on the struggle to prevail, in the face of deprivation beyond your control, can be good for the soul; hardship based on a breaking down of society's values and structures can be more cancerous than productive.

So they're not against a bit of hardship, far from it. But they are perplexed by the ravages of unemployment in the midst of such prosperity. They are bewildered by young people willingly taking to the drug scene, as if they don't understand the consequences. They fear there's a lack of discipline among the young. (Not all of them think that, of course: some are dazzled by the drive and initiative of the young, but 'discipline' is a recurring theme when they try to explain what they see as an excess of permissiveness, or when they try to account for the depth of despair that leads to drug abuse and even suicide.)

Somehow there was a lot of hope in the Depression. Even the blokes that were on the track and humping the bluey felt that times would change. There was a better spirit. You didn't have drugs and thieving and the rest of it.

The other word they'd like to pass on, with a recommendation, is 'self-reliance'. Facing hardship with a determination to overcome it depends, in their view, on being self-reliant and they fear the consumer society has made us all rather too passive. The computer craze, in particular, troubles them, because they see their grandchildren relying too heavily on video games to entertain themselves. They see boredom as having become the great bogey of the young, to be avoided at all costs, but they wonder whether boredom should sometimes be left to run its course, as a stimulator to more self-reliant activity.

(This attitude is echoed in advice given to parents by the Master of one of Sydney Grammar's preparatory schools, Bryan Pennington: 'If your son tells you he's bored in the holidays, then he's not bored enough. When he's really bored, he'll find something to do.')

'Children shouldn't be overindulged'

There's a touch of guilt in this piece of advice. Seniors know they were the first generation to introduce their children to the joys and hazards of consumerism, and they sometimes wonder whether they put enough emphasis on the hazards.

They accept as a virtual law of nature the proposition that 'you always try to do more for your children than your parents did for you'. They acknowledge that they gave their children so much that it might have amounted to 'indulgence', but their excuse, if they needed one, was that they were making up for their own deprived childhoods, that the consumer society was abuzz with new life—and a dazzling array of new products— in the Fifties and Sixties, and that the symbols of middle-class prosperity were mainly material symbols. This, after all, was the generation for whom expressions like 'keeping up with the Joneses' and 'status symbols' were invented.

Whatever failings they might admit to in their parenting (and they typically claim to have been far better parents than their own parents had been), the seniors would like us to know that, on reflection, they think children suffer from being overindulged—not just in material ways, but also in being treated *too* carefully and taken *too* seriously.

Kids are starting to think they are too important.

Schooling has changed dreadfully. When I was with the Department, kids jumped when you spoke. Now the attitude to teachers is almost contemptuous. The kids have challenged the discipline of parents, schools and the community ... and the kids have won.

Seniors would urge young parents not to 'bend over backwards' for their children, but also not to use material possessions or other forms of indulgence as a compensation for lack of parenting, or as a substitute parent:

Children need their parents, not computers.

My daughter talks about her quality time with the children, but she makes too much of a big deal of it. She takes them to restaurants to make time to talk to them. I tell her you just have to be around more ... but she simply hasn't got the time.

'Retirement? Go for it'

As long as they are in good health, people in retirement generally find it to be a pleasant surprise. Though some find the adjustment painful, the more typical story is for people to experience unspeakable relief at finding they are free to do what they want to do, not what they have to do.

Few retirees believe they were fully prepared for the pleasures of the retired state. 'If I'd known it was going to be this good, I would have done it years earlier' is a typical remark—usually retracted after doing some quick financial calculations. Men often contrast their retirement with their fathers' experience: the previous generation seemed to work for longer, and die younger, so retirement wasn't the prolonged state that it turns out to be for so many contemporary retirees.

My old man never really enjoyed his retirement—he worked like a dog, right to the end.

I don't think my father could afford to retire, and the pension wasn't nearly as generous in their day. In fact, I'm not sure they even had one.

My father never had the luxury of a happy retirement like I'm having.

There are some conditions that have to be met, of course, such as reasonable health and financial security. Though the aged pension seems to be regarded as adequate—particularly by those who don't receive it— many pensioners and some self-funded retirees are acutely aware that they are marginalised in all the talk of growth and prosperity. Some self-funded retirees even claim to be wondering whether they would have been better off 'living it up' while earning an income, and then going on the pension. (Perhaps this is where the Boomers got the idea.)

A common view is that it's a mistake to move too far away from friends and family and that if you're determined to retire to some little town on the coast, you should ideally establish a base there and create a social network a few years before you make the final move.

Here's another of the arts of retirement: picking the right moment for moving out of a family home into something smaller or into a retirement village.

The hardest decision of all is knowing when is the best time to move out of your home into something a bit more manageable. If you leave it too long, it can be a real hassle, and it can feel as if you are basically finished.

Though people in retirement say eulogistic things, like 'every day is the best day', and 'I don't know how I ever found the time to go to work', and 'there's so much to do and so much to see—I'm much more active than my parents were at this stage of their lives', it's not all beer and skittles.

Three recurring complaints:

Personal safety. Older people feel they are peculiarly vulnerable to personal assault and robbery, and they often become afraid of going out at night, or alone. 'Security' and 'peace of mind' are big issues, not only because they are an immediate worry for seniors themselves, but also because their loss is perceived as a symptom of the gradual breakdown of society.

Superannuation. It's often described as 'a nightmare' and some self-funded retirees feel as if they have been penalised for making proper provision for their retirement. The main complaints: 'The rules keep changing'; 'You're at the mercy of interest rates'; 'You still pay tax on it, even though you've already paid tax on all the income you earned while you were providing for your retirement'.

Recognition. Seniors feel that they are well supported by pensions, health benefits, Seniors' Cards and the like, but they wonder whether less respect is accorded to older people today than in the past. Young people don't give up seats on public transport; society seems to be in the grip of a 'cult of youth'; it's easy to feel as if you're regarded as a drain on resources—a generation who have outlived their usefulness. (There are many exceptions to this view: some seniors report the great pleasure they take in young people's conversation with them, and those who are involved in voluntary work are gratified by the recognition they receive.)

Not surprisingly, seniors love special treatment: cut-price days at the movies, free coffee from McDonald's, concessions in restaurants, on public transport and in their dealings with many business organisations, 'as long as you're prepared to admit you're a senior'. So that's another piece of advice: don't be afraid to reveal your age—it might do you some good.

'Avoid looking in mirrors'

One of the most persistent attitudes among seniors is that 'I don't *feel* old'. It is only when they look at their own children and grandchildren that people are forced to acknowledge that they must be 'getting on'.

There's widespread belief that they look younger, feel younger and act younger than their parents did at the same age. (By the way, their children—the Baby Boomers—are already saying the same thing about themselves, so perhaps that's what every generation says.)

The big thing, as you get older, is to avoid mirrors.

The other big thing—if only you could control it—is not to live too long:

My mother is 91 and she's beginning to fail. I don't want to be 91, I've decided.

I know you can't choose, but I'm sure most of us would like to go quickly, when the time comes.

A cautionary footnote: 'I am granny, hear me roar'

There's a growing rumble of discontent, still only faintly perceptible, emerging from some members of the contemporary generation of grandmothers. Faced with the prospect of becoming their working daughters' unpaid staff, they are making noises which seriously challenge the stereotype of the serene, gracious, benign—and acquiescent—older woman.

It's not at the stage where we're likely to see an army of grandmothers storming the barricades of a new counter-revolution, wearing Grannies'

Lib cardigans and chanting, 'What do we want? Our promised freedom! When do we want it? Now!' The movement is more genteel than that, and less focused. It springs from a classic dilemma: women who have strongly supported their daughters' drive for greater freedom and independence are now wondering whether they have sacrificed too much of themselves in the process. Even those who have longed for the joy of grandchildren occasionally find themselves wishing for some relief from the burden of caring for them ... or hoping, at least, for a more generous acknowledgement of their contribution.

I go all round the globe for my daughter, picking children up and taking them places and going to school when their mother can't be at Parents' Day. That's one reason I couldn't move away. She says to me, 'You won't leave me, will you Mum?'

Such grumbling is done very, very quietly—and mainly to other grandmothers in the same boat—because these women are fiercely proud of their daughters and full of admiration for the way they have fought for equality in education, in the workplace and in marriage. They like the feistiness of many of their daughters' generation of women; they admire many of the ways in which feminism has found its voice and transformed our society.

So they are rather embarrassed about their lurking sense of resentment; they don't want it to be misinterpreted by their daughters, and especially not by their grandchildren. There is no question of whether they love their grandchildren: the only question is whether they really wanted to be a parent all over again.

Yet, recognising that their daughters have neither the time nor the energy for full-time parenting—and recognising, too, that the demands of children can sometimes be the last straw when a marriage is sagging under the burden of both partners' jobs—they see no alternative. They hear horror stories about 'the dreaded child care' from other grandmothers who are not close enough to their daughters, geographically or emotionally, to be able to offer help, and they are thankful that in spite of the effort involved, they can play a useful role.

They are also glad of the opportunity to exert some influence on the development, especially the manners and moral development, of their grandchildren, because they harbour secret doubts about the real value of the 'quality time' so loudly trumpeted by their daughters.

In previous generations, a grandmother playing an active role in the raising of the young might have been accused of unwelcome interference; today, the grandmother's help having been actively recruited, a daughter can hardly complain if her children show signs of adopting their grandmother's standards ('Grandma says we shouldn't have so much takeaway'). Indeed, many grandmothers—and grandfathers, too, of course—welcome their inclusion in something approaching an extended family set-up, though, as they frequently say, 'you soon develop the knack of knowing when to make yourself scarce'.

Given all the advantages of more active grandmothering for the grandmothers themselves, what's the problem? Partly it's a question of expectation: they—and especially their husbands—had assumed that retirement would offer less structure and more freedom than is possible when they take on the role of 'secondary carer'—or, in some cases, primary carer—for their grandchildren.

A far more vexing problem lies in their daughters' attitude to them. The greatest of all the paradoxes of the women's movement is that some of the very daughters who criticised their mothers for being doormats, or slaves to their children, are now relying on those same mothers to continue shouldering the domestic and parenting load for the next generation as well.

While grandmothers will ruefully remark, with some pleasure, that 'you never stop being a mother' they might also say, in the next breath (or, perhaps, under the next breath): 'I'm a slave to my daughter's liberation.' The daughters themselves rarely acknowledge this, though some can be heard to remark that 'I'm lucky to have my parents on tap' for regular, or even emergency, child care.

It's that 'on tap' that's the real sticking point for these grandmothers. The sense that they are taken for granted, rather as a paid cleaner or nanny might be, is irritating and sometimes distressing. And when they hear their daughters declaring that, in the future, 'there's no way I'm going to give up work to be a grandma', they wonder whether they are simply being exploited.

That, certainly, is one of the inconsistencies in Baby Boomers' attitudes as they hurtle towards their own retirement and possible grandparenthood.

I'm so grateful to my mother for all the support she's given me. But I've told my daughter that she can't expect to have the same support from me. I've been a working mother, and I'm going to be a working grandmother. My husband isn't talking about giving up work so he can be available for looking after grandchildren, if we ever have any, so why should I?

None of our children is showing the slightest sign of wanting children of their own. Not yet, anyway. And it's just as well. I have no intention of giving up work. Now that they are grown up and gone, I'm really getting into my stride. It would be very awkward if they asked for my help.

The thing that might well 'save' the next generation of grandparents is the combination of the falling birthrate (many couples will have no children; many will settle for one; few will have more than two), the acceptance of 'child care' as the new norm for preschoolers, and the increasing variety of after-school care facilities—sporting programs, coaching, music lessons, supervised play—for children of primary-school age.

But today's generation of grandmothers would say, almost without exception, that if their daughters are not careful, they will miss out on one of the great pleasures of seniority.

I've looked at my daughter all the way through and wondered if she is really getting the balance right. She is perpetually tired, and I don't think she has really had the time or energy to enjoy motherhood as much as my generation did. Now she's talking about working up to age 60 or beyond. I hope she knows what she's doing.

Not all Boomer women will choose to work until 'retirement age'—

though in many organisations and industries there are no longer mandatory ages of retirement. Some of them are pleased to withdraw from the workforce, either because they've made their point and now feel it's time for a breather, or because the financial pressure on the household has eased and they can look to other forms of gratification and fulfilment. (The idea that, in the end, it is still the man's responsibility to be the ultimate breadwinner is still deeply ingrained, even in the thinking of many women who would otherwise describe themselves as fully-fledged feminists.)

But whether grandparenting is on their agenda remains to be seen. The older generation hope it will be. Some of them might quietly 'roar' about the excessive demands that have been made on their own time—and they sometimes wonder whether a better balance mightn't be possible, in their daughters' lives as well as their own—but they still hope that their daughters and sons will find time for the special pleasure of being an active, involved grandparent.

CHAPTER EIGHT

Heroes

The New Frontier

Turning Point: A common complaint at century's end is that we are short of old-style heroes. But perhaps we're looking in the wrong places. The world has changed, and so has heroism. The media throws up new celebrities every day, but no-one is fooled into thinking that fame—or even success—is the same as heroism.

What are we hoping for? A new style of hero—less remote, more here-and-now—who will lift our spirits and expand our sense of our own heroic potential at the new frontier of personal relationships.

Sir Charles Kingsford Smith had a big year in 1928. He became the first pilot to fly across the Pacific Ocean, the first to fly non-stop across Australia, and the first to fly across the Tasman. Two years later he cut five-and-a-half days off Bert Hinkler's London–Australia record.

Sir Charles Kingsford Smith—'Smithy'—was also famous for drinking a glass of beer while standing on his head, for flying a plane under Cowra Bridge, for founding the original Australian National Airways and for being insulted by an Australian Prime Minister (Billy Hughes, who called him a 'damned dreamer' and vetoed Smithy's plan to attempt a Britain–Australia flight in 1920).

Smithy was hailed as the world's greatest aviator, yet he was also pilloried by the press for an alleged publicity stunt which resulted in the deaths of two of his friends who were searching for him when he was lost in Western Australia.

He worked as a barnstormer to earn money. He pioneered the concept of airmail. He accurately predicted jet engines, airspeeds of 800 km/h, and stratospheric flight.

He took risks. He infuriated people. He was criticised for arrogance and egotism. And yet, he was unquestionably a hero: not just an adventurer, not just an achiever, but a true hero.

And what is that?

Personal sacrifice + Inspiration = Hero

For what it's worth, I'll give you my interpretation of the two essential ingredients that are to be found in the kind of people Australians regard as genuinely heroic:

They make personal sacrifices—in the form of risk or sustained, devoted work—in pioneering new frontiers of human endeavour.

They stir in the rest of us an expanded sense of human potential; they heighten our sense of *what we can do and who we can be.*

In other words, the true hero opens new frontiers, not only in aviation, or exploration, or medical science, or technology, or even sport, but also *in our imagination.*

Heroes inspire us because they show us what we humans are capable of doing. They are, in an old-fashioned sense of the word, our champions: they stand for us. They represent our capacity to prevail. They defend us against our own tendency to be sucked down into despair, depression or even boredom. They raise our sights, our hopes and our spirits. They inspire us.

Heroes have generally been regarded as remarkable people who do remarkable things. But their true greatness lies in their power to make us *all* feel more remarkable; to encourage us to share in their excitement, their challenges and their triumphs.

In the broad sweep of history, the greatest heroes have tended to be explorers and scientists. When you think of figures like Christopher Columbus and James Cook, you realise that it is almost impossible to imagine the depths of their courage and bravery. (Even those latter-day explorers, the astronauts, enjoyed the support of sophisticated technology: Columbus and Cook had no such support.)

Columbus and Cook carried with them on their voyages an ancient European dream: the dream of the New World, a utopia which would be discovered or established beyond the oceans. Their heroism is recorded in the legacy of entire nations created in their footprints. They *literally* expanded our sense of human potential by opening up the possibility of a new social order: the American Dream and, subsequently, the Australian Dream.

By the way, not everyone in Europe saw the Australian Dream in positive or potentially heroic terms. James Froude, an Englishman, visited Australia in 1885 and remarked that 'they will have good lawyers among them, good doctors, good men of science, engineers, merchants, manufacturers, as the Romans had in the decline of the Empire. But of *the heroic type of man*, of whom poets will sing, there will not be so many, when the generation is gone which was born and bred in the Old World. Such men are not wanted, and would have no work cut out for them.'[1] Still, for many other Europeans, the idea of an antipodean utopia was very appealing indeed, and still is. (And presumably even James Froude would be prepared to eat his words when confronted by the varieties of heroism displayed by Australians as diverse as Macfarlane Burnet, Howard Florey, Edith Cowan, Alfred Deakin, W C Wentworth, General John Monash ...)

It takes time to know who the real heroes are: stunning achievements may impress us, but there are deeper qualities in a true hero that are sometimes only fully grasped over time. A person may do something that looks like the stuff of legend, but the way they handle fame might be an even greater test. Still, there are plenty of latter-day heroes, more modest in scope than Columbus or Cook, yet inspiring in their own ways: Edmund Hillary on Everest, Neil Armstrong on the moon, John Landy on the track (not for winning, but for upholding the noblest standards of sportsmanship when he stopped in the middle of an important race to help a fallen competitor). All of them—and many others—demonstrated that all-important capacity to inspire us; to unlock our imagination; to encourage us to believe in the potential of the human spirit to aim higher, to go further, to do better ... to achieve something beyond our dreams.

Media exposure can easily overcook a hero

But those are all names from the past. What about today? Where are the heroes in this media-saturated, culturally destabilised, anxious, neurotic, postmodern world?

Has TV—as it is so often accused of doing—diminished the possibility of heroes, and devalued the very word, by feeding us too many stories about too many celebrities, surrounded by too much hype? Have the media created too much fame? And is it all too fleeting?

Does TV inhibit the emergence of true heroes by making them too accessible, too human, too immediate in their presence among us? (Fred Hollows was a heroic figure in the minds of many Australians, but we came to know more about his warts than we really needed to, and perhaps his death saved him from overexposure.)

Almost every day's news brings a fresh sporting 'hero' to our attention, but while sporting prowess is admirable, and many sporting feats require enormous determination and courage, few players of any sport would regard themselves as heroes. It is hardly heroic to win a game, though the manner of playing may sometimes constitute heroism. Don Bradman, for example, was possibly the greatest batsman the world has ever seen. He is undoubtedly a legend, but he would be the last person to claim hero status for himself. He was an exceptional cricketer, and that is sufficient to ensure his place in the sporting pantheon.

Roger Bannister, the first man to run a mile in less than four minutes, kept his sporting feats in perspective. He rejected an offered knighthood at the time, only becoming Sir Roger many years later when his services to medicine were recognised.

It is getting harder to be a traditional hero in the postmodern world. This is the age of subjectivity, in which we make very ready judgments about each other and in which everyone's opinion is taken to be equal to everyone else's. This is a period when we seem to be losing respect for authority, when the process of deconstruction—in everything from literature to heroism—often seems like a kind of belittlement.

Everything is moving too quickly—and instant legends are too easy to create—for heroes to be established in the public mind. Today's potential hero (or was he/she a mere celebrity?) is soon pushed aside by tomorrow's headline.

Are we even corporatising heroes?

Two things seem to be changing in the world of heroism.

On a big scale, 'heroic' organisations seem to be replacing the idea of individual heroes. Greenpeace and Amnesty International, for example, have acquired a quasi-religious status in the minds of many people and their work—like that of the Red Cross and countless other aid organisations—is done by essentially anonymous workers. Many of those workers are undoubtedly heroes. We will never know their names but their work has made the organisations themselves seem heroic.

Mark Taylor, the recently-retired Australian cricket captain, spoke movingly and compellingly of the heroes he most admired. When he was nominated as Australian of the Year in 1999, he said this: 'The people I generally most admire are the volunteer workers. I think they're probably the real heroes in our society. They don't end up on the back pages or the front pages like I do but they work harder than I do.'[2]

Public broadcasting organisations like the ABC, research organisations like the CSIRO, medical research foundations and philanthropic trusts do wonderful work that sometimes rises to the heights of heroism. Perhaps we are corporatising and bureaucratising our heroes.

Unsung heroes have always been part of us, of course; not necessarily buried in an organisation, but possibly just chipping away, year after year, making personal sacrifices that enrich our lives and encourage us to aspire to something beyond the everyday in our own lives. Volunteers of all kinds, teachers, creative artists, counsellors, medical practitioners in financially unrewarding hospital appointments, clergy, even some politicians—people can be found in all kinds of unlit corners of society, working unselfishly to improve the lot of the rest of us.

Heroism is a response to a more noble ideal than adventure

But there's a second shift in the character of turn-of-the-century heroism—a shift that fits with the emerging culture of postmodernism. The heroic focus is narrowing. The new breed are the heroes of the inner life; the tools of the new hero are more likely to be *values* than maps and compasses, test tubes or spaceships. Sacrifice is still a central theme, but we are more likely to be impressed by sacrifice made in the name of social progress than in some grand feat of human endurance.

One reason for this shift is that the distinction between old-style heroism and the 'heroics' of self-indulgence has blurred. Mountaineers, round-the-world sailors and pilots undertaking long solo flights, for example, may engage in exploits of great difficulty, requiring huge reserves of courage, skill and bravery, but when they are doing it for fun, or simply as a way of achieving some personal goal, the impact on others is far from heroic. Particularly when they are following in the steps of a genuine pioneer, there is a disturbing element of mock-heroism—game-playing—about their activities that makes them seem entertaining rather than heroic.

Such adventurers certainly run into all kinds of difficulties, sometimes as a result of irresponsibility, and they create controversy about the amounts of public money required to be spent in order to pluck them, for example, from a capsized yacht in a boiling ocean. Some of the sagas of survival under such conditions—such as the extraordinary rescue in the Southern Ocean of British yachtsman Tony Bullimore in 1997—are undeniably impressive and inspiring. The resilience of the human spirit is amply demonstrated in circumstances like those.

But sacrifice? Heroism? The will to live is one of the strongest of human urges, especially when an untimely death is threatened. Survival against such overwhelming odds is remarkable but not, of itself, the kind of thing we would normally call heroic, or even brave.

Captain Lawrence Oates, a member of Scott's ill-fated Antarctic expedition of 1910–12, exemplified heroism: he chose death, rather than a struggle for survival, in deference to the welfare of the other members of the team. His words on leaving the protection of their tent in a blizzard—'I am just going outside and I may be some time'—have rung down the century, reminding us that the essence of bravery, and heroism, is sacrifice, not foolhardiness.

Given that so many people are now retracing the steps of former heroes, it is perhaps not surprising that heroism itself is being redefined. Responsiveness, not to the urge for adventure but to the needs of others, has become the crucial test of heroism in the postmodern world. When all around are bent on serving their own ends, and when materialism has a society in its grip, it is the small voice of service—the whispered expression of non-material values—that begins to sound heroic.

Relationships are the new frontier

Heroism has entered the domain of Everyman. In the present cultural climate, we are no longer expecting giants: we are alert to the possibility of encountering heroism in ourselves and each other. We seem less inclined to accept the humdrum in our own lives; less inclined to settle for the inspiration of other people's stories. Increasingly, we want real fulfilment for ourselves.

We have entered an era of acknowledging *the hero within* . . . and that might turn out to be a very healthy development.

For example . . .

If you search our recent history for real pioneers who have inspired us, you need look no further than the feminists who led the women's movement of the 1970s. They redefined the role of women in our society and, in the process, revolutionised the meaning of gender. Many of the women who have taken up the cause of feminism have been nothing less than heroic in their painful journey to establish their right to full, independent personhood. Such women, nameless to all but their own small circle of family, friends and work colleagues, have, indeed, explored new frontiers and expanded our understanding of what it means to be human.

But so have those—women *and* men—who have taken parenting seriously and tried to discharge their responsibility to minimise the damage they do to their children. (All parents damage their children, of course; that's life. But the heroes are those who actually shoulder the awesome, and often tiresome, responsibility of trying to get it right, day after day.)

And so have those who have shown leadership in the development of a more tolerant, more ethnically diverse society.

So have managers who have tried to break new ground in the organisations they lead, by being more sensitive, more consultative, more responsive to the needs of their employees and more accommodating of the changing values and responsibilities of those who work for them.

Today's heroes are, almost by definition, destined to be unsung. They are the people who are pioneering new frontiers of personal development; exploring new approaches to social responsibility; finding richer meanings for words like 'marriage', 'success', 'community' and even 'culture'.

They are the people who are fighting intensely private battles against ignorance, prejudice, intolerance and apathy.

This is *the new order of heroism*. People like Smithy inspire and thrill us—but, at the turn of the century, most of the challenges that face us have moved to a different frontier:

The challenge of learning how to deal with life in an inherently unstable society (how to stay sane, even, in the face of the growing temptation to retreat into one neurosis or another);

Learning how to cope with pervasive stress of a kind unknown in the era of people like Smithy;

Learning how to manage relationships between people whose roles are increasingly complex and who, as a result, are constantly refining and adapting their values;

Learning how to keep in touch with each other, when the pressure to fragment our social networks is almost irresistible.

These are the challenges that demand a new kind of hero. The old kind isn't dead—and we'll always know them when we see them—but a postmodern world creates the possibility of a gentler, more intimate, more accessible brand of heroism.

CHAPTER NINE

Information

Can We Know Too Much?

Turning Point: Information has never been cheaper, more plentiful or more accessible. But we're becoming uneasy about the flood of information, much of it from electronic sources we don't understand and don't fully trust. Parents, in particular, are worried about their children's exposure to the new world of cyberspace and its effects on their judgment, their social skills and the use of their time.

What are we hoping for? A way of 'owning' and enjoying all this information without being either addicted to it or overwhelmed by it.

As a result of Allied bombing raids during the Second World War, 80 per cent of all buildings in Hamburg were destroyed, generating 40 million tonnes of rubble.

That's a lot of rubble—and that's also a piece of information. So now you have it, what are you going to do with it?

Will you recycle it over morning tea tomorrow, for something to say?

Will you store it up, in case an opportunity arises to demonstrate your grasp of information about the impact of bombing raids?

It seems such a graphic piece of information—80 per cent of buildings destroyed, 40 million tonnes of rubble—that you might imagine it would be hard to forget.

It's possible that you will remember it and that you might even find a way to make use of it, but I doubt it. After all, many TV viewers can't recall a single item they saw on the evening news, just an hour or two after they saw it, and that information is beautifully packaged and professionally presented.

Most of the information which reaches us every day is neither recalled nor reused. Some bits of it may momentarily distract us because they are quirky or arresting in some way, but most of it is destined to be sucked into the black hole of psychological oblivion. And so it should be, if it has no relevance to our personal circumstances. Our mental attics are already sufficiently cluttered with memories based on our direct experience, without trying to store lots of other people's stuff.

And yet, this being the Information Age, we struggle courageously to try and get our minds around as much information as possible. We have come to believe that it is our civic duty to know as much as we can and, indeed, to hold opinions about as many subjects as we possibly can.

In fact, I'm not sure that we shouldn't be talking about the Age of Opinions, rather than the Information Age. Not only are we expected to have opinions about everything from the prospects for peace in Kosovo to Bill Clinton's impeachment, but we expect our opinions to be taken seriously, and we train our children to expect the same.

Hugh Mackay

As a social researcher, I have to admit that our obsession with knowing a lot and having opinions about everything has been at least partly fuelled by the public opinion research industry itself. We'd better keep topping ourselves up on all these matters, in case some wandering survey interviewer accosts us and demands to know what we think—or, even more alarmingly, what we feel. Imagine being caught short; imagine being found to be *devoid* of an opinion about Northern Ireland or East Timor or the fate of the Palestinians. Imagine not being able to express appropriate indignation about the behaviour of the International Olympic Committee, or the Bosnian Serbs, or the improprieties of yesterday's discredited celebrity. Imagine saying that you're withholding judgment!

The problem is that we are being overwhelmed by information, and by an absurd expectation that we should have opinions about things that don't remotely concern us. Why are we so afraid to say 'don't know' or 'no opinion' or even 'don't care'?

The explosion of news and current affairs programming on radio and television and the dramatic emergence of computer-based information networks has created a shift from a world in which we once responded primarily to each other and to our immediate environment, to a world in which many of us now respond primarily to *mediated* information: not reality, but representations of reality or messages about reality.

What is emerging is a kind of 'information club' whose members can be identified by the range of subjects about which they are suitably informed and on which they can readily express opinions. If literacy was once the passport to acceptance in educated Australian society, being opinionated about current affairs may well be the emerging alternative. Where will it all end?

I have a vision of the ultimate info-victim: tap, tap, tapping on his keyboard, headphones clamped over his ears, with a bank of monitors flickering before him and cellular phones to right and left of him. This is a man who knows everything there is to be known. He can tell you what the weather's like in Kansas City right now; he can tell you Tony Blair's precise winning margin in the British general election of 1997; he knows where the most lurid pornography can be accessed, but he can also tap into a bland stream of innocent stockmarket information when someone else is looking over his shoulder.

He knows how to access the catalogue of the library of the University of Minnesota ... but he doesn't know where his own kids are, or what they're doing. He'll probably only realise his wife has left him when he receives an e-mail message from her. After a moment's reflection, he'll probably decide that a virtual-reality woman would be less trouble, anyway.

You don't have to be an *opponent* of technology to be a techno-sceptic. (See Chapter 20.) We need to be fully alert to the impact that this incessant flow of information is having on our lives and, in particular, on our relationships. Unless we carefully monitor the impact of the information revolution, we will become victims of it as surely as those who were sacrificed as factory fodder became victims of the Industrial Revolution.

A good starting point might simply be to remind ourselves that information technology is unnatural. No matter how sophisticated, brilliant, convenient or effective it might be, it is inevitably taking us further and further away from the kind of society in which humans have traditionally felt most comfortable.

Paul Burton, in his book *Information Technology and Society*, reminds us that 'technology has effects which go beyond those originally planned'.[1] We have only to look at the motor car or even the telephone—to say nothing of the printing press—to observe how radically technology can change the way we live and how, even when we are convinced of its value, it may produce unintended effects which we scarcely realise are happening.

Did we realise, for example, that mass literacy—made possible by the invention of the printing press—would create the climate in which the present information revolution could happen: a climate in which we had already learned to separate the message-sender from the message, and to interpret inky symbols as if they actually contained meaning? Did we realise, when we embraced the astonishing convenience of the telephone, that it would encourage us to stay away from each other and to rely on contacts which eliminate all the visual messages which normally play such a critical part in a person-to-person encounter?

No-one would suggest that we should do without the printing press or the phone—or the car, for that matter—but we have to acknowledge, as Burton suggests, that there is a complex interlinking of society and technology, 'in which cause and effect are ... difficult to disentangle'.

It is inevitable that information technology will change the way we live. It has already done so. This is a revolution, after all, and we can't expect to be unaffected by it. But that doesn't mean that we are irrevocably destined to become its unwitting victims.

We're better than machines at communication

It is easy to be seduced by the dazzling performance of the electronic media and to ascribe almost magical powers to them. But the truth is that machines can only move information around. They do it very well, but that's all they do. Data transfer is their one trick. No matter how brilliantly they do it, they can't approach the complexity, subtlety and richness of person-to-person communication. Communication is not simply the exchange of information: it is information attached to a personal relationship.

> A father is slumped in a chair, watching TV. His young daughter comes in to say goodnight. Why would we be outraged if we saw him ignore his daughter and remain glued to the screen? Why is it infuriating when you visit someone and they leave the TV on?

Communication is something we do *with another person*: we share meaning with them. Information, whether in the form of words, facial expressions or a particular tone of voice or rate of speech, is merely the set of signs and symbols we use for expressing and exchanging our meanings. (What a pity we ever coined the term 'mass communication' to describe a process which is really only the mass dissemination of information.)

When you're caught up in the excitement of the information revolution, it's easy to be seduced by the idea that moving information around is the same thing as communication and that, since machines can obviously move information around more quickly, more accurately and more efficiently than people can, machines are superior communicators. Here is a chilling quote from George Miller, an American academic, who wrote an essay—way back in 1967—called 'The Human Link in Communication Systems':

It is quite clear that man is a miserable component in a communication system. He has a narrow bandwidth, a high noise level, is expensive to maintain, and sleeps eight hours out of every twenty-four. Even though we can't eliminate him completely, it is certainly a wise practice to replace him whenever we can ... our society has already made the first steps towards eliminating human bottlenecks from communication systems, and the years ahead are sure to bring many more.[2]

You might hope, from the tone of those remarks, that Miller was being ironic or whimsical but, in fact, he was making a serious point which is often made by people who confuse the process of communication with data-transfer systems.

It's our failure to distinguish between data transfer and communication that explains why so many employees complain that, in the organisations for which they work, 'there are too many messages but not enough communication'. What they are complaining about is the data stream which flows endlessly, and sometimes torrentially, through the organisation, but which seems to exist quite independently of *personal relationships* up and down the management line. Everything from the printed staff newspaper to e-mail has its proper place in the total information system of an organisation, but whenever we fall for the trap of thinking that the dispensing of information *is* communication, we are in serious trouble. Communication rarely occurs in the absence of face-to-face contact.

In an interview with Thomas Moore, the American psychotherapist and author of *Soul Mates*, a journalist mentioned the growing popularity of computer-based information networks as a means of 'socialising' and, in particular, seeking friends or even spouses. He asked Moore this question: 'As the Internet is an invisible world, is there a better chance for people to know one another online and less chance of being judged for superficial qualities?'

Moore's reply was emphatic: 'As a therapist, I've heard this same story repeated a dozen times. Two people talk for months and imagine their relationship is deepening. They meet in person and—bam!—they can't relate. Something has changed. We are not just ethereal presences, or disembodied voices in cyberspace. Our faces and bodies express an enormous amount of data about who we are that can't be reduced, not if we want a real flesh-and-blood relationship. We need soul and body to communicate truly. You can't get around this.'

Bill Gates, the Chairman of Microsoft, has made the same point in relation to e-mail. He regards e-mail as a very good preparation for a meeting, and a very good way of summarising the outcome of a meeting, *but not as a substitute for a meeting.* Among other things, he remarks that 'e-mail is not a good way to get mad at someone, since you can't interact'.[3]

There's a clear message in all this: make as much use as you like of information technology for moving information from one place to another, but never assume that what you are doing is communicating.

The new face of materialism:

information is good; more is better

According to Neil Postman, the author of *Amusing Ourselves to Death*, the central thesis of information technology is that 'the principal difficulty in solving problems stems from insufficient data'.[4] You can see where that line of thinking takes you. Before long, you start to believe that the mere receiving of information—any information—is a worthwhile activity: 'Don't disturb Daddy; he's surfing the Net.'

Information has become cheap and plentiful. We live in the middle of an information supermarket, and, inevitably, we are responding by developing a huge appetite for more and more information. Info-greed is the latest eating disorder.

We are in danger of evolving into a *culture of information*: a culture where information is treated as if it's a valuable commodity of itself, whether it is relevant to us or not, and whether or not we have the time or the inclination—or the need—to interpret it.

The longer we sit in front of that TV set or that computer monitor, the more we find ourselves justifying our behaviour: information must be good for us, so the more we know, the wiser we will inevitably become. The American media commentator George Gilder raised some doubts about that cosy line of thinking when he echoed and embellished the famous lines of T S Eliot:

> Where is the wisdom we have lost in knowledge?
> Where is the knowledge we have lost in information?
> Where is the information we have lost in data?[5]

Some recent writers about information technology have tried to turn all this around and suggest that there is an inexorable progress from data to information, from information to knowledge, and from knowledge to wisdom.[6]

Perhaps there is, but there's another possibility. Under the influence of the information revolution, we are being so overloaded with information that our journey towards wisdom and maturity may actually be slowed by our dalliances with data.

If we allow ourselves to be swamped by too many messages, will we lose our sense of what is relevant under the weight of such massive amounts of data? If we immerse ourselves in a continuous flow of information, mightn't this actually diminish our capacity to sift and evaluate it? Mightn't there be a risk that we will be drawn into the information process in a way which excludes contemplation of it?

Those who allow themselves to become preoccupied with information—the people who have become unbalanced and addictive in their response to the information revolution—often turn out to be using information as a *distraction from thinking* (as long as I keep absorbing this information, I won't have to make sense of it); or as an *insulation from reality* (as long as I'm immersed in information, I don't have to confront what is actually going on around me); or as a form of *constant stimulation* to create the illusion that something is always happening (I'm never bored ... there's always the TV or the Internet, or the latest CD-ROM).

If you let the information keep coming, you will practically guarantee that your capacity to make sensible judgments about it will be dulled. We already have the example of the TV junkie to show us how uncritical we can become if we abandon ourselves to constant stimulation.

But there is another danger inherent in the idea that if information is good for us, more of it must be even better. Once we are trapped on the escalator of that argument, we might begin to think of information as something to *possess* in quantity; as a new expression of old-fashioned materialism. Before long, we'll be thinking of the *amount* of information we can access as a symbol of our status, in precisely the same way as certain material objects have in the past conferred status on their owners. (We already talk about the information-rich and the information-poor, and there is a real risk that information may well come to divide us—and stratify us—as surely as any other kind of possession.)

We simply need to remind ourselves that information is not the pathway to happiness, enlightenment or wisdom, any more than material prosperity is the pathway to any of those things. Information, of itself, sheds no light on the meaning of our lives. Indeed, like other possessions, too much information can conceal the meaning of our lives from us and can positively impede our progress towards wisdom. We can *know* too much, just as we can *have* too much.

My favourite primary school teacher, Miss King, knew her pupils were easily seduced by the idea that information was just another possession to be flaunted, and she was particularly tough on those children who were inclined to spout information for information's sake. She called it 'airing your knowledge', and she left us in no doubt that airing your knowledge was no different from any other form of showing off.

If you suffer from info-greed, even a piece of information about the rubble of World War II can seem valuable, until you start trying to work out what you're going to do with it.

Don't let information keep us from each other

The most significant of all the dangers associated with the information revolution is that we might become so preoccupied with sending and receiving messages—and so accustomed to interacting with machines— that we allow ourselves to become personally isolated from each other, even while we are cascading electronic information all over each other.

It would be simplistic to blame information technology for the sense of alienation which troubles so many Australians, especially young people, but it would be equally foolish to deny that information technology is making its contribution to that problem. The time we spend interacting with *mediated* information is time we are not spending with each other. If our media-focused time becomes excessive that poses a threat to our personal connections with each other.

Here's how the Harvard philosopher James Wilson describes this problem in relation to television:

> The real problem with prolonged television viewing is the same as the problem with any form of human isolation: it cuts the person off from those social relationships on which our moral nature in large part depends.[7]

So the danger of information overload is both social and moral. Once we recognise that moral sensitivity is a product of social interaction, we can appreciate the importance of nurturing our personal relationships and our communal life. (See Chapter 21.)

The most precious resource we have for coping with life in an unstable, discontinuous and revolutionary world is not information, but *each other*. Wisdom is not to be found in a database; it grows out of the experience of living the life of the human herd and absorbing the lessons which that experience inevitably teaches us about who we are. Thomas Moore puts it rather poetically in *Soul Mates*:

Every relationship, from the intense closeness of parent and child or partners in marriage to connections with co-workers, is an entanglement of souls. The gift in this entanglement is not only intimacy between persons, but also a revelation of the soul itself, along with an invitation to enter more deeply into its mysteries.[8]

A mere transfer of electronic data can't do that.

CHAPTER TEN

Job Insecurity

Changing the Way We Think About Work

Turning Point: Unemployment—especially youth unemployment and long-term unemployment—is a symptom of a deeper
problem: our failure to find an equitable and sensible way of
distributing the available work among the available workforce.
Ironically, the psychological problems created by unemployment
and underemployment are very similar to those created by overwork, so all is not well at either end of that spectrum. Attitudes
to work are changing, and women—taking a fresh look at the
pressures of life at the top—are forcing us all to rethink the place
of work in our lives. Many young people have already reached
the turning point.

What are we hoping for? A society that values work, but keeps
it in perspective by encouraging people to incorporate their jobs
into properly balanced lives.

Women typically don't have much testosterone in their bodies. But they do have just enough, apparently, to produce a typically male response to the stress of working in a traditionally male domain.

And what is that 'typically male response'? Baldness, of course.

Dr Hugh Rushton, a consultant trichologist at the University of Portsmouth, England, has conducted research in which he finds that women who adopt aggressive and competitive working styles, in an attempt to match traditional masculine approaches to work, may develop an increased sensitivity to their own testosterone, resulting in what Dr Rushton euphemistically describes as 'thinning of the hair and wider centre partings'. Dr Rushton found that 30 per cent of women in his study were experiencing hair loss.

He is not alone. A second opinion—from another British trichologist, Dr Glen Lyons—suggests that many women who are succeeding in fields previously dominated by males, such as law, medicine and journalism, often work much harder than men, not only because they are competing on turf previously considered men's' domain, but also because they are still juggling the demands of their traditional female roles, especially mothering.

Says Dr Lyons, in a statement which will resonate with working mothers everywhere, with or without hair: 'These career-minded women are placing enormous demands on their bodies.'

Is this what women's liberation promised? Is this the new world of work ... for women? Is the pay-off for sexual equality to be that women striving to succeed in direct competition with men will end up with wider centre partings? Do women who want to succeed in business, the professions or politics have to act like men? Is there no way of being equal, but different?

Does this mean that, when it comes to female employees in the upper echelons of business and the professions, we are incapable of revising our approach to the structure and the demands of work, in order to take into account some of the *other* demands made on women (and, increasingly, on men as well) because they happen to be complete human beings with families and private lives?

Is it the case that we are so unimaginative—as a society, as a corporation, as an employer—that we can't develop a more flexible notion of how to be a lawyer or a managing director or, indeed, a prime minister?

Women have sought the gratifications which flow from success at work for precisely the same reasons as men have sought them. It is true, of course, that women have only recently arrived in large numbers in the ranks of the professions and management, and it is true that, for many women, paid employment—and, in particular, *success* at work—is inextricably linked with the symbolism of the women's movement.

This is the first generation of senior women who, *en masse*, have used paid work as a symbol of their independence, of their determination to take control of their own destiny, and of their resistance to the idea of dependency on a male (with all the implications that flow from that, including the implication of second-hand identity and second-class status in our society). We are now looking at a workforce which is rapidly moving towards a 50–50 split between the sexes, so whatever we might say about women's search for satisfaction at work will not be radically different, and may not be different in any degree, from what we might say about men's motives.

For both men and women, work creates a pleasing sense of identity—or, at least, adds a significant dimension to our sense of identity. Even mundane work can provide, each day, a welcome structure, a pleasing sense of accomplishment and, of course, some quantification of the value of what you've done, in the form of wages.

This used to be one of the best kept secrets of a male-dominated workplace culture. But the secret is out: women now know that paid employment is one of the most satisfying and therapeutic ways of filling in your day. (By contrast, days spent at home, particularly for mothers of young children, are disorganised to the point of being chaotic, vaguely unsatisfying—in spite of the many joys of mothering—and, to make matters worse, unrewarded in a direct and quantifiable way.)

But hair loss wasn't supposed to be part of the deal, for women *or* men. Liberation wasn't supposed to mean a new kind of enslavement. The feminisation of the workplace wasn't meant to imply the masculinisation of women.

Did 'equality' have to mean that women would make the same

mistakes as men? Fall into the same traps? Did it have to mean that women would get their priorities just as wrong as all those men who are killing themselves with stress, while neglecting the parts of their lives—like their families—that could have kept them sane, and perhaps even hirsute?

Or is the problem more insidious than that? Is there something about the contemporary world of work that is bound to challenge the health, above or below the hairline, of any man *or* woman? I think there is.

The epidemic of job insecurity

We are living at a time when even people with apparently secure jobs in successful corporations feel as if the axe might fall at any time. The workforce has now become so used to the idea of downsizing that it is no longer taken for granted that performance guarantees employment.

In 1998, for example, people watched as the chief executive of BHP *and* the newly graduating class of Qantas apprentices all lost their jobs. From the top of the ladder to the bottom, it seemed, no-one was secure. Indeed, one of the deepest sources of uneasiness in Australia at the end of the 20th century is the growing conviction that government and private employers are intent on employing as few of us as possible; not as many as possible, as we might wish, but as few.

The folklore of work has changed, perhaps irrevocably. Workplace humour has turned black: 'If you've got a job, it's because they haven't yet worked out a way to get rid of you.' Research on the problem of job insecurity shows that *anticipation* of redundancy is at least as distressing as the experience of unemployment itself, and often more so. During economically unsettled times, even when the economy is said to be booming, many more people worry about the prospect of losing their job than the number who will actually be retrenched, which means that the sense of insecurity becomes a kind of epidemic.

My husband was so tense about the possibility of being made redundant that he was losing sleep, and getting cranky with the kids. I said to him, 'For goodness sake, resign. You'd be better off

*knowing your fate than putting yourself and your family through
all this anxiety.' But of course he wouldn't. Then the axe fell, and
it was actually a relief. He's found another job on less pay and with
less stress, and he's as happy as Larry.*

It is no longer assumed that primary, secondary and tertiary industries
exist for the purpose not only of supplying the needs of customers but
also providing work to the members of a prosperous society with an
optimistic outlook. Work is becoming associated with risk,
meanspiritedness, uncertainty and anxiety, because it is increasingly seen
in the context of corporations that, when forced to choose, will favour
short-term returns to shareholders over the provision of secure
employment for their employees.

When so many Australians either have no work or much less work
than they want, the apparent intractability of the problem of unemployment and underemployment has inevitably become a major social
issue. This is not only because unemployment or underemployment limits
the gratifications available through work, but also because they fuel the
process of redistributing household income to the alarming extent
described in Chapter 5. As that chapter shows, the great paradox of the
current distribution of work is that we are simultaneously creating a
rapidly-growing rich class and a rapidly-growing poor class.

But job insecurity is not only about the level of unemployment and
underemployment, or even the impact of the fear of retrenchment on
people's wellbeing; it is also about the pressures on those who have a job.
Australian researchers David Fryer and Anthony Winefield have
discovered that the mental health consequences of employment stress are
remarkably similar to those created by unemployment. Writing in the
Australian Journal of Social Research, Fryer and Winefield quote a
number of studies which point to anxiety, depression, psychiatric
morbidity, cognitive failure, headaches, sleep loss, burnout, skin disorders,
hypertension, chronic fatigue, substance abuse, aggression, coronary heart
disease and many other conditions—to say nothing of job dissatisfaction—
which have been reported as manifestations of psychological and
physiological strain arising from stressful employment.[1]

Stress at work can be induced by many factors: employment conditions, time pressures, role conflict and ambiguity (not being sure where your responsibilities begin and end), inadequate support, limited scope for decision-making, as well as an excessive workload. However it is induced, stress is the enemy of peace of mind; high levels of stress are the enemy of productivity.

It is ironic that, in the name of productivity and economic efficiency, we are imposing such a heavy load on our full-time workforce that, quite apart from their fear of the prospect of unemployment, they carry the burden of overwork.

Job insecurity has already become a factor in the reshaping of our workplace culture and values. Job insecurity means that the workforce begins to think about work *in a new way*. For a start, they assume disloyalty as part of the employer's value system, and so they develop a corresponding predisposition towards disloyalty in themselves. Why give your loyalty to an employer who is going to shed you if commanded to do so by the tyranny of the bottom line?

One of the greatest of the ironies of job insecurity is that, at the very time when management practices are becoming more enlightened and when there have been significant breakthroughs in our understanding of the world of work, the relationship between employees and many of the organisations who employ them has become strained. No amount of management enlightenment can compensate for the sense of job insecurity. It is hard for an employee to trust an employer when, lurking beneath the surface of good management practice, is the threat of having to look for another job, or having to retreat to part-time work, or having to shoulder an even greater burden of work to compensate for departed colleagues who are not going to be replaced.

Will the Baby Boomers reorder their priorities?

There are major generational differences in Australians' attitudes to work and the future of work. Those differences are most starkly revealed when we compare the baby-boom generation (born in the 15 years after the end of World War II) with the rising generation of young Australians who are now approaching, or have recently crossed, the threshold of the workplace.

As Chapter 2 suggests, one of the greatest problems the Baby Boomers have had to face is that their expectations of the future were created in the Fifties and Sixties. As they have moved into the middle years of their lives, it has dawned on them that the Nineties were never going to feel like the Sixties. The nuclear holocaust has not happened, but neither has that rosy future promised by the Sixties. Plunged into a period of social, cultural, economic and technological change, the Boomers have found themselves cast in the role of social pioneers. They have set a new record for the divorce rate; they have redefined gender roles; they have watched while Australia split into the haves and have-nots (contradicting their fondly-held belief in egalitarianism).

Not surprisingly, the Boomers' favourite word has become 'stress' and one of their most common cries is that 'it is all turning out to be much harder than we thought it would be'.

Under the strong influence of its female members, this generation is now rethinking its values, its goals and its aspirations. In particular, Boomer women (typically, women who have combined motherhood with paid employment outside the home) are beginning to ask why things are not turning out the way they expected. Their 'liberation' is not always as fulfilling or gratifying as they thought it would be. (See Chapter 23.)

Many of them are looking at the top of the jobs ladder and asking themselves whether it is worth the climb. Some are reaching positions of great seniority and responsibility and deciding that enough is enough. Either they are prepared to stay at that level, where they know they can just manage the juggling act that is their lives, or they are contemplating a retreat to part-time work or a move right out of the workforce, at least for a while.

A high-profile example of a remarkably successful businesswoman deliberately taking a sideways step is Jill Hickson. Announcing in May 1999 that she had sold her thriving literary agency, Hickson said, 'I just want to spend some time with my husband [former NSW premier, Neville Wran]. I want to be able to read to my children. I want time to clear my head. But I am not disappearing ...'

In a remark that will have given pause to overstretched senior executives, male and female, all around the country, Hickson said, 'When you want to go on, when you know you could go on, that's the time to go.'

Women who have come with a relatively uncluttered and unprejudiced view of the workplace have not always liked what they have seen. It goes without saying that they don't like to see men trying to protect their own power but, more significantly, they also don't like the prospect of doing a job which is going to take too heavy a toll on their own lives and, quite possibly, destroy the balance they have struggled to achieve between their work and their domestic and private lives.

Under their influence, many men—often the spouses or close colleagues of these sceptical women—are being encouraged to rethink their own attitudes to work. Reflecting on their own problem of stress, some of them are prepared to entertain the possibility that they might have been prepared to run too hard and to accept, without critical reflection, whatever demands were placed on them by the job. Then they, too, start to hanker after the goal of 'balance'.

A related factor in such reappraisals has been men's growing awareness of the emotional importance of fatherhood and the enrichment of their own lives, as well as their children's, that can flow from greater involvement in the process of parenting. Such thoughts create further pressure to pull back from blind, relentless ambition, and to consider—perhaps for the first time—the possibility that less responsibility at work might mean a more fulfilling life at home.

The tension between work and home is at least as excruciating for politicians—especially those holding ministerial rank—as it is for business executives and overworked professionals. What politician doesn't feel an immeasurable sense of debt to the family that accepts the demands of political life and is prepared to absorb the punishment that politics inflicts on its players? And what politician's family hasn't sometimes wished that the flame of political ambition would die? So it was no surprise when, in the middle of 1999, the Deputy Prime Minister, Minister for Trade and Leader of the National Party, Tim Fischer, announced his resignation from all three positions. He had decided to stay in parliament, but to return to the backbench. Mr Fischer attributed his decision to a combination of political and personal factors, though subsequent media commentary focused almost exclusively on the personal (and the political factors remain largely unexamined).

His wife, Judy Fischer, spoke of her enormous relief at his decision: 'To have a chance of having a family life and do all the things that we've said we'd do is really exciting.' But she went further than that: 'There is a lot of pressure [in politics] and I wouldn't think that our family could have stood it for another five years.'

In the community at large, the most common response to Mr Fischer's decision was approval. The idea that people should strike a balance between their working and personal lives is gaining currency. Even five years ago, if a man had stood up in a business meeting, looked at his watch, and announced that he had to leave in order to catch his daughter's performance in the school play, the eyebrows of his colleagues might well have been raised. The thought might have crossed their minds that his heart wasn't really in the job if he was prepared to put a school play ahead of an important meeting.

Today, there's some chance that their response would be closer to encouragement and support (and possibly even a little envy). Parenthood is becoming fashionable and although many men are still paying mere lip service to the idea of 'balance', at least the subject has been placed firmly on the agenda by the courage of those—women *and* men—who have seen what damage a job can do to their psychological wellbeing if its demands are allowed to run wild.

So far, these are merely hints, early signs that we might be approaching yet another turning point. If they become more widespread and more entrenched, then we will see more than the present trickle of senior people out of the executive suite: it will become a steady stream that won't slow down until employers begin to reconstruct executive packages in ways that take account of 'the whole person'.

Either way, we are heading for a new way of thinking about work and its place in our lives. I suspect that in 20 or 30 years' time, it will be generally acknowledged that the greatest single impact of the women's movement on the culture of this society was that it caused us to take seriously the need to strike a more sensible balance between the various roles that we are all obliged to play—in particular, the balance between our work and our personal lives.

The rising generation are keeping their options open

The children of the Boomers see all this rather differently. They are the generation who have grown up in the Seventies and Eighties and who are reaching adolescence and young adulthood in the Nineties.

Growing up in a period of accelerating change, the main lesson learned by the rising generation of young Australians has been to *expect change*. Because they expect tomorrow to be different from today, they are inclined to postpone commitments, to wait and see, and to 'hang loose'. Whether it's a set of religious beliefs, a political party, a sexual partner, a commercial brand, a course of study or a job, this is a generation that is saying, 'let's keep our options open'.

The turbulence that so destabilised their parents' generation is simply normal for them. Being the children of change, change is not much of an issue: it is the air they breathe; it is simply the way the world is. So they incorporate it quite naturally into their outlook. The prospect of continuous change is inherent in their approach to everything.

And why not? For this generation, 'the women's movement' was already history by the time they became aware of gender issues. The girls have always known that girls can do anything! (What is there to discuss? Why do their mothers go on about it?)

They have grown up with a high divorce rate. They accept one-parent families as normal—after all, about 20 per cent of them have lived with only one of their natural parents. They see the working mother as part of the normal social landscape.

They know that every piece of new technology is superseded by the time they get their hands on it.

They are even unimpressed by high unemployment—not that they like it, but it has become an integral part of their world. (At present, about 800 000 dependent children live in households where no wages are earned at all, and somewhere between 25 and 30 per cent of the work-seeking children of Boomers are currently unemployed).

While none of these things is remarkable in the eyes of young people, their attitudes and behaviour are inevitably affected by them. A high divorce rate, for example, changes their attitudes to marriage. They are marrying later, resisting marriage entirely in larger numbers, and having babies at a later stage in their lives than their parents did. (See Chapter 13.)

Similarly, living with high unemployment changes their attitudes to work. This is a generation that has largely abandoned a straight-line approach to work. They know that the jobs they want might not exist in ten years' time; they might end up doing jobs that don't exist now. Not many of them expect to get a job and keep it for life. They don't expect that an employer will take them on and stick with them forever, so they expect neither to give nor to be given loyalty in the workplace.

On the contrary, they accept that their working lives might turn out to be a kind of patchwork; a jigsaw puzzle; a series of jobs that, over time, fit together to create their world of work. Among young women who have been criticising their mothers for confusing 'having it all' with 'having it all-at-once', the goal of a more balanced life adds further impetus to the idea of moving in and out of the workforce as it suits them.

Some members of the Options generation have already begun to absorb this idea into their thinking about the value of work. They have relegated work to a less significant place in their lives than the place it occupied for their parents or grandparents, especially their grandfathers. (As an unemployed 20-year-old said in one of our recent studies: 'I tried work, but I didn't like it,' and, since half his mates were out of work, dropping back onto the dole seemed a natural alternative to an unpleasant job.)

Because they are interested in keeping their options open, they are looking for greater flexibility in the work that is offered to them. They want to know, more explicitly than their parents did, 'What's in it for me?' They are increasingly concerned about the way in which work will enhance their lives, rather than destroy their 'lifestyle'. Some of them have already decided that, whether they want to or not, they are unlikely to be as materially well off as their parents have been. Looking at their grandparents and seeing that they are less prosperous than their parents, some of them are saying, 'I wouldn't mind being like them: they seem more contented than my parents'.

Of course, all such brave predictions and intentions may be modified under the influence of actual experience of work—and, particularly, the experience of parenthood. But there is no doubt that the rising generation *think* that they are going to be more in control of their lives and more determined to keep their options open than their parents ever were. Choice—like change—is an inherent part of their world view.

So it would be a mistake to assume that at a time of high youth unemployment, young people will automatically be scrambling to accept whatever job is on offer. On the contrary, employers will have to woo them, because they have already decided that work is not going to be as important to them as it was to their parents. The rising generation of young Australians are likely to be the sharpest, most assertive, most sceptical and most demanding employees we've ever seen.

'Human Resources': a sign of the times?

It is an unfortunate coincidence that at the very time when Baby Boomers are beginning to rethink their attitudes to work, and members of the Options generation are becoming more sceptical about work and more determined to lead well-balanced lives, the term *human resources* has come into the language.

If anything is calculated to diminish an employee's sense of self-worth, surely being regarded as a 'human resource' would be it. Photocopiers, chairs, paperclips, computers, humans—are these merely the various resources that employers will exploit in order to get the job done? 'Human resources', as a term, must be one of the most offensive labels ever to be attached to people. It is also one of the most potent symbols of the tyranny of the bottom line.

To the question, 'Do you want to work for me?', the answer will increasingly be, 'Not if you're going to treat me like a human resource!'

If there is, indeed, a culture shift taking place in the world of work, in which people are more determined to be treated like human beings and to strike a better balance between their private and working lives, then employers will need to explore creative ways of ensuring that they are putting more—not less—emphasis on employees as *whole persons*, not resources.

An important sign of that will be the creation of more family-friendly workplaces. Whether the birthrate rises or not, there are still going to be plenty of mothers, and a growing number of fathers, too, who would like to be able to bring their young children to a workplace creche, or to have more flexible working hours, or to negotiate job-sharing arrangements. What they will not be looking for is the kind of insensitivity implied by an employment policy that treats them as an expendable resource.

Those women who took part in Dr Rushton's study of hair loss might have experienced stress as a result of competing with men on their own patch. But if you had been conditioned to feel like a 'human resource', wider centre partings would be the least of your worries.

Hugh Mackay

CHAPTER ELEVEN

Kooris

Reconciliation and the Good Ol' Aussie Values

Turning Point: After years of feeling that 'the Aboriginal question'—whatever it was—was either beyond them or irrelevant to them, Australians have begun to focus on the native title issue, the tragedy of the Stolen Generations and, more fundamentally, on the issue of reconciliation. There is still widespread disagreement about the most appropriate response, but the issues are on the agenda at least. Yet our history suggests that when we speak of 'traditional Australian values', we have rarely questioned whether they also apply to our relationship with Aboriginal people.

What are we hoping for? A non-divisive approach to reconciliation, with strong political leadership; an end to the sense of shame (for those that feel it), and a willingness to tackle Aboriginal issues—health, welfare, education, alcohol abuse—with understanding and compassion.

Martin Krygier, Professor of Law at the University of New South Wales and the ABC's 1997 Boyer Lecturer, recently had this to say about the plight of Aborigines since the arrival of European settlers in Australia:

> In our short history, there is nothing else that is equivalent to what happened to Aborigines. Those of us whose identity is bound up with this nation, and like to think well of it, can at least be relieved, even proud, that there are no other tragedies of this order. But the history of Aboriginal/settler relations is so full of incivility, indecency, injustice, poverty, not even to mention murder, dispossession and more, that we have every reason to feel shamed. Not usually, today, because of what we individually have done, nor as an extended version of personal guilt. Rather because of what our community has in its record and is responsible for, that community of which we are a part and which is part of us, in which we are bound up, whose successes and virtues please us and whose vices sadden us, which gives us elements of our identity, and for which we might feel affection, might even admit to feeling love. And since what we do now *is* our responsibility, it is hard to say we are good enough until we have adequately faced the challenge of that shame.
>
> Moreover, if we react with a determination to ignore the grounds of that shame, or to insist that it is simply cancelled by the good of our past and present, or to blame the victims, or to insist that what they regard as injustices were merely misfortunes, and anyway it was all in the past and we weren't here then, we have another—and more directly personal—reason to be ashamed.[1]

Professor Krygier puts the reconciliation question into perspective for us. Until we face and deal with the truth about Australia's treatment of its Aborigines, we can't begin to relax with the idea that we are a 'Good Society' (the title of Professor Krygier's article in *Eureka Street*, from which the above quotation was taken). This is part of our history, therefore it is part of us.

Professor Colin Tatz of the School of Humanities at Macquarie University has consistently maintained that unless we were prepared to make an official

Hugh Mackay

apology for the injustices done to Aboriginal people, we couldn't really claim to have understood or acknowledged the enormity of those injustices. The symbolic gesture is important, if only because, as Professor Tatz puts it in *Genocide in Australia,* 'apology is acknowledgement'. By contrast, mere acknowledgement is no sort of apology.[2]

Realpolitik, 1999 style, meant that there could be no formal apology, but only an expression of 'regret' by the Howard Government.

An apology would have been a potent symbol, but there are still problems in the administration of Aboriginal affairs, by both blacks and whites, that require bold, creative solutions. All the money spent on Aboriginal health, for example, has failed to narrow the gap between black and white mortality levels: that gap is, in fact, continuing to widen. And the various experiments in Aboriginal self-determination have had mixed results. Lowitja O'Donoghue, the former chairman of ATSIC, has called for radical reform of that body; Aboriginal leader Noel Pearson has acknowledged that welfare dependency among Aborigines is an issue that needs to be carefully addressed and thoroughly investigated; alcohol abuse and domestic violence are still rife in Aboriginal communities.

Even the issue of the so-called Stolen Generations strikes some Australians as vexed. There are certainly cases of Aboriginal children who were rescued from conditions that posed a threat to their wellbeing and who, on reflection, feel grateful to the white families who cared for them and the white communities that gave them an education and a secure place in white society. But such cases are outweighed by the horrific tales of forcible removal of children from their weeping mothers, and of the lifetime of anger, anguish and bewilderment suffered by people on both sides of those separations.

In any case, if we were to argue that the end justified the means, we would be on a moral slippery slope. The *principle* of forcible removal of children from their parents in order to 'civilise' them and socialise them into a Eurocentric culture, is an indefensible principle—unless you accept genocide as a legitimate strategy under certain conditions. 'Genocide' sounds like a harsh judgment on our own quite recent history, yet when the purpose of a policy is to eradicate, over time, the culture of a people, what else can you call it?

But these issues have been canvassed elsewhere by experts and authorities in the field. I am neither of those things.

Yet, as a social researcher who has spent his life listening to Australians talking about life in Australia, I have been driven to an additional conclusion about the matter of shame. I believe it is time for all of us—Aborigines and those who have settled here more recently, from Europe, Asia and elsewhere—to admit to each other that, in one particular respect, we have all failed; on both sides of the black/white divide, we should *all* be ashamed of ourselves. And this is not because of the appalling history of white Australia's treatment of Aborigines (from which many Australians are still able to keep their emotional distance), nor the appalling history of Aboriginal violence, drunkenness or any other socially disastrous behaviour.

No, our shame should be more immediate, more personal and more contemporary than any of that. We ought to be ashamed of our failure to understand each other's needs, each other's heritage and each other's aspirations. I'd go even further than that and say that we ought to be ashamed of our *lack of will*—on both sides—to understand each other's positions.

'Freedom' includes freedom from prejudice

and racism

We constantly hear Australians celebrating their faith in the Australian nation. Oh, they bleat, they whinge, they moan and they criticise everything from politics to the media and the performance of our national sporting teams, but, in the end, they want you to know that they wouldn't want to live anywhere else; that Australia is the best country on earth; and that Australia is—above all—a place of freedom.

But freedom for whom? And freedom from what?

When white Australians talk about the freedoms they enjoy, they mention religious freedom, sexual freedom, cultural freedom, freedom of speech, freedom from political tyranny—as well as the freedom which comes from living in a spacious continent with landscape and climate encouraging our enjoyment of the great outdoors.

An occasional cloud drifts across this blue sky of freedom. We have to admit that, sometimes, we are a bit intolerant towards the latest wave of immigrants, whether they happen to have come from Greece and Italy in the Fifties or Vietnam in the Nineties. We experience a frisson of anxiety when we hear that Buddhism is the fastest-growing religion in Australia or that it is conceivable that, by early in the next century, there will be one million Muslims living here.

But when it comes to Aboriginal freedom, Australians tell a very different story. Or, to be more precise, they tell no story at all. For years, they have expressed bewilderment, uncertainty and confusion. They have said, 'We don't know what Aborigines want'—as if that is the fault of the Aborigines. They talk as if Aborigines somehow lie outside the vision of freedom that inspires white Australians. If they mention Aborigines, it is likely to be in the context of a racist slur, taunt, or a joke in the most appalling bad taste.

When Australians talk about our multicultural society—or, as they prefer it, our cosmopolitan society—they rarely include Aboriginal culture in that discussion. When they talk about religious freedom, they rarely include Aboriginal religious life in their discussion. When they talk about the attractive diversity of Australian life—and the ability of Australians to choose their styles of living—they rarely acknowledge the diversity of Aboriginal people and the complexity of *their* different ways of life.

This is a curious state of affairs, considering three core values that most Australians would regard as being essential to any understanding of an Australian ethos.

Mateship, egalitarianism and the 'fair go'

As a word, 'mateship' has practically had its day. It has become too blokey, too political and too evocative of a bush culture that scarcely connects with the life of urban Australia. (As the former Labor leader and former Governor-General, Bill Hayden, once remarked: 'Being called "mate" by the NSW Right [of the Labor Party] is a bit like being given a bunch of flowers by the Mafia.')

When the Prime Minister attempted to incorporate 'mateship' into his draft of a new preamble to the Constitution, he was roundly criticised for using an outmoded word that, by its masculine connotations, excluded half the population.

The word might be dead on its feet, but the concept lives on. Although we have often used the word in ways that devalue its earlier meanings, it still has some currency as a shorthand way of describing a particular cluster of values: loyalty, a sense of mutual obligation, a willingness to respond to need *simply because it exists*. (Even white feminists understand that kind of mateship!) Mateship, converted into formal language, really refers to the noblest ideal of *good citizenship*. It implies the idea of embrace; connection; accepting that each of us is part of the same whole; acting as if we are all on the same team; accepting responsibility for each other's wellbeing.

Isn't it curious, therefore, that a society which is supposed to esteem the concept of mateship so highly should not have paid more careful attention to the Aboriginal people whom it displaced during the period of settlement and establishment in an alien land? Which of us white Australians could say, with integrity, that we have accepted Aborigines as if they, and we, are part of the same whole? Which of us could say that we are prepared to respond to Aborigines' needs *because they exist* without any thought of entitlement, or any question of whether Aboriginal people *deserve* this or that level of support.

And what about *egalitarianism*? Isn't Australia a place where we have dreamed of a broad, comfortable middle class which would be the envy of more rigidly stratified societies around the world? Isn't this the place where, during the Fifties and Sixties, the promise of universal economic prosperity was so strong and seductive that we believed in a society where we would *all* be prosperous? Even within the white community, the dream is turning sour as we observe the growth in rich and poor households, and a dramatically shrinking middle. (See Chapter 5.)

But while the ideal of egalitarianism itself begins to evaporate, we need to reflect on the fact that it never seemed, in practice, to be an ideal which

Hugh Mackay

was stretched to include Aboriginal people. Did we ever think, when we dreamed of our middle-class prosperity, that this should imply no sense of superiority to Aborigines whose values were so patently different from ours? Did we understand that egalitarianism was never intended to mean that we would all aspire to the same values; all want two cars and a swimming pool in the backyard? Rather, it should have meant that all people are equal, and must be given equal opportunities to pursue their own goals, within the limits of a just and fair society.

If we ever did have that understanding, I think we might have forgotten how to apply it to Aboriginal communities. Especially when it comes to the question of pastoral leases and their potential conflict with native title, we seem to have had great difficulty with the concept of egalitarianism, as if pastoral leasehold land is *ours* in a way which could not possibly be true for Aborigines who also want to claim it as *theirs*. (But there are signs of hope, especially in South Australia, where successful arrangements have been negotiated in which native title and pastoral leaseholds coexist, on the basis that each party respects the other's right to use the land in their own way.)

Australia has made itself famous as the land of the *fair go*. This is supposed to be the place where everyone is entitled to a hearing; where tolerance is elevated to the status of high virtue; where anyone who has a point of view can be sure that it will be heard.

So what about a fair go for Aborigines? Whatever happened to the idea of harmonious coexistence of different cultures?

Why can't we educate pastoralists to understand that their right to use the land as an economic resource does not cancel out Aborigines' right to use the very same land as a source of identity? And what about Aborigines, for their part, agreeing to act, in using the land, in ways which respect pastoralists' rights as well? Closing gates, extinguishing fires, being careful of stock and so on.

Is there nothing in the concept of the fair go which allows us to resolve land claims which are, in fact, competitive only at the most superficial level—since pastoralists and Aborigines don't want to do the same things on the same land?

But perhaps the concept of the 'fair go' is suffering the same fate as egalitarianism—and, indeed, mateship. It is not only in relation to Aborigines that we are becoming resistant to the idea of giving everyone a fair go. We are failing to attack the problem of youth unemployment, thereby denying any sensible meaning of egalitarianism to an entire generation of young Australians and, in the process, denying many of them a fair go. Already, the 'haves' in our community have become obsessed about their status, their security and their personal safety. The 'have-nots' are increasingly angry about their inability to gain a toehold on the ladder of the fair go.

But somewhere in the distance, not even within cooee of that ladder, are Aborigines for whom the idea of a 'fair go' is about as realistic as the story of the goose that laid the golden eggs. For people like Melbourne footballer Jeff Farmer, who once complained that he had to cope with racist taunts every day of his life, the idea that 'a fair go' might be fundamental to Australian values would seem laughable.

That is our failing. That is the source of the shame we should properly feel. We have simply failed to understand that the values we profess to hold seem to stop at the end of our own cultural backyard.

The need for leadership

On Friday, 30 April 1999, Justice O'Loughlin of the Federal Court rejected the Commonwealth's application to strike out the civil action brought against it by two members of the Stolen Generations, Lorna Cubillo and Peter Gunner.

Setting aside the legalities of the Judge's decision, and the grounds for the Commonwealth's application, the very fact that the application was made raises important questions about the Federal Government's moral leadership in the process of reconciliation between white and Aboriginal Australians.

Robert Manne, Associate Professor of Politics at La Trobe University, remarked at the time of the Federal Court action that if the Commonwealth's application had been upheld and Cubillo and Gunner had been denied their day in court, this would have had a disastrous effect on Aboriginal perceptions of the Howard Government's sincerity in its talk of reconciliation. 'What effect did [the Government] think it would have,' Manne asks, 'on the millions of non-Aboriginal citizens for whom the question of Aboriginal child removal is a matter of bafflement and shame?'

Manne's assessment: 'The question of how this country now deals with the surviving members of the stolen generations has become central to the process we call reconciliation'. He also draws our attention to the bizarre situation that existed in the Prime Minister's Department, where one group of advisers was working to advance the process of Aboriginal reconciliation while another group in the same Department, working on the application to have the Cubillo-Gunner case struck out, had 'developed a legal strategy potentially lethal to the reconciliation cause ... In the case of the stolen generations, it is not the law but the Government which has been behaving like an ass'.[3]

Although Aboriginal issues are now on the national agenda to an extent they have never been before, it would be quite wrong to assume that they are in the forefront of the public's mind. Considering the long history of prejudice and hostility between whites and blacks, it would take very little to plunge our society back into a morass of racism directed at Aborigines. Weak or ambiguous leadership on the issue would be enough to do it. This is the moment for national leaders, across the political spectrum, to add momentum to the community's wish to see justice done.

In his 1998 election victory speech, John Howard committed himself to a process of 'very genuine' reconciliation with the Aboriginal people. In August 1999, he rejected the powerful symbolism of a formal apology, moving only that the Parliament express its 'deep and sincere regret' for injustices suffered by Aborigines 'under the practices of past generations'.

The issue of reconciliation needs to be understood in the context of the demographic fact that Aborigines represent about *two per cent* of the Australian population. This is not America. We do not have a 'race problem' which is numerically large. Aborigines are one of the smallest cultural and ethnic minorities in our society. If we can't find a pathway to reconciliation between the 98 per cent and the two per cent, there is no hope for us. The way we define that pathway, and the speed with which we move along it, will be the measure of our civilisation.

All we have to remember is that each of us wants to be taken seriously. Each of us wants to be heard. Each of us wants our needs, our values, our points of view, to be taken into account. That is all reconciliation has ever been about. The challenge is actually tiny, and it has little to do with 'past generations': it is a matter of insisting that the values we hold up as being characteristic of our society should be extended to embrace *all* Australians.

Hugh Mackay

CHAPTER TWELVE

Leadership

Please Explain Us To Ourselves

Turning Point: When people are feeling insecure and uncertain, they yearn for strength and vision at the top. They dream of a leader who can articulate a clear sense of Australia's destiny but who hasn't lost the common touch; a person who combines integrity with humility; a person whose own ambition doesn't get in the way of understanding and responding to the needs of the people. Australians are disappointed with the quality of national leadership at the turn of the century, but they know what they want.

What are we hoping for? Leaders who instil confidence in us by their strength of purpose, their ability to paint an appealing picture of the kind of society we could become, and their capacity to inspire us—to bring out the best in us.

There's a telling little anecdote, tucked away in the Old Testament's Book of Exodus (chapter 32, if you want to follow this up) that casts some useful light on the problem of leadership and helps to explain the psychology of that most dangerous of all political phenomena: the *leadership vacuum*.

In this story, Moses has disappeared up a mountain, as he was wont to do. When he fails to reappear, the Children of Israel grow impatient—not only with Moses, but also with his God. Like leaderless people everywhere, they look around for something to fill the void. Aaron is pressed into service and asked to manufacture a god that is more to their liking. Aaron obliges with a golden calf, fashioned out of the Israelites' jewellery.

The people are so pleased with the result, they settle down to some serious feasting. The next day, they rise early and sacrifice burnt offerings and, as the day wears on, involve themselves in a little harmless revelry. (Well, not harmless so much as predictable.)

God doesn't approve of any of that, needless to say, and threatens to destroy the lot of them. But Moses, back in action, intervenes on behalf of his people and all is finally set to rights.

Here's another story: different time, different genre.

There was once a top-rating American TV series called *Lois & Clark: The New Adventures of Superman*. An important ingredient in the success of each episode was the sexual tension between Superman/Clark Kent and Lois Lane; a kind of 'will-they/won't-they?' tease that kept viewers intrigued long after the Superman thing had worn off.

This program, like most top American TV shows, was subjected to regular audience research, so the producers could be sure their formula was still working and so they could detect any sign of viewer fatigue that might precipitate a slump in the ratings. (Success is a fragile thing in the world of TV ratings, and the approach is very scientific; big money is at stake.)

But when *Lois & Clark* was put to the test, there was no sign of viewer fatigue. No sir! Quite the contrary. Its devoted viewers were so emotionally involved in the series that they said they'd quite like the sexual tension to be resolved one way or the other. They were curious to know whether Superman finally gets the girl.

The producers scratched their heads. If they gave the viewers what they wanted, they would have eliminated the magic spark that lay at the heart of the program's appeal. Would viewers really want to stick with a TV series about a guy who saves the world while his wife is worried sick about what might befall him? Would Superman's domestic arrangements be interesting? Would he have to be home at a certain time? Would his wife insist on him wearing his red shorts *under* his flying suit? Would he ever take off that crazy cape—and would it fade in the wash? Surely there was only one way to go: keep the tension.

You might think this apparent dilemma was no dilemma at all. You might assume that, no matter what the market research was saying, someone in authority would have thumped the desk and simply said, 'Hey! The formula is working! The reason people keep looking, week after week, is that they don't know whether these schmucks will get married or not. They don't even know whether, when it comes to the point, Superman is, you know—normal. So they keep watching. Of course they'll say they want to know how it will turn out. That's why they're watching. So if we tell them how it turns out, they'll stop watching. Pow! Just like that. No mystery, no tension—no viewers. Now, what's next on the agenda? Taking Jerry out of Seinfeld?'

But no-one said any of that; or, if they did, no-one listened. The market research won: give the viewers what they *say* they want (almost always a very different thing from what they actually want). So the decision was made to let Lois and Superman/Clark marry. The result— do I really need to tell you?—was that the program's popularity plummeted and, soon after, the series was cancelled by the American ABC network.

It's easy to underrate the importance of strong, visionary leadership—in politics, in business, in sport, in the arts, in the neighbourhood and even in the family. It's possible for strong leaders to be bad, of course, but weak leadership, or no leadership at all, is a surefire prescription for the kind of nonsense the Children of Israel got up to. Leave people leaderless and, sooner or later, they'll make a mess of things and fall into the trap of self-indulgence—almost always including the appointment of a new, unofficial leader of their own.

This sort of talk is not universally popular. It has occasionally been fashionable to talk about leadership as though it is a kind of malaise in human society: a symptom of a serious lack of inner direction that makes us vulnerable to leaders who, once they've acquired power over us, will inevitably exploit that power for their own murky purposes, psychotic or otherwise. On this view, the very phenomenon of leadership arises from the dependency of weak humans who are not yet fully evolved. And leaders are all bad guys in the end, because they are bound to be corrupted by their power over the rest of us.

Yet our yearning for visionary leadership, and our capacity to respond to it, looms large in human history. Ordinary people have been encouraged by visionary leaders to do extraordinary things, both wonderful and terrible. In Australian history there have been magic moments, like 1972, when a leader has captured the imagination of the nation and encouraged us to expand our vision of what Australia might become. Much of the nostalgia about 'the Whitlam years' is about wanting to recapture that intensely personal feeling of energy and optimism. (Not everyone responded warmly to the policies of Gough Whitlam, of course, but the euphoria of the early months of his government's first term strongly reinforced the belief that, after 23 years of Coalition rule—in the words of Labor's election campaign slogan—'It's time'.)

A new kind of tyrant: the polls

In more recent politics, there has been an ugly development: the emergence of the opinion poll as a substitute for leadership. Let the polls tell me what people want to hear, and that's what I'll say. Let the polls tell me what I can get away with, and that's how far I'll go. Let the polls tell me how to be popular, and I'll be all those things.

During the last years of the century, when Australia has been debating the question of Aboriginal reconciliation—and the broader questions of the rights and needs of indigenous people—there have been several occasions when it has appeared as if government attitudes might have been shaped by the opinion polls.

In 1997, for example, in response to calls for an official apology for past injustices to Aboriginal people, the Prime Minister, John Howard, baulked, partly on the grounds that there was insufficient community support for an apology. Mr Howard also offered the defence that an apology would open the way for expensive compensation claims on behalf of dispossessed and abused Aboriginal groups and individuals.

There is little doubt that his research at the time would, indeed, have been telling him that the community was divided on the question of a formal apology. Polls were still saying what they had been saying for some years: that white Australians didn't really know what Aborigines wanted, and they were wary of being exploited—*exploited!*—by various Aboriginal claims for special treatment. Mabo and Wik were still rather mysterious. Their relevance to ordinary Australians was still unclear and their possible implications—like native-title claims over suburban backyards—uncomfortable and disturbing.

But so what? Injustice is injustice, whether the community feels personally and directly responsible for it or not. As the previous chapter has suggested, our response to injustice committed on our behalf, or by our forebears, says a great deal about our values and the kind of society we are trying to create. When we say that we believe in the 'fair go', for instance, the proof of whether we mean it will always be found in our response to the most difficult cases, not just the easy ones.

The challenge for any prime minister faced with an important social issue is to read the research, assess the mood of the people and then, in response to all that, develop his or her strategy. Doing what the polls say is not a policy: public opinion is not the final arbiter of moral issues, nor of how political challenges should be met. If Mr Howard had wanted to offer an official apology to the Aboriginal people, the polls should not have discouraged him from doing so. Conversely, his subsequent decision to stop short of an apology could never be justified solely on the grounds of its presumed congruence with public opinion.

Leadership is the art of encouraging us to bring out the best in ourselves;

unlocking our potential to do the decent thing; defining a goal we can recognise as being worthy of us—even if it isn't the one we might have come up with if left to our own devices. True leadership never involves pandering to ignorance, prejudice or self-interest, even though that might bring short-term popularity. The community's existing attitudes are the raw material of a leadership strategy; they are not the leader's script.

If a prime minister is faced with a lack of community support for a course of action he believes is right and in the community's own best interests, his task is to explain his vision to the people, show them why it is worth aspiring to, and encourage them to share in it. (This, indeed, is precisely the strategy adopted by Mr Howard when he wanted to persuade the community to accept his controversial taxation proposals, including a goods and services tax. Not only did he suggest that such changes were in the national interest, but he further encouraged those who might be adversely affected to accept that some sacrifices would have to be made.)

In 1999 there was another chapter in the story of Aboriginal reconciliation and the opinion polls. When the Prime Minister drafted a possible new preamble to the Constitution—in anticipation of the other changes that would need to be made if Australians voted to become a republic—he rejected the advice of the Constitutional Convention by refusing to use the word 'custodianship' to refer to Aborigines' prior occupation of the land. His defence was that the use of such a word would offend large sections of the community who did not support that view of history. (This was in spite of a High Court decision confirming not just Aboriginal custodianship, but ownership.)

Precisely the same leadership issue arises here: if Mr Howard believed that the Aborigines were, as the High Court had determined, the prior owners of the land, then he had an opportunity to encourage all Australians to take the important step of acknowledging that. Knowing what the polls said on the subject simply gave him an understanding of the magnitude of the task he faced.

If, on the other hand, he disputed the High Court's decision and genuinely believed that Aborigines were not the prior owners, nor even the custodians, of the land before European settlement, then the leadership challenge was to say so, and to explain the grounds of his belief. Merely to suggest that many people, or even 'most people', would not support a particular view is never a reason, on its own, for a prime minister to reject it. (Again, the GST example serves: 'most people' were opposed to aspects of the GST package, as proposed by the government, but that was not interpreted by Mr Howard as grounds for walking away from it, since he genuinely believed it was the correct strategy.)

Dick Morris, American spin doctor extraordinaire, claims to have masterminded US President Bill Clinton's presidential campaigns, and to have used poll results to formulate other crucial strategies for Clinton in his relationship with Congress and the American people. In *Behind the Oval Office*, he says this:

> I have a lot of faith in polling. But polling shouldn't determine what a political leader does. Much of the time he has to go against what the polls say the people want. But polls can help a leader figure out which arguments will be the most persuasive.[1]

Polls are no substitute for leadership because, at its very essence, leadership is about giving people what they *don't* already have—a sense of vision, inspiration, or even an adequate grasp of a particular subject. The theory that we rely on leaders because of our own deficiencies is partly right. We need leaders to explain us to ourselves, to offer us ways of understanding our situation and to propose creative solutions to our problems.

The polls can't supply any of that. But they can certainly show leaders—in politics, but also in business or any other arena—what's worrying the people. They can tell leaders whether their policies are understood and accepted and, if not, what more needs to be said. They can hint at the potential that lies within the people, waiting to be unleashed.

Wanted: a mirror to our nobler selves

Part of what we want from leaders is that they should give us something of themselves. We yearn for *strong* leaders so we can borrow their strength.

We want leaders with *integrity* because we know their example can inspire us and expand our own capacity for honesty and moral clarity. We admire leaders with *passion* because they radiate the kind of commitment, the charisma, the emotional force and courage we wish we had.

Leadership, at its best, won't just inspire us but will somehow compensate us as well.

This is one reason why great leaders are sometimes diminished and finally spent by the demands of office: it's not just the workload, it's also the endless giving of themselves. Those political leaders who shed tears at the moment of defeat may well be weeping over the knowledge that they gave us all they had—and it still wasn't enough.

It is the misfortune of contemporary leaders, across the whole spectrum of Australian life, that the community's demand for strong leadership is growing in direct proportion to our lack of confidence in ourselves. The end of this century is an unusually difficult time to be a leader in Australia. This is a society in the throes of redefining itself, and it urgently needs a sense of vision. It is a society deeply unsure of itself, and it needs inspiration. It is a society suffering the pangs of a deep-seated insecurity, and it needs an injection of confidence.

Australians have been trying to cope with three revolutions at once: the gender revolution (see Chapter 23), the information revolution (see Chapter 9) and the cultural-identity revolution (see Chapter 4). So it's no wonder people are feeling anxious and edgy. And it's no wonder they are calling for strength, steadiness and clarity at the top. (They also wouldn't mind a laugh occasionally, just to lighten proceedings.)

But what do people mean when they say they want strong leaders?

At one level, they want to feel as though someone is 'taking charge' and restoring our sense of control. For some people, that means leaders who will impose more rules and regulations; judges who will impose tougher sentences; leaders in education and the church who will get 'back to basics', especially in morality.

That interpretation of strength can easily lead a society into extremism and the pursuit of false hope and empty promises. An important part of the appeal of One Nation has been the perception that it has a 'get tough' social policy agenda. (See Chapter 24.)

But there is more to strength than toughness. The yearning for strong leadership is more about *strength of purpose*—clarity of vision—than about 'getting tough'.

Destabilised by the recent past and unsure of the future, Australians are nevertheless sure that 'Australia's time will come'. Their present blend of optimism and pessimism is confusing and uncomfortable, and they keep hoping that a leader will soon emerge who can rekindle their faith in Australia's future and, in the process, make them feel better about themselves. (Until the Victorian election in 1999, the closest they could get to their ideal was Premier Jeff Kennett—a man who was widely seen as combining a clear sense of vision with a personality that has some of the attractive features, including the passion, of the Australian larrikin.)

The present mood is tinged with disappointment. That's partly because of our frustrations over the apparently intractable problem of unemployment, especially youth unemployment; partly because of the growing divisions between rich and poor that have soured our dream of an egalitarian society; partly because of our failure to balance our stated values with the way we actually lead our lives.

But it's also because the perception of a leadership vacuum, in politics and elsewhere, has created the uneasy sense that, on the very threshhold of the 21st century, there is no real blueprint—apart from tax reform—for our national future. Or, if there is, it hasn't yet been expressed in a powerful theme with a clear focus, to which ordinary Australians can relate.

We need a 'guiding story'

What seems to be lacking is a 'guiding story' that connects leaders and people: a set of coherent ideals, values and beliefs, imaginatively couched, that gives us a framework for making sense of our national life, and encourages us to take more confident steps towards controlling our future.

One of the most important responsibilities of governments and of tribal elders in any setting, including business organisations, is to tell us our own story; to help us weave some meaning and purpose into the fabric of our lives; to illuminate our understanding of where we have come from; to paint word pictures of our future onto which we can project our aspirations.

That process can be negative as well as positive, as Adolf Hitler demonstrated when he told the German people a story about themselves that reinforced and released some of their darkest prejudices. As the psychoanalyst Carl Jung put it at the time: 'Hitler is the loudspeaker that magnifies the inaudible whispers of the German soul until they can be heard in the German's unconscious ear.'[2] The American social analyst Walter Truett Anderson sees Hitler as one storyteller among many, who prevailed because he created a story about the German people that they couldn't resist:

> Adolf Hitler made his mark on the world not as a political theorist, certainly not as a military tactician, but as a dramatist. He was a story-maker. Other story-makers were in business in the German-speaking society at the same time: Freudians, existentialists, theologians, scientists, and ideologues of all kinds were offering their own versions of what was happening. Hitler outdid them all, at least for a while, and he did it because he was able to place the German people in an awesome story that thundered through their blood and bones.[3]

Closer to home, Pauline Hanson was the loudspeaker—or perhaps the lightning rod—for the disgruntled murmurs of almost one million Australians in the 1998 Federal election. (See Chapter 24.)

Winston Churchill told an uplifting story that sustained an entire nation at war. John F Kennedy did it for America in the Sixties, and Franklin D Roosevelt did it in words that still live in the American psyche:

> I see a great nation upon a great continent, blessed with a great wealth of natural resources ... I see a United States which can demonstrate that, under democratic methods of government, national wealth can be translated into a spreading volume of human comforts hitherto unknown, and the lowest standard of living can be raised far above the level of mere subsistence.

But here is the challenge to our democracy: In this nation I see tens of millions of its citizens—a substantial part of its whole population—who at this very moment are denied the greater part of what the very lowest standards of today call the necessities of life ... I see one-third of a nation ill-housed, ill-clad, ill-nourished.

It is not in despair that I paint you that picture. I paint it for you in hope—because the nation, seeing and understanding the injustices in it, proposes to paint it out. We are determined to make every American citizen the subject of his country's interest and concern; and we will never regard any faithful, law-abiding group within our borders as superfluous.

The test of our progress is not whether we add more to the abundance of those who have much; it is whether we provide enough for those who have too little.[4]

Inspirational storytelling—explaining us to ourselves—would never be enough, of course. We will always need courageous decisions to be taken. We will always need brilliant policy development. We will always need politicians to concentrate on the grinding work of government, and to refine the political, economic and social structures that allow us to lead fulfilling lives.

Managers can always be found to work out the logistics, but leadership is a very different thing from management. Only leaders can tell us the story of where we're going, how we will get there, and why that's the right path and the best destination for us.

Footnote: how to be a star without getting 'the treatment'

Australians being Australians, the most visionary and inspirational leader in the world would come unstuck here if he or she appeared arrogant. Arrogance is still the cardinal sin among Australian leaders and potential heroes, whether in politics, business, sport, the arts, academia, religion or the professions.

Australians love success. They admire accomplishment. But they hate arrogance. (And that's the real source of the tall poppy syndrome: it's not the tall poppies we slash; it's the ones that *act* tall.)

So, to the list of other desirable attributes in a leader—strength, integrity, passion—we must add the important modifier: humility.

With humility, strength can be expressed with dignity and grace; integrity can be assumed, without needing anyone's attention to be drawn to it; passion can be focused on the task in hand, without spilling over into lust for power. (Some older Australians recall Curtin and Chifley—as some older Americans recall Truman—as leaders who displayed true humility.)

Australians want to feel optimistic; they want to believe the country is poised to realise its potential—socially, culturally and economically. If they had to pick just one out of the several factors they would most like in a leader at the turn of the century, my guess is that they would choose passion, enthusiasm, a zest for having a go. When you're reaching a turning point, that's the kind of energy you need.

The pollies get incredibly worked up about things like travel rorts or some slip of the tongue by someone on the other side. I wish they were equally passionate about some of the real issues, like poverty, or unemployment or the environment.

CHAPTER THIRTEEN

Marriage and the Family

Is Marriage Going Out of Fashion?

Turning Point: With the marriage rate at an all-time low and the ABS predicting further falls, we are approaching a turning point in our view of the institutions of marriage and the family. The concept of marriage has undergone an irrevocable change—from being an expression of faith in the future, to being a 'test' of a relationship. The low rate of marriage will continue to drive the birthrate down, and the high rate of divorce means that more than 20 per cent of dependent children now live with only one of their natural parents. Is this an experiment, or a process of evolution into a different kind of society?

What are we hoping for? A way of approaching partnerships and cohabitation that gives people the freedom and flexibility they demand, but doesn't disadvantage or damage children in the process. Older Australians would like to see more emphasis on loyalty; younger Australians are hoping to find a relationship that 'works'.

Tear up your estimates! Get your head around a completely new way of thinking about the place of marriage in our society. Most people eventually get married; that's true. But what does 'most people' mean? If the latest estimates from the Australian Bureau of Statistics are right, it will soon mean 'a bit over 50 per cent'.

Even if you eliminate the years of the postwar marriage boom—the Forties and Fifties—and look at the broad sweep of the 20th century, these new estimates are stunning. On average, for most of this century, about 75 per cent of Australians married. So the 25 per cent who didn't—though some cohabited outside the formal institution of marriage—were a significant minority, but still easily recognised as a minority. Perhaps they were gay; perhaps they were so committed to the care of elderly relatives that they never had the time or opportunity to marry; perhaps they were fiercely independent, or too busy; perhaps they were shy; perhaps they were simply disinclined. Whatever their circumstances, most of them wore the labels 'spinster' and 'bachelor' more or less lightly.

Now we're facing a future where, in the rising generation of young adults, the ratio of marrieds to never-marrieds will be approaching 50–50, where 'partners' will be as common as 'spouses', and assumptions about the dynamics—and likely duration—of other people's relationships will be more dangerous than ever.

This doesn't mean that fewer people will live together in sexual relationships. It means that partnerships (including a growing proportion of those that produce children) are moving out of the public domain where they are formally recognised and 'registered', into a more private domain where *freedom and flexibility* become new virtues, to be added to the list that includes loyalty and commitment.

Sceptical? Take a look at the figures.

The ABS tells us that the number of marriages registered in 1996 was the lowest since 1979, and that the crude marriage *rate* was the lowest recorded in Australia this century.

Based on age-specific marriage rates for 1997, the Bureau is now estimating that about 42 per cent of men and 44 per cent of women will *never* marry.

Low marriage rates—and an increasing proportion of couples choosing *de facto* relationships—aren't the only index of the fashionability of marriage. Those who *do* marry appear to be as keen as ever. John Haslam of Wildfire, a company that specialises in publishing wedding magazines, reports that, in Sydney, the average wedding and honeymoon package now costs about $26 000.

Here's another indicator: only about 65 per cent of contemporary marriages are first marriages, so those who take the plunge seem to enjoy it so much that they are increasingly inclined to have a second or third go. The average age for divorce is 40 in men and 37 in women, but 11 per cent of divorcing people are under 30. The average duration of a marriage that ends in separation or divorce is seven years. (The most popular month for marriage in Australia is November. January is the most popular month for divorce, perhaps confirming the theory that Christmas is the most testing time for shaky relationships.)

The swing from marriage-as-institution to marriage-as-relationship

We'd be making a big mistake if we assumed that when people say 'marriage', we know precisely what they mean. Of course, we know they mean that the knot has been tied in a legal sense, and for some people, there will be a dimension of religious significance as well—reflected in the fact that about 50 per cent of marriages are still conducted by ministers of religion, down from 68 per cent in 1977 and 89 per cent in 1967. But marriage, as an institution, has been undergoing such profound cultural changes, even beyond those revealed by the official statistics, that we are entitled to wonder, when someone speaks of marriage: what *kind* of marriage?

The generation of Australians who were born in the Twenties, for example, had a completely different approach to marriage from that of their children and their grandchildren. They were the children of the Depression, and the adolescents and young adults of World War II. They grew up in an atmosphere of hardship and deprivation (characterised by record high unemployment among their parents' generation and very poor social welfare provisions) but, looking back, they say that they learned some fundamental and enduring values from the experience of those formative years.

They learned about the importance of loyalty—to a spouse and a family, especially, but also to a community, an employer, a church, and even to a bank. They learned about the value of hard work and the need to take whatever work was on offer; about the importance of mutual obligation, and the need to share resources with other, less fortunate members of a community; about the importance of prudence and caution, having observed that debt was a burden which crushed many of their parents' generation.

Based on that foundation, this generation found themselves establishing their families and careers at the very moment when Australia was entering a Golden Age of economic growth and prosperity. World War II was over, and *marriage became one of the most potent symbols of the confidence and optimism of that period*. That generation's hope for a bright, prosperous and peaceful future was expressed in the record marriage rate which they established. At the same time, they set a new record for the birthrate: the highest recorded birthrate in Australia was in 1952–3. (Incidentally, the lowest was in 1996–7—is this a symptom of our current pessimism?)

Because marriage was a symbol of confidence, and because it was an institution based on the values of loyalty, commitment and obligation, marriage also became a symbol of a particular way of life for the burgeoning postwar suburban society. Marriage was not primarily about the quality of a personal relationship between a man and a woman; it was primarily *an institution* whose stability was taken to be necessary for the stability of society at large.

To that generation, marriage was—and still is—largely about the raising of children and the maintenance of stable families.

We never talked about relationships. We just got married and got on with it. You had your happy times—especially with the children—but you had your difficult times, as well, and you knew everyone else did, too.

I suppose I never really thought about whether I'd get married or not. You just did. Everybody did. It was the done thing, and you felt sorry for people who couldn't find a husband or a wife.

Once the children came along, you knew where your duty lay.

In the transition from that generation to its children's generation, a radical shift occurred in attitudes to marriage. The children born during the postwar baby boom were shaped by a very different set of influences from those that shaped their parents' early lives. Inevitably, this affected their attitudes to marriage, along with everything else.

The Baby Boomers' formative years have been described in detail in *Generations*, and summarised in Chapter 2 of this book. The key point is that they were raised in a world of contradiction. On the one hand, it was a time of such economic growth and development that the future seemed rosy. On the other hand, they were the children of the Cold War—a generation who grew up with the possibility of nuclear holocaust fixed in their minds. They knew that any regional conflict, like Korea or Vietnam, had the potential not only to go global, but thermonuclear as well. And they believed that this could happen either deliberately or accidentally, if some general in the USSR or the USA happened to push the wrong button.

The key to understanding the Baby Boomers is to recognise that, in response to that paradox, they embraced *instant gratification* as a way of life. They wanted to reap the rewards of being young Australians in a period of growth, excitement and rising prosperity, but they were in a hurry to do so. Their horizon was up close; they didn't want to contemplate the long-term future, let alone plan for it. At some half-conscious level, they thought they might only ever be young.

So they rushed marriage in the same way as they rushed everything else. Thirty-three per cent of Boomer women were married by the time they were 20, compared with only 5 per cent of contemporary women who are married by that age. The median age of Boomer mothers at the birth of the first child was 23, compared with 29 today.

Because they weren't disposed to be long-term planners, they approached marriage, pre-eminently, as a here-and-now *symbol of romantic love*. This is not to suggest that their parents were immune to romantic love, but their parents' pre-eminent view was of marriage as an institutionalised, permanent symbol of stability and commitment that would survive long after romantic love had faded. They knew, going into it, that marriage would require hard work and persistence, and that the personal rewards might be neither obvious nor continuous. The Boomers, by contrast, had heard The Beatles: 'All you need is love,' they sang, and the Boomers were disposed to believe them.

'We're in love. Let's get married.' That's what we said. That's how easy it seemed.

As the Boomers moved into their middle years, some unexpected things happened. For a start, they survived. But the economic rosiness had faded and it was clear that life would be harder, for many of them, than the Sixties had led them to expect. Disappointment loomed.

But there was an additional challenge: they found themselves on the leading edge of social change. This appealed to their Sixties idealism, but it also meant that they would have to absorb a new set of strains that were typically not imposed on their parents' lives—or on their parents' marriages.

This became the first generation of Australian women to fully embrace the messages of feminism, and to incorporate a new understanding of the role of women in their daily lives and in the quality of their personal relationships. Gradually, as men began to adjust to these messages, the new emphasis on *relationships* produced a fundamental shift in the Baby Boomers' attitudes to marriage and, in the process, began the redefinition of the institution of marriage itself.

The revolution in Baby Boomers' thinking about the centrality of 'the relationship' meant that marriage was no longer just about children, or families, or stability, or mutual comfort. It was no longer even so much about romantic love. It had evolved, in their thinking, to the point where it was primarily about *the quality of a relationship between a man and a woman*. In this climate, when one or other partner said 'This is not working for me', that came to sound like a death knell for the marriage.

Not surprisingly, as this profound change of orientation occurred, the divorce rate climbed to the point where we can safely estimate that more than 30 per cent of Boomers' marriages will end in divorce. And, for the first time in our history, most divorces are being initiated by women.

Of course, the dramatic increase in the divorce rate was triggered by the Family Law Act of 1975, and it is by no means confined to Baby Boomers. But it has been powerfully fuelled by Boomer women's new view of themselves and, in practice, by the strain imposed on many marriages where both partners are working. (See Chapter 23.) Those have been, generationally speaking, Boomer issues: the Boomers have been the pioneers.

Marriage, for the baby-boom generation, has been caught up in the larger process of men and women redefining their roles and responsibilities. For older Australians, the male breadwinner ('head of the house') and the female housewife and mother were not always fulfilling—or appropriate—roles for both parties, but they were established to such a stereotypical degree that there was little debate about that way of sharing the paid and unpaid work.

For Boomers—and for the generations that are following them—the whole question of roles and responsibilities became open not only to debate but to negotiation. Marriage, in many cases, became a casualty.

Glacial patience or fear of commitment?

The young are saying, 'Let's wait and see'

Like all generations before them, the next generation of young Australians will recreate marriage in their own image.

We looked in on the rising generation in Chapter 10, and we'll visit them again in Chapter 15. So we don't need to examine them in detail here, except to the extent necessary to illuminate their attitudes to marriage.

Born since 1970, they have grown up in a period utterly different from the formative years of their parents and their grandparents. They are the children of the Age of Discontinuity; the children of their parents' Age of Anxiety. The rate of change is so rapid that it is producing a very wide range of individual responses. It is harder to generalise about today's adolescents and young adults than it was about previous generations, especially on the subject of marriage. (Young Australians themselves staunchly resist our attempts to make generalisations about them, and they are right to do so.)

They aren't alarmed by the dramatic social and cultural changes going on around them—changes that have so disturbed their parents and grandparents—because change is the air they breathe.

They have always known that girls can do anything. They know that more than 50 per cent of university students are female, that 45 per cent of the workforce is female, and that both figures are still rising. (See Chapter 23.)

They have always known that a high divorce rate is 'normal'. They may not like being the offspring of divorced parents, but the experience has certainly shaped their own attitudes to marriage—encouraging them, in particular, to enter *de facto* relationships before—or instead of—marriage. They have grown up with the one-parent family as part of the natural landscape. (Roughly one million dependent children now live with only one of their natural parents, though sometimes with a step-parent as well.)

About 60 per cent of their mothers have had full-time or part-time paid work outside the home, so 'working mothers' are normal, though not always admirable. (See Chapter 23.)

They know that whatever piece of new technology is placed in their hands today will have already been superseded. They are not astonished by e-mail, mobile phones, personal computers, the Internet, or the concept of virtual reality: these things are part of the standard technological landscape. (Remember, this was the generation who managed to program the VCR without reading the manual.)

They are a generation who have grown up with an awareness of AIDS; with the knowledge that there is a drug culture in their school or suburb which they could access if they wanted to. The street-kids phenomenon is a product of *their* generation. The rate of youth suicide has doubled in their lifetime, making Australia the only country where the suicide rate peaks in the under-30 age group.

They are our most highly-educated and, in a media sense, our most overstimulated generation. And they might be one of our most over-indulged generations as well, since their rather stressed and preoccupied—and highly divorced—Boomer parents have often tried to compensate for all that with material indulgence.

What has all this done to the rising generation? It has taught them to *keep their options open*; to keep an open mind; to wait and see; to hang loose; to postpone commitment. (See Chapter 15.)

Not surprisingly, they see marriage in these terms, as well.

For a start, marriage is for 'when we are ready'. They say that they want to be both emotionally and financially 'established' before they tie any legal knots, and some of them are already saying that a joint mortgage is a more potent symbol of commitment than a marriage certificate. Some of them will even go to the extent of testing their capacity as parents before deciding whether or not to get married: 27 per cent of Australian babies are now being born to unmarried parents. (Others will try themselves out on a dog or cat before going for the real thing.)

They say that their parents got married and *then* worked on establishing themselves financially and emotionally. They want to do things the other way around.

Like their parents, though, they are quite clear about the idea that a good marriage means *a good relationship*. Their view is that no marriage is worth persisting with unless the relationship is working—and they are probably even more demanding on this point than their parents are.

They also have a more pragmatic view about the likely duration of a marriage. It would be a rare person indeed who would approach marriage without the hope that it will last for life, yet the rising generation are prepared to say that 'ten years would be a good innings' and that divorce is not the big deal it once was.

And yet, for all this pragmatism, and for all the new meanings being attached to marriage, it remains true that when you ask young Australians about their expectations of life, almost universally they expect to marry and have children. (Caution: when they use the word 'marry', they increasingly take it to mean *de facto* marriage: that ABS estimate that about 43 per cent of the rising generation will never marry is certainly borne out by the tone of their conversation.)

Still, however it is defined, marriage remains part of most young people's ideal view of a healthy, stable society—much as it was two generations ago.

There is obviously a growing gap between the ideal and the way things are working out. On this point, as on so many others, Australians are both disappointed and confused. They know that the current state of marriage is a long way short of their ideal, but they don't know what to do about it. They know we are approaching a turning point, but they don't yet know whether that might involve a return to a more stable, more institutional view of marriage, or an even more transient one than at present. The evidence, so far, favours the latter.

Who are the *real* guinea pigs?

Once you revolutionise the institution of marriage, the family is next in line. And when it comes to the family, it looks as if Australia is in the midst of a vast social experiment, the results of which won't be known for another generation, at least. The guinea pigs are our children, and many parents are already becoming nervous.

In the wild gallop of social change, we sometimes make choices that don't really feel like choices at the time. They just seem like responses to new circumstances. Later, when we reflect on how things are turning out—especially for our children—we might wish we'd had the opportunity to think through the consequences a bit more thoroughly.

So, without necessarily intending to, we've become a society in which more than a quarter of all babies are being born to unmarried parents. Only 40 per cent of preschoolers are being cared for at home by a parent. The majority are either being looked after by a grandparent or other relative, or by a professional child carer, either at home or at a child-care centre.

There's nothing wrong with any of that, of course, as long as it fits comfortably with our concept of the kind of society—and the kind of families—we want to become. If it doesn't, we might need to re-examine some of the choices that got us to where we are now.

The choice to be so busy, for instance. When both parents have paid jobs, children have to be carefully slotted into the routine. That's one reason why so many parents have arranged such highly structured activities for their offspring. If the children are at ballet, basketball, violin lessons or maths coaching, at least they are under supervision. And that relieves their parents of one source of pressure—while, ironically, adding more pressure to earn the money to pay for all these varieties of child care.

Occasionally, parents pause and wonder whether they are robbing their children of their childhood, and themselves of some of the more relaxed pleasures of parenthood. They wonder whether they are teaching their children, from too early an age, to juggle time; whether there is a danger of overstimulation in all this frenetic activity that might lead to heightened anxiety, depression or other disorders in the young.

Still, it's a decision parents are making and it may well turn out to be the right one. Perhaps life *is* turning into a series of video clips. But that shouldn't stop us reflecting on the lessons our children are learning from our busy schedules, our fast food, our incessant chatter on our mobile phones, and our impatience to spend our disposable income.

Watching us, will they be concluding that parenting is more about organisation and administration than cuddling and listening? Will they be thinking of the kitchen as a kind of pit stop; a place to heat a cup of coffee in the microwave or to tip some cereal into a bowl, rather than a place where complete meals are prepared? Will they think of sitting up at a table to eat as something you only do when you go to McDonald's? (And does it matter?)

Another example, dealt with more fully in Chapters 9 and 20: if we've chosen to expose our children to computer technology from the start (and it might well seem that we had no choice), what will this be doing to their perception of the value of information, their ability to discriminate between the useful and the useless, and their capacity to make judgments about the integrity and authority of different sources of information?

If we allow them, or even encourage them, to spend more time in front of a screen (another form of child care?) than they spend with family or friends, should we be surprised when they start to confuse data transfer with human communication? Should we be concerned if they think that tapping out messages to someone in a chat room on the Net has the same value as making friends with someone down the street?

And when we take our children shopping, should we worry when, from the beginning, they behave like fully-fledged consumers, demanding a particular brand of everything from shoes to chocolate bars? (Did they actually spring from the womb with brand images already in their heads?)

Such things only matter if we think they do. But when we experience a twinge of uneasiness about what we're doing to our own children, we probably shouldn't ignore it. The experiment isn't over, and there are still plenty of choices to be made.

CHAPTER FOURTEEN

Nostalgia

'Let's Get Sex and Violence off TV and Back on the Streets, Where They Belong'

(Headline from *Mad* magazine, circa 1965)

Turning Point: As the future promises more change, more stress and more uncertainty, one short-term defence is to seek refuge in the past. When we are facing the unknown, the known is a comfort. In everything from housing to cars and supermarket products, Australians are seizing on styles and brands that say 'heritage' and, by implication, offer the reassurance of being tried and true. Nostalgia is the undertow of social change, and it can distract us from the possibilities offered by the next wave.

What are we hoping for? A future that won't involve sacrificing too many of the values that link us to the past.

The ferocious outbreak of nostalgia in the Nineties is one of the surest signs that Australians know they are facing some difficult choices about their future.

When the future looks daunting—even if it is exciting as well—it's natural to take a nostalgic glance over the shoulder. We're all experts on the past, because we've all survived it. We are all, in a manner of speaking, 'past masters'. The future is untested—or, more correctly, our capacity to respond to it is untested.

Nostalgia is the undertow of social change—an inevitable reaction to the turbulence that is created when a society is reinventing itself, and when the crosscurrents are at their most confusing and disturbing. The undertow makes it hard to tell which way the tide is running, and even if we want to catch the next wave, the undertow might drag us down and hold us back.

But while nostalgia can have an inhibiting effect on us—making us reluctant to embrace change, even when it might be to our benefit—it can also have the positive effect of restraining us from hurtling unprepared into the future, believing that all change is progress. It can remind us that some things work perfectly well as they are; that some values ought to be respected; that we need to think carefully about the likely effect of change, particularly technological change, on our way of life.

One way of doing that is to look back, and see what we're prepared to give up and what we're not.

In Melbourne, for instance, nostalgia for the institution of tram conductors, now replaced by ticket machines, has caused many Melburnians to think carefully about why they are so unhappy about that change. They reflect on the security provided by a conductor, especially at night; the guidance available to people who don't know their way around; the convenience of being able to buy a ticket from someone who can give change. But something less tangible, as well: the sense of wellbeing created by a cheerful conductor; the reassurance of seeing a familiar face; even, occasionally, relief from loneliness or distress provided by a conductor's sympathetic ear. At their best, conductors, like corporate tea-ladies of yore, seemed to provide a kind of social glue. So their disappearance raises questions—too late to save the conductors—about the things we value and the things we wouldn't easily give up in the future.

Nostalgia, in such circumstances, can be the catalyst for social action. More and more, Australians are turning to the past not simply for sentimental reassurance, but also as a resource for making sense of the future and, indeed, for deciding if some proposed futures make any sense at all.

'What if … ?'

We hear the forecasts of strong economic growth, but we don't know if that's a wave that will dump us or if we'll be able to ride it all the way in. Our nostalgic perspective warns us that strong growth, Nineties-style, tends to create casualties—unlike the growth of the Fifties and Sixties when the economy was booming in a way that seemed to benefit almost everyone. (Can that be right?) 'Downsizing', 'deregulation' and 'out-placement' were not in our lexicon, back then. So we ask nervous questions:

We know the rich will get richer, but will the poor get richer too?

Does economic growth eventually guarantee a drop in unemployment?

Will big companies keep boosting their profits by employing fewer people? How is that good for society?

Were we wrong to think that being middle class meant being safe? Is egalitarianism finished?

We hear about the next wave of the information revolution and its impact on work, shopping, entertainment and interpersonal communication. Heady stuff: broadband, convergence, e-commerce, smart cards. Will we soon be shopping on the Internet? Will the television set really become a multi-purpose data transfer station, right there in the lounge room? More questions:

Will we be able to attract our children's attention for long enough to get them to talk to us?

Why can't old people keep their bank passbooks, if it makes them feel better?

Shouldn't we think about what to do with all the people whose jobs will be replaced by machines, before we replace them?

How affordable will all this technology be? Are we dividing ourselves into information-rich and information-poor?

We hear about the reluctance of the young to marry and have children. What will that do to the institutions of marriage and the family?

Will we receive any credit for having stuck to our spouses for such unfashionably long periods?

Will I ever have any grandchildren and if I do, will I be expected to look after them while my daughter advances her career?

We hear about globalisation, and wonder, nostalgically, if this means we will lose even more control over our own destiny. Will mega-companies have more power and influence than some countries, like Australia, and will they attract a new kind of patriotism from their workforce—or will there be so much outsourcing that workers, drawn from the cheapest available pool, will be even more expendable than now?

If globalisation means that the world is one big market, won't that mean the stronger countries will exploit the weaker, as the strong dominate the weak in most markets, from media to retailing?

Does globalisation really mean neo-imperialism?

If one country has a cheaper labour force, won't they get more

work than a country like Australia with higher labour costs? Does
this mean Australian wages will inevitably be dragged down to meet
the global market? Or will we be the lucky ones, exploiting rather
than exploited?

Give us a break!

'Reform fatigue', a term coined by Singapore's former Prime Minister, Lee Kuan Yew, has many Australians in its grip. The pace of change through the Eighties and Nineties has destabilised so many people that nostalgia has become a kind of psychological defence mechanism.

Feminism and its implications for gender relations and for the status of women, upheavals in the institutions of marriage and the family, industrial relations and workplace reform, the impact of electronic technology, a new attention to the fragility of the physical environment, multiculturalism, republicanism—there's been a long list of challenges to our way of thinking about Australia. Virtually all the conventions, the reference points, that were once used for defining the Australian way of life have been modified, reformed or replaced.

Some of us have taken all this in our stride. Some have been overwhelmed by it and reduced to helpless neurosis. Most of us, between those two extremes, have experienced occasional pangs of nostalgia: why does everything have to change? Why do things have to change so quickly? Why does it have to be so hard? Why are there so many adjustments to be made? Couldn't we pause for a while and just take stock? What was wrong with the old way of doing things anyway?

On reflection, we know that the process of change can't be arrested, but we resent the sense of losing control of our own lives. Nostalgia gives us a welcome respite from all that.

Old movies, re-runs of old TV programs, listening to the endlessly recycled hits of our adolescence, even going through old photo albums— all these things offer harmless relief from reform fatigue and they also help to remind us of the things we once thought were important, so we can decide whether they still are.

I remember when ...

One of our favourite, and most effective, forms of nostalgia is the recital of rose-tinted memories.

I remember when people could leave the front doors of their houses unlocked all day. The neighbourhood kids always knew they could come in if their own mothers were out. It's a different story today. You wouldn't trust half the kids around here. They'd trash the place if they knew the door was unlocked.

I remember when kids were more innocent than they are today. My seven-year-old gets under the bed with Woman's Day, *looking at the girls' boobs—in bikinis, of course. When you were that age, or even a bit older, did you know about sex or even have any interest in it? I've even had 'What's a condom?' from my five-year-old.*

I remember when Cabramatta was a nice Italian suburb.

I was talking to this old guy on Anzac Day. He had fought for Australia and he was saying the problem is that young people can't recognise what good morals are because everything keeps changing. There's no standard for people to hang their hat on.

Remember National Service? Everyone who did nasho ended up a disciplined person and they contributed to the community. All this riff-raff we're talking about today—they've done no national service.

I remember, as a kid, coming home with too much change in my pocket and I got belted all the way back to the shop where I was made to hand it over. I'd do the same with my kids. But my sister works in a retail store and she's seen kids who are actively encouraged to steal—the mother keeps the sales person occupied while the kids stuff things up their jumpers.

I remember lovely holidays down on the Bay. These days people seem to think they have to go up to Noosa or somewhere—or even Fiji or Bali. I reckon we had just as much fun, or more.

People these days are so concerned about their relationships. 'The relationship wasn't working for me,' they say. Or, 'We couldn't make our relationship work.' When we were bringing up the kids, no-one talked about their relationship. You had a blue, and that was it. You got on with it.

We got married to settle down and have kids and pay off your mortgage. These days, you hear people saying they won't have kids until they've paid off the house. I feel you've got to live—not just put everything into paying off the house.

Let's face it, there hasn't been any decent music since The Beatles.

Did we have more fun when we were young? I think we did. We made our own fun. These kids expect everything to be laid on for them—TV, video games, all the latest gear. They go off to sport looking as if they are miniature professionals. And look at the way the girls all wear black all the time—it's so gloomy.

I feel uncomfortable in this world. If you have an old-fashioned set of values—or a religious set of values—you are regarded as a bit of an oddity in today's world. These days, people just assume you're in it for whatever you can get out of it.

You can't turn the clock back. I know that. But sometimes I wish you could. Life was more simple, somehow.

Heritage houses, heritage brands, retro design ...

and *The Truman Show*

We know we can't go back to the past, but there are symbols everywhere to remind us of how it was—or how we imagine it used to be—and a marketing industry keen to respond to our desire to preserve some of the values of another era.

The American *Business Week* reported the launch of the new, retro-styled Volkswagen Beetle like this:

> To viewers watching the ad for the new Volkswagen Beetle, it is like squinting into the past. A vague image begins as a small circle set against a stark white background. As the picture sharpens, the circle becomes a flower—with seven daffodil-yellow New Beetles as its petals. The cute-as-a-Bug cars drive away, and a zippy black Beetle careens into view and skids to a stop. The tag line: 'Less flower. More power.'[1]

As *Business Week* says, 'Volkswagen is not the only marketer mining the warm associations of baby-boomer youth and the Age of Aquarius to sell consumer goods.' And while we're in America, here's a related comment from a futurist called Watts Wacker (a neighbour, perhaps, of Faith Popcorn): 'We are creating a new culture, and we don't know what's going to happen, so we need some warm fuzzies from our past.'

Warm fuzzies from our past are in heavy demand in Australia as well.

Take a look at the new housing market, and see all the project homes that have little architectural flourishes—gables, finials, wrought-iron lace, stained glass—tacked on to modern houses to remind the buyer of more leisured times and more substantial houses. As the centenary of Federation approaches, there is seemingly no end to the fashion for housing that echoes the Federation style. The verandah is back, too, as part of the homestead style, reminiscent of our legendary bush heritage.

But the car market is even more revealing. The Volkswagen Beetle appears set to repeat the success of its American launch in Australia, and sports cars like the BMW Z3 , Porsche Boxter and Ford Thunderbird have the kind of retro styling that causes a Baby Boomer's heart to skip a beat. These cars look as if they were conceived in the Fifties or Sixties and kept on ice, just waiting for the surge of nostalgia that would hit the Boomers at precisely the time when they would be rich enough to be able to afford them.

Even Audi's highly acclaimed TT coupe sedan was described by Australian motoring writer Tony Davis as looking like a late Twenties/early Thirties version of a 'car of the future'. The Mercedes A-class and Citroën's new 2CV are, in fact, two of very few models to succeed with a design that genuinely looks like something out of the next century.

But stroll along the aisle of any supermarket and you'll be struck by the number of products that have returned to their original labelling and packaging style—like Coca-Cola with its classic 'hourglass' bottle and Arnott's rosella parrot. 'Since 1884' is prominently featured on Sunlight soap's packaging, and Bickford's prune juice has been doing its thing since 1874.

Many new products, even those that rely on high-tech production processes, strive to create their own 'instant heritage' with pack designs that look both traditional and natural, usually with a distinctly rural flavour: Uncle Toby's new 'Country Cup' range of soups in high-tech packaging designed to look positively rustic, or Country Harvest's bread mix, Farm Pride's egg mix or the broadacre-style labels of the Always Fresh (fresh from Hungary, that is) range of pickled cucumbers.

Brands like Vegemite, Sanitarium and Schweppes have all used packaging and advertising to associate themselves with an unashamedly nostalgic image. But you don't have to be an old-established brand to get in on the act—in 1999, McDonald's borrowed the nostalgia surrounding Anzac Day in support of its hamburgers.

The tendency to take a lingering look back before we surge into the future is by no means confined to Baby Boomers. Some younger Australians are also embracing images from the past. Complaining that there are no pop icons of the Nineties to compare to those of the Fifties, Sixties or Seventies, teenagers are diving back into those periods for some recycled style: platform soles and flares, miniskirts and French-roll hairdos are reappearing alongside even more distantly retrospective fashions, like the Goths. Abba is riding another wave of popularity, and in 1999 people in their twenties and thirties were reporting that they were looking forward to the musical *Fame* as a 'real nostalgia trip'.

Romantic lingerie is back. Collette Dinnigan, though fresh and new as tomorrow, has revived a style that recalls the Fifties and beyond. And the return of satin and lace has been celebrated through the Nineties by the advent of the slip dress and other items of outerwear indistinguishable from underwear. (Actually, the Dinnigan look is also the quintessence of postmodernism: the frills and lacy decorations perfectly express the 'object-as-narrative' philosophy rather than the plainer 'form-follows-function' philosophy of classic modernism. The revival of traditional symbols is also characteristic of postmodern design, as is the blurring of categories. Is it a slip? Is it a nightgown? Is it a dress? Who cares?)

Some nostalgia runs deeper than fashion, though, or even the reassurance of heritage symbols. The appeal of *The Truman Show*, Peter Weir's movie about a man whose whole life is lived on a movie set, was partly due to the intriguing idea of life lived in a fully controlled environment, but partly also to the nostalgic presentation of an idealised version of small-town life in the Forties and Fifties, where neighbours were neighbourly, where life was predictable, the sun always shone, and everything had a cardboard-cutout simplicity about it.

The Walt Disney Company has developed an entire town—Celebration, Florida—on the assumption that Americans are pining for the look and feel of Forties neighbourhoods, and there are many new housing developments in Australia—Golden Grove in Adelaide and Forest Lake in Brisbane, for example—that capture, in a contemporary setting, the serenity and security of the suburbs of 50 years ago.

Moral nostalgia

It's not just the cars or the biscuits or the houses of the past that give focus to the current nostalgia boom. Old-style values are also back on the agenda for many people who are using the Nineties as a kind of moral retreat, in preparation for a future in which they fear that a coherent, traditional approach to morality could turn out to be one of the casualties. To them, the twin pillars of postmodernism—subjectivity and relativity—don't look like pillars at all, more like moral time bombs, in fact.

The swing towards right-wing conservatism in politics, religion and ethics is a reflection of the widespread sense that the pace of cultural change has been too rapid and its impact too radical. Anti-abortion, anti-euthanasia and pro-censorship movements are all early signs of a gathering resistance to liberal ideology.

While many people are coming to terms with a more pluralistic society—a society in which many moral systems coexist without necessarily coinciding—others are fighting back. Though undoubtedly being part of the wave of nostalgia, this moral backlash is far from being a dreamy, misty-eyed reminiscence. It is a strongly supported, clearly targeted counter-punch, directed at anything that smacks of moral laxity, from heroin trials or safe injecting rooms for drug addicts to any perceived 'softness' in the punishment of convicted criminals—especially where it is based on the criminal-as-victim mentality.

Moral nostalgia is closely connected to the push for tougher sentencing in the courts, and to the 'law-and-order' debate in general. It is also linked to religious conservatism and fundamentalism, and to a strongly pro-regulation attitude. It is generally hostile to the sort of change that has accompanied the increase in the divorce rate and the growth in the number of single-parent families. In looking back, the moral nostalgists are now simply hankering after the way things were: they want to insist that that is the way things should be again.

Far from believing that their stance will allow them to resist the wave of cultural and religious liberalism, with its emphasis on a vague 'spirituality' rather than on inflexible doctrine, they believe that the fervour of the emerging religious Right—Christian and otherwise—will create its own wave of social conservatism. They believe they not only have truth, but also history on their side.

At the other end of the moral spectrum, there is a quite different group of more subdued 'nostalgists': these are the people—often victims of a rather pathetic sentimentality that may have been aggravated by years of drug use—who hanker after the permissiveness of the Sixties and Seventies and who are perplexed by what they regard as an unattractive tendency for other people, including some of their own former playmates, to become too sensible, too cautious, too responsible and boring. They yearn for the pre-herpes, pre-AIDS days of sexual liberation and they fear that short haircuts are a nasty sign of things to come.

Apart from the moral and religious counter-punchers, most of those with an eye on the past are content to wallow in their nostalgia for a while longer, knowing that, sooner or later, they will have to catch a wave and head for the shore. To switch metaphors: they may acknowledge that we are all speeding towards a future that will reshape our society in unimagined ways, but they would prefer, for the time being, to watch the view through the rear-vision mirror. And if it's a little rose-tinted, so much the better. For them, nostalgia is a harmless, self-protective distraction.

For others, it is a more deliberate retreat; a time for gathering emotional resources in preparation for a fresh assault on the future.

For the serious and committed moral nostalgists, though, the very label 'nostalgia' would be repugnant. They are determined to impose on society a set of moral absolutes they see as timeless—even eternal—rather than springing from any particular time in the past. They are ready to join battle with the relativists and liberals who, in their view, have already sold out to postmodernism. For them, even the powerful symbolism of retro Beetles will not be enough.

Hugh Mackay

CHAPTER FIFTEEN

Options

'Hanging Loose' May be a Health Hazard

Turning Point: The postmodernists tell us that 'reality' is a social construction—just like language or morality—and that we are free to choose the 'reality' we want. As the pace of life increases and the range of options broadens, we find ourselves needing to make choices—about personal identity, and about our way of life—that were never available (or never apparent) to previous generations. Should we consciously adopt a particular world view, as a foundation or a fixed reference point in the midst of postmodern chaos, even if we know it's only a 'social construction'? Or should we browse and drift through the postmodern bazaar of culture and subculture, resisting commitment to any one framework? Experience suggests we are morally and emotionally safer when we don't 'hang loose' for too long, but how are such choices made? A turning point for many people is when they realise that a moral position doesn't have to be based on moral absolutes in order to be valid.

What are we hoping for? A sense of meaning and purpose that will sustain and stabilise us, in spite of the shifting sands of a postmodern world.

The modern era was a long period of transition, now nearing completion. As it ends, we are all thrust rudely into a new climate of freedom and stress. In the postmodern world we are all *required* to make choices about our realities. You may select a life of experimentation, eternal shopping in the bazaar of culture and subculture. Or you may forego the giddy diversity of contemporary life-style swapping and fall into step with some ancient heritage: be an Orthodox Jew or a fundamentalist Muslim or a Bible-toting Christian. The range of such choices is enormous, but the choice is still a choice and requires an entirely different social consciousness from that of the Jews, Muslims or Christians who knew of no alternatives ... Today we are all 'forced to be free' in a way that Rousseau could not have imagined when he coined that famous phrase. We have to make choices from a range of different stories—stories about what the universe is like, about who the good guys and the bad guys are, about who *we* are ... [1]

That's a quote from *Reality Isn't What It Used To Be*, Walter Truett Anderson's book about the postmodern character of contemporary society. Anderson suggests that our response to the apparent uncertainty of everything might be either to live with that idea itself as our 'guiding story' or, alternatively, to adopt a belief system that will protect us from the ravages of uncertainty. Either way, uncertainty and complexity are the realities we face, and we must choose our response to them.

Anthony Giddens, the BBC's Reith Lecturer for 1999 and author of *Beyond Left and Right*, argues that our lives are now so dominated by choice that we construct our own identities. 'Individuals now make decisions which society previously made for them: whether to have children, what kind of sexual relationships to engage in, what form of class relationships to engage in.'[2] That's another way of saying that we construct our own 'social reality': the decisions we make about the character of our lives create, in effect, the worlds in which we shall live.

The question is whether, in the face of such freedom to be whoever we wish to be—and in the face of a complex world in which the alternative realities continue to multiply—we are better off embracing a set of transcendent beliefs as a fixed reference point, or hanging loose, going with the flow, and keeping our options open. Or is there a 'postmodern' way of combining both alternatives?

When bad means good

When young people say something is 'really, really sick', you would need to listen carefully to the tone of voice, and attend to the context, before you could be sure what meaning was intended. Sometimes sick means bad; increasingly, sick means good (as 'terrific' once meant terrifying, and now, usually, means wonderful; as 'cool' once meant colder than warm, but now means, well ... terrific, or even bad). But by the time this book is printed, 'sick' might mean funny, dead, or excessive ... or even unwell.

The thing about colloquial speech is that its meanings are always slipping in and out of the linguistic mainstream—sometimes through constantly-evolving codes devised by the young to exclude adults from comprehension of their arcane exchanges; sometimes as derivatives of the jargon of the tribe (accountants, graffiti-writers, religious zealots); sometimes as part of the deeper shifts that occur as language responds to changes in the culture itself.

So if you're looking for the most obvious, most everyday example of the ways we construct our own realities, why not start with language? Language is both our description of 'reality' and our prescription for it. It provides our framework for making sense of the world, but we ourselves create that framework, and that's how we impose our 'sense' on the world.

When the feminists of the Seventies wanted to shake us out of an old gender reality and force us into a new one, they began with language: inclusive language became a battle cry as well as a simple request to the rest of us to look at the world in a new way, through the eyes of 'she-and-he' rather than merely 'he'. Even the dread 'chairperson'—a word devoid of legitimate etymology—did its job. Though many organisations have wisely shifted to the use of the less cumbersome 'chair', or the more elegant 'president', the very awkwardness of 'chairperson' drew our attention to the way we had been assuming that, in the natural order of things, leaders would be men.

Words like 'good' and 'bad' are notorious framers of reality. What is a 'good woman'? There was a time when we all knew that a good woman was either a virtuous virgin, or a mother who attended faithfully to the needs of her husband and children. Today? A 'good' woman is, perhaps, one who has struck a blow for feminism by being feisty, outspoken and rebellious against male-dominated institutions; or, perhaps, one who devotes equal parts of energy to studying, jogging, drinking and dating. It all depends on your cultural framework, your construction of reality. For some people, even today, a 'good' woman is still vestal, chaste, submissive and obedient.

The Bible is a valuable reminder of the ways in which constructed realities have influenced, and been influenced by, the meanings our forebears have attached to words like good and bad. As Bishop John Shelby Spong notes in *Rescuing the Bible from Fundamentalism*, 'Moses was a murderer, but this was not [presented as] a character flaw because his victim was an Egyptian'. Spong cites many examples of an inconsistent Biblical morality that reflects shifting social realities:

> Tribal hatreds are extolled as virtues in parts of the Hebrew Scriptures. Captive people, if spared from death, were reduced to slavery. Captive women were used for sexual sport by their Hebrew conquerors. Judah treated his daughter-in-law Tamar as a prostitute and then proposed to kill her when she became pregnant ...
>
> I could quote passages condemning witches and mediums that were used until the eighteenth century to justify the murders of countless women. I could point to passages that condemned homosexuality that were used to justify the burning at the stake of many a person either thought to be living or actually living a respectable gay or lesbian life. I could quote passages glorifying war used to justify the nationalistic ambitions of many a political leader who, under the guise of patriotism, used war to build fortunes.[3]

So good becomes bad, and bad becomes good. And that's really all the postmodernists want us to acknowledge: as with language, so with morality, religion, philosophy. But also with literature, art, the cinema, politics and personal relationships: we construct our social reality and then operate as if it is *the* reality. Some of them want to make us feel uncomfortable about that, as if every reality we construct is a mere delusion that will somehow limit and constrict us; others are perfectly content for us to adopt our reality and stick with it. Their crucial point is that *we have to choose.*

But how do we choose?

'I chose my husband at the migrant hostel.

I had a look and there he was!'

Many of the biggest decisions we ever make—the choices that determine our life's work, for instance, or our sexual partners, where we will live, or our religious beliefs (if any)—are scarcely recognisable as decisions at all. They just seem to happen.

Lower down the scale of significance, our decisions are the result of an often vexed interplay between the rational and the emotional (the next chapter develops this theme in the context of consumer behaviour in the commercial marketplace). So it's not surprising that the easiest choices are those that lie closest to the emotional end of the spectrum. Nothing is easier than falling in love.

Decisions that evoke our deepest feelings, or offer us a new way of seeing ourselves, can feel like emotional breakthroughs that sweep us along on a euphoric tide. No matter how much we might try to justify such choices on rational grounds—just as some consumers will try to justify the purchase of a luxury car or an extravagant fashion item on rational grounds—the truth is that such 'decisions' are usually more to do with having our emotional needs met than with making rational assessments. Being swept away is exciting, engrossing and emotionally rewarding ... at least in the short term.

My husband was tall, dark and handsome ... before he became fat and bald.

It would be terrible to be completely hard-headed about buying a house, wouldn't it? You have to feel some emotional involvement in it ... you have to feel as if it is the kind of place that could be your home.

When I started going out with the girl who was going to become my wife, my family said, 'what does he see in her?' but that's not the point, is it?

Being irrational can be fun, and we often admire unrestrained outbreaks of emotion in each other. Our friends like to see us caught up in the excitement of a wedding, the purchase of a new house, the nervousness of a new job, the adventure of travel to a destination we have just 'discovered'. It's as if such moments reveal an aspect of ourselves that is normally hidden. We revel in the sense of freedom and power that goes with making such apparently life-enhancing decisions (even if they seemed to make us, more than us making them: 'I just felt as if it was the only thing I *could* do').

Occasionally, such episodes feel positively ecstatic. In her study of *Everyday Ecstasy*, Marghanita Laski describes them as revelation experiences: 'The relevant characteristic of these experiences is the discovery, for the first time, of a more or less lasting focus of value.'[4]

And, mostly, such experiences are therapeutic. There is a danger, though, and the voice of postmodernism alerts us to it. This is the danger that, as we construct these new social realities, we will make such a huge emotional investment in them that we will inevitably be not only disappointed, but devastated. Their failure to live up to our expectations will bring about its own form of 'deconstruction'.

Where did the romance go?

I fell in love with the new house. I really thought we could make a fresh start, but things only went from bad to worse. Home really is where the heart is, and there was no heart here.

When I look back on it, I can't believe how extreme my views became. I was never particularly religious before, but I just seemed to go overboard. Now I feel embarrassed when I see those people.

When I looked at that sunset over the lake, I thought I understood the meaning of life. I was nice to everyone for a whole night.

People attempting to compensate for a state of instability or deep insecurity can make themselves vulnerable to emotional excess— repeatedly falling in love with wildly inappropriate partners, plunging uncritically into unfamiliar forms of religious experience, or discovering new and miraculous 'therapies', or even investing unwarranted faith in a 'messianic' political leader. The end point of such intense commitment is, all too often, despair and even depression.

Even for people not obviously disturbed, peak emotional experiences can become dangerous if overinterpreted. Laski cautions that the more extreme the experience, the more likely we are to think that it has revealed 'the truth' to us—a truth so grand that it may not be testable against our broader experience. 'Delightful as such experiences are,' she says, 'I think it prudent to regard them as at least slightly pathological.' (Pathological, maybe, but not to be missed, most lovers would say.)

For those of us battling with 'normal' levels of insecurity and with the pinprick disappointments of everyday life, emotional breakthroughs—in response to love, beauty, triumph, tragedy, loss—add much-needed colour and intensity. More importantly, they remind us that we are capable of idealism and commitment; that passion can generate a powerful sense of purpose in us; that life might seem to be nothing more than a sequence of meaningless events if it were not illuminated by bursts of emotional intensity, both positive and negative.

Paradoxically, such moments can supply the necessary surges of energy to develop a set of beliefs, ideals or convictions that will sustain us when the inevitable disappointments come. Although we would be well advised to construct our solid core of values, our world view, out of the totality of our experience—including the humdrum—'breakthrough' moments often provide the insights that allow us to put several learnings together into a unified whole. (*Aha!*)

> *I thought I had my priorities straight, but when my father died, I realised that I was treating the wrong things as important.*

The syntheses we construct in those breakthrough moments are important stages in the construction of our moral and emotional compass (so it is fortunate that youth is usually associated with so many moments of emotional intensity!). As long as that compass is in working order, we can find our bearings—even in an emotional blizzard—and move forward.

That alerts us to one of the hazards of embracing postmodernism as a personal philosophy, rather than merely as a way of describing the present stage of our cultural evolution. If we were to decide that a 'constructed reality' is literally *all* there is—that there is no genetically-determined reality, no inherent value in a set of transcendent beliefs, no possibility of a shared set of realities, no 'real world', no 'cosmic' reality—we would make ourselves vulnerable to nihilism.

To deny that there are moral absolutes is not to deny the value of a moral position, even a relativistic one. We can acknowledge the impermanence or relativity of values while still embracing a set of values that work for us. If we adopt *no* system of belief as an underpinning for all our chosen 'realities', where will we find the sense of meaning and purpose that pulls us back from the abyss of unknowing?

The recovery of meaning

It is clear that some views of 'reality' induce feelings of despair in us, and some bring a degree of peace or optimism or meaning to our lives. The experience of certain *ways of life*—stable partnerships, voluntary community service, regular time spent in creative and aesthetic pursuits, the rituals of yogic meditation or mystical contemplation, or the practice of religion—produce gratifications that are typically described by their practitioners as more enduring and worthwhile than those reported by people who regard the making of money as the highest priority, or who adopt a lifestyle of addiction to hallucinogenic drugs, or bed-hopping, or binge drinking (a practice now engaged in by about half of Victoria's senior secondary-school pupils, according to a March 1999 report in *The Age*[5]).

A heroin user interviewed for *Time* magazine's April 1999 story on drug abuse makes it clear that once addiction takes hold, heroin doesn't bring ecstasy, just equilibrium. 'Having a hit makes you feel normal.' The same addict tells of his despair at watching his girlfriend taking her first hit: 'It's the worst thing I've ever done ... Heroin's all bullshit, mate, it's all crap, it's all fucked. We look happy, but we're not. We're not happy.'[6]

Altered states of consciousness are one option, if you're in the market for a construction of your own reality. But the evidence from those who've experienced it isn't encouraging. Still, to repeat the remarkable words of New South Wales Premier, Bob Carr, quoted in Chapter 3: 'Life is an inherently disappointing experience for most human beings. Some people can't cope with that.'

One challenge in a postmodern world is to offer each other, and especially our children, experiences that alleviate that disappointment; experiences that create the sense of meaning which helps us to make sense of a world of overlapping and interacting realities. For some people, that emerges from spiritual exercises of one kind or another. For others, the sort of convictions that inspire and sustain us may arise from education, or from a political, social, cultural or philosophical agenda—or from the sublime moments of an occasional emotional breakthrough.

This is not to deny the artifice of 'social reality' but only to acknowledge that having constructed a reality that meets our own needs and resonates with our own experience, we need to work at it; to nurture it; to protect it. To let it slide away in the face of every new possibility, or in response to a nihilistic denial of the value of any belief, is to risk losing the moral compass.

The growing interest in spirituality in Australia—reported in Chapter 19—may be one sign of our need for a counterpoint to the shifting realities of postmodernism. In *Care of the Soul*, American psychotherapist Thomas Moore suggests that 'the great malady of the twentieth century, implicated in all of our troubles and affecting us individually and socially, is "loss of soul". When soul is neglected, it doesn't just go away; it appears symptomatically in obsessions, addictions, violence, and loss of meaning.'[7]

(Don't be too alarmed by Moore's use of the word 'soul'. He doesn't attempt to define it, but says it has to do with 'genuineness and depth'—as when we say music has 'soul'. Soul, for Moore, is revealed in attachment, love and community, as well as 'inner communing and intimacy'. Think of it as the essential you; your spirit or, perhaps, the nobler part of yourself.)

Moore urges us to find a place for more ritual in our lives, partly as an anchor in the crosscurrents of postmodernism, and partly as a way of deepening our spiritual lives:

> The soul might be cared for better through our developing a deep life of ritual rather than through many years of counselling for personal behaviour and relationships. We might even have a better time of it in such soul matters as love and emotion if we had more ritual in our lives and less psychological adjustment. We confuse purely temporal, personal and immediate issues with deeper and enduring concerns of the soul.
>
> The soul needs an intense, full-bodied spiritual life as much as and in the same way as the body needs food. That is the teaching and imagery of spiritual masters over centuries. There is no reason to question the wisdom of this idea. But these same masters demonstrate that the spiritual life requires careful attention, because it can be dangerous. It's easy to go crazy in the life of the spirit, warring against those who disagree ... or taking narcissistic satisfactions in our beliefs rather than finding meaning and pleasure in spirituality that is available to everyone.[8]

Hugh Mackay

Such sentiments will sound strange to those who can't conceive of a spiritual life, yet Moore's message need not be interpreted in exclusively religious terms in order to be useful. He is stressing the need for order and ritual in our lives; for time to be set aside for contemplation of life's great mysteries (of which there is no shortage); for proper attention to be paid to our non-material needs; for us not to neglect the very thing that makes us uniquely ourselves.

From a different perspective, Charlene Spretnak comes to similar conclusions. In *States of Grace*, she bemoans the loss of 'religious literacy' as a tool for making sense of a postmodern world:

> Even among people who have a rudimentary knowledge of the major religious traditions ... spiritual concerns are experienced as increasingly incongruous with the dynamics of a relentlessly orchestrated consumer society in which 'you are what you buy' ... Clearly, modern society is out of touch with the insights of the great wisdom traditions, those rich cultural repositories of thousands of years of human development of relationship with the sacred. Some call them 'the great religions' but the Buddha's teachings, for instance, do not fit the standard definitions of a religion ... and the deeply rooted wisdom of native peoples' spirituality is generally denied a place among 'the great religions'.[9]

It's safe to say, as other chapters of this book have also suggested, that another of our most precious resources for surviving the uncharted territory of postmodernism is our personal relationships. Loneliness is a dangerous prelude to alienation, and alienation is a stepping stone to despair. When the things you wanted to believe have been devalued—'deconstructed' to the point of meaninglessness—emotional connections with the people who are important to you become even more important. Through our personal relationships with each other, we have the capacity to enrich the meaning of each other's lives.

We construct our networks of friendships, just as we construct the other parts of our social reality. Having chosen our friends—and they us—we might well heed Shakespeare's advice, via Polonius:

The friends thou hast, and their adoption tried,
Grapple them to thy soul with hoops of steel;
But do not dull thy palm with entertainment
Of each new-hatch'd, unfledg'd comrade.[10]

As with friends, so with our values, our beliefs and, indeed, our rituals: their adoption tried, grapple *them* to thy soul with hoops of steel, as well. Thus armed, stroll through postmodernism's bazaar, by all means, but be prepared to resist, until tested, 'each new-hatch'd, unfledg'd' possibility.

'Never give up'

That was the inscription added by John Howard to an old campaign poster unearthed in May, 1999, for the celebration of his 25 years in Federal Parliament. It is certainly a valid career summary. After having been dropped as Liberal Party leader in 1988, and overlooked in subsequent leadership ballots in 1990 and 1994, Mr Howard famously asserted that for him to make a comeback as leader would be like 'Lazarus with a triple bypass'—unlikely, but not impossible. Sure enough, after basking in the glow of a period of 'elder statesmanship', he was reinstated as leader in 1995 and elected Prime Minister in 1996.

Even Mr Howard's political foes praise his persistence, and it's certainly the characteristic that voters most admire in him. So although no-one would be likely to describe him as a postmodern figure—in the manner of a Blair or a Clinton—Mr Howard's 'never give up' approach, combined with his unshakeable faith in his own agenda, is actually an instructive example of how to prosper in a postmodern world.

Research on prisoners of war throws up similar examples. The overwhelming evidence is that the people who survive the most testing privations are those who have a clear set of beliefs to which they can cling; those whose values give a sense of meaning and purpose to their lives; those who will never give up because their convictions sustain them.

In a postmodern world, when the alternatives presented to us are more numerous and more complex than ever, and when we have come to understand so clearly that we are the architects of our own realities, the strong temptation is to 'hang loose', wait and see, keep your options open.

This is the very temptation that has faced the generations of young Australians born since 1970. The past 30 years have been such a time of constant change, upheaval, dislocation and redefinition that young Australians could be forgiven for thinking, as many of them do, that there is no point in making a commitment—to a course of study, a job, a sexual partner, a political party, a set of religious beliefs, a rock music group, or even a brand. After all, something else will come along tomorrow, and who knows how you'll feel then? Why commit, when life is a shifting series of realities and you want to experience them all?

This is why fashion trends are so hard to pick in the young. It is why so many students abandon one course, unfinished, and proceed to another. It is why dramatic changes of direction in employment are made without a backward glance. And it is why older people sometimes question whether there's any loyalty, any capacity for commitment, in today's young adults.

My own research (reported in *Generations*) supports the idea that the rising generations are determined to keep their options open: their commitment is to *flexibility* and *freedom*. And why not? Those are the very lessons that their world has taught them. They have grown up in a cultural kaleidoscope, and they are more likely to be transfixed by the *changing* of the patterns than by any one of them.

Yet the evidence does not encourage the idea that the best response to a postmodern world is *simply* to hang loose. The level of despair among teenagers is itself distressing—'The Big Picture' at the beginning of this book listed some of the dark truths about young Australians: 20 per cent of them will have had an episode of depressive illness before the age of 18; about 40 000 of them are attempting suicide each year; the level of cannabis use is approaching 50 per cent among teenage girls.

Experts in the field of suicide and drug use have not yet been able— and may never be able—to agree on a set of definite causes for the epidemic of depression in the young. Parental neglect is sometimes cited, but some suicides occur in loving and supportive families. Rejection by peers can be a trigger, but some well-liked and socially nurtured adolescents fall into depressive pits. Everyone's despair is unique.

The John Howard prescription, anchored to a set of strong personal beliefs, does seem to offer a pathway of hope, at least for some. Truett Anderson says, correctly, that we can choose, if we wish, to be mere shoppers at the bazaar of culture and subculture, and Harold Bloom wrote in *The Closing of the American Mind* that postmodern relativism recognises 'no enemy other than the man who is not open to everything'. Students, said Bloom, have been taught 'to doubt beliefs before they believed in anything'.[11]

Living in the postmodern age exposes us to all kinds of possible realities we might once have ignored (or of which we might simply have been ignorant). Even if we choose one of those, we are conscious that this *is* a choice, and that, at some point in the future, we might make a different choice. In everything from marriage to careers, young Australians are adopting a more tentative, flexible approach than their grandparents and parents did.

But some members of the Options generation are showing us that a synthesis is possible. It might be possible to be open to all kinds of new ideas, new fashions, new 'constructs', yet remain grounded in a core belief—or a core system of thought—that sustains us. It might be possible, after all, to shop at the cultural bazaar—and even to pluck bits and pieces from a wide range of stalls—while still operating within a serviceable framework of enduring attitudes, values and beliefs that we have discovered, from our *own* experience, will give meaning and purpose to our lives.

Here's a remarkable piece of wisdom from a 13-year-old, Christopher Honnery, interviewed by Diana Bagnall for a 1999 *Bulletin* cover story on contemporary teenagers: 'The most important thing is to act as if you really believe in something.'[12] Acting *as if* you believe in something is the first step towards believing it, and once you believe it, you are on the way to a sense of purpose.

CHAPTER SIXTEEN

Persuasion

The Meaning of Brands is Changing

Turning Point: Brands are far from being the most important things in the universe. Yet so much money and talent is spent on marketing them, it's no wonder they seep into our culture. Brands add colour to our lives, enhance our sense of identity, reinforce our tastes and preferences and, sometimes, even clarify our values. (When someone says, 'I'm a Holden man', we know what he means.) But brand integrity is being eroded, and consumers are becoming more sceptical ... and that's part of a broader culture shift.

What are we hoping for? Brands we can trust. Brands that genuinely expand our range of choices. Brands that don't deceive or confuse us. (And we'll keep switching until we find the transparency we're looking for.)

'If I am what I eat,' the peripatetic former Senator from the Northern Territory, Bob Collins, once remarked, 'then I must be Ansett Catering.'

He was closer to the mark than he might have intended: it's not just the food we eat, but the *brand* of food we eat that in the full flowering of consumerism, helps to define us. Capitalism is at the height of its powers, and brands are its handmaidens.

Hardly anyone just buys any old car: the brand of car you buy says something about the kind of person you are—and not just the thickness of your wallet. Even when you convince yourself that a car is, after all, just a means of getting from A to B, or that, in any particular segment of the market, competing brands are offering essentially the same features, certain makes and models are still likely to appeal to you more than others. The basis of that appeal will be a complex (and possibly impenetrable) amalgam of rational and emotional factors.

Virtually no purchase is entirely rational. People seeking gratifications of any kind—from a private school for their children, to a packet of breakfast cereal—rarely turn out to have been exclusively concerned with quantifiable, physical features, or even with perceived value for money. Emotions play a part in every purchase decision: from shoe polish to underwear, a purchase decision is a decision about *me*—me and my needs, me and my style, me and my values—and when am I ever entirely rational about myself?

On the other hand, very few purchases are entirely emotional. Cheap, impulse buys are sometimes made on an emotional spur of the moment, but the more money you're spending, the more you'll need some rational support for even the most outrageously emotional purchase. (Luxury cars are the classic case: if I'm going to spend all this money, convince me, at least, that it's for the superior brakes, or the 25 on-board computers, or the zero-offset steering, or the thickness of the body panels, or the five air-bags ... or the ingenious cup-holders. Anything! But don't leave me stranded, looking as if I was nothing better than a sucker for prestige and status—not when I'm spending three times the price of a Holden Commodore.)

Your clothes, your drinks, your shampoo, your magazines, your favourite stores—all these are likely to be branded with names and logos that, to some extent, have come to reflect (and sometimes to shape) your tastes, your values, your style. Even the people who say 'I'm not interested in brands' will usually make brand choices that express that very attitude in some way (for example, by buying brands that are packaged and advertised in a no-nonsense way). We use brands to make us feel better about ourselves.

But things are changing in the world of brands. At a time when the techniques of mass persuasion are at their most sophisticated—and are being harnessed to market not only conventional brands, but also football codes, political parties and road safety—you might think that consumers would be at their most vulnerable. Not so. The message from the market is that *consumers are taking charge*: they are becoming more demanding, more assertive, more ready to complain about poor service or poor quality, more able to see through a clever advertising strategy, more inclined to 'cut a deal'—and more mistrustful of brands whose integrity they once took for granted.

This more sceptical, less acquiescent attitude to brands (like the growing scepticism about the credibility of the mass media) is part of a broader culture shift: it is consistent with the rise of 'grass-roots' politics, and it reflects a new determination to become involved in everything from decisions about urban planning, property development or the privatisation of government enterprises, to debates about censorship and immigration. As old prejudices begin to break down under the influence of cultural and economic change, a greater degree of open-mindedness leads people to want to have their say, at every level. (This is one of the outcomes of the trend towards so-called postmaterialism, and it is most marked among the young.)

If greater consultation—in government and the workplace—is the way of the future, starting with the primary school classroom, then people will become accustomed to flexing their muscles and expressing their needs in every setting. The supermarket, the department store or the car showroom are the easiest places to start. 'People power' has arrived in large numbers.

A new scepticism about brands is closely related to increasing scepticism about the church, the law, politics, big business. Wherever they look, Australians find reasons to question the integrity of 'the establishment': police corruption, child sexual abuse by priests, corporate tax avoidance scandals, political chicanery, dubious marketing techniques, sexual harassment in the armed services—every fresh revelation increases the tendency to re-evaluate the political, religious, professional and commercial institutions that were once regarded as pillars of our society.

'Who can you trust?' is a question Australians no longer find it easy to answer. In response to their own disappointment, they have gone onto the front foot—and that includes their behaviour as consumers.

Consumers are revolting against
a new kind of deception

It's obvious that consumers don't want to be deceived by brands—in packaging, advertising, or in pricing that exploits them. But, thanks to government regulation and the operation of agencies like the old Prices Surveillance Authority and the Australian Competition and Consumer Commission, there is a widespread belief that the marketing and advertising industries have largely cleaned up their act.

Now there's a new problem. It was easy to be outraged by blatant dishonesty; the latest criticisms imply that something has been stripped away from the traditional significance of brands that has caused consumers to become more cautious, more wary, in their response to the blandishments of the marketplace.

To understand this new wariness, we need to appreciate the historical role of brands. Brands have traditionally served as a maker's mark: a way of associating a product with the company that makes it. Even where a company might produce two or three brands in the same product category—as Colgate or Unilever have so often done in the soap and detergent market—the consumer was generally able to establish the manufacturer's identity from the pack.

The idea of multi-brand marketing by one company could be accepted by the consumer as long as it had the effect of offering the consumer a wider range of choice: each new brand was designed with its own unique

Hugh Mackay

features, at its own pricepoint in the market. Although consumers knew these were products coming out of the same factory, the differences between them provided some justification for consumers regarding them as being in competition with each other.

That identifies another important feature of the legitimacy of brands: that each brand should offer something unique; each brand should extend the consumer's range of choice; each brand should be clearly different, in some way, from other brands—in terms of ingredients, price, packaging, perfume, performance, or any other factor the consumer might take into account in reaching a purchase decision.

Today, product categories are being swamped by so many brands, including brands whose manufacturer is simply unknown, that the legitimacy of many of those brands is being questioned, as is the authenticity of the competition between them.

In other words, consumers are now being confronted by a proliferation of brands that look to them as if they are only *pretending to compete*, either because they are, in fact, identical products with different labels, or because the differences between them are so insignificant as to be undetectable. Whether they happen to be made by the same manufacturer or not is no longer the issue. The issue is: *who* makes them, and are they really different from each other?

When there was a salmonella scare in 1998 involving peanut butter, the media published a list of the brands of peanut butter that were all produced in the offending factory, which happened to be the Kraft factory. Consumers were staggered. Here were a dozen brands of peanut butter, all produced by Kraft, appearing on the market under a dozen different names. Some of them were so-called 'house brands'—that is, the private labels of retail stores—and this confirmed consumers' belief that if you could find out exactly who was making what, you might well be able to buy the products of major manufacturers for a cheaper price under a different name.

When Holden and Toyota began model-swapping (a strategy they have since abandoned), they spoke of 'badge engineering' which meant just what it said: the only significant difference between a Holden Commodore and a Toyota Lexcen was the badge (and how significant could that be?). Of course, there was no deception involved: everyone knew that the

Lexcen was really a Commodore, just as they knew the Holden Apollo was really a Toyota Camry. But that wasn't the point.

The point was that two major manufacturers were fundamentally altering the meaning of their brands and, in the process, failing to meet the consumer's two cardinal criteria for assessing the legitimacy and authenticity of brands in any market. First, the badge engineering strategy meant that the consumer's choice was not, in fact, expanded at all (so one brand was superfluous); second, brand names even as well-established and muscular as Holden and Toyota were declaring they were prepared to sell, under their own names, cars produced in someone else's plant.

The same thing is happening in the financial services market, where banks and insurance companies, for example, offer each other's products under their own brand names, often with the consumer only dimly aware, if at all, that the insurance policy being issued by a bank is actually the product of another financial institution altogether. Where the true identity of these 're-badged' products is not made explicit, consumers will be understandably irritated when they find out (wondering, inevitably, if they would have been better off going to the originating company in the first place). Where the identity is made explicit, the issue of brand integrity arises again. What does it mean to say that this is a Bank X product, if it is really the product of Insurance Company Y?

There's not much of cosmic significance in all this, and the deception, if it exists, is pretty insignificant, since consumers are still buying the products they want, whichever guise they happen to be marketed under. But it all makes its contribution to the consumer's growing perception that brands don't mean what they once did; that many product categories are being crowded by products that don't expand the consumer's choice at all; that branding is often little more than a hoax; that brand loyalty might turn out to be misplaced.

Particular brands of shampoo I run with for a certain time, and then try something else. It's such a commodity market out there, it's rare that you would think, 'I'll be sorry if that goes off the market' because there's a substitute for almost everything—except Vegemite.

There's all these brands, but no real competition. Look at petrol companies.

Are they deliberately trying to confuse us?

It's not just spurious competition that irritates consumers; they are also challenged by competitive offers which are so complex that they are difficult to understand.

In the telecommunications market, for example, consumers swap irritated stories of their attempts to sort out the real differences between a Telstra deal and an Optus deal. Part of the problem is 'the fine print'; part of the problem is that the companies themselves are seen as constantly moving the goal posts:

> *All the phone companies are the same and there's so many of them now ... we changed to Optus because we were sick of Telstra, but they didn't treat us any better so we ended up going back to Telstra. ... We did the same thing, but someone from Telstra actually rang up and convinced us we'd be better off switching back. How would you know?*

The deregulated milk market is another classic:

> *There are so many new milk brands now—Hi-Lo and Lo-Cal and all those fancy names—you don't know where to start. If you're informed enough, it's good to have choice. But if you are not, it's just bewildering.*

(Early in 1999, New South Wales consumers were further confused about the supposed advantages of deregulation by a press report in which Max Ould, managing director of National Foods, was quoted as saying that, as a direct result of deregulation of the milk market, prices in New South Wales would inevitably rise.)

The housing loan market is another common source of confusion. Consumers are now thoroughly conditioned to the idea of shopping around—in person, on the phone and, increasingly, via the Internet—but they are often frustrated by their inability to decide which offer is really best. They would not wish to return to the days of customers acting like supplicants, tugging their forelocks at paternalistic bank managers, but they don't enjoy being bewildered by the complexity of offers they are trying to compare.

There is also some bewilderment about the corporate manoevrings that see brand names change hands, as if they themselves are merchandise. Given the consumer's traditional view of brands as a maker's mark, switches in the identity of a brand's parentage almost guarantee that there will be some loss of respect for that brand in the consumer's mind.

By the time Volkswagen has bought Bentley, BMW has bought Land Rover, Ford has bought Jaguar, General Motors has bought Saab and Mercedes-Benz has merged with Chrysler, the meaning of luxury car marques—once the purest and most rarefied of all brand names—will have been irrevocably changed. Mystique will gradually give way to pragmatism ... in the consumer's mind, as it already has in the manufacturer's.

Consumers will have to adapt to the idea of brands as 'properties' that can be bought and sold by corporations, but in the process the whole idea of brand integrity will be further eroded.

Buying more than the product

As product categories become more crowded, products more homogenous, and brand identities more confusing and less transparent, the consumer is driven to look beyond the brand name for some other reason to buy.

It is as though consumers are now saying: 'Well, the products themselves are all much of a muchness, so what else are they offering me?' Increasingly, the market is supplying plenty of answers as marketers, too, struggle to distinguish their brands from their competitors'.

Three discriminators, extrinsic to the products themselves, are currently popular. The most obvious are the so-called 'incentives and rewards' that offer inducements—like Fly Buys—to buy a particular brand or to patronise a particular retailer. As the benefits they provide are usually unrelated to the branded product itself, the immediate effect of these programs is to distract consumers from the benefits supposedly inherent in the brand and to focus instead on the deal. (Whether this 'iron-lung' approach to supporting a brand will work in the long term, nobody yet knows.)

Another extrinsic discriminator is the product's country of origin. Although Australians are favourably disposed towards the idea of 'buying Australian', controversy rages endlessly over what is *truly* an Australian product. Does it depend on Australian ownership? (That would rule out Vegemite and Holden, for a start, and put Qantas on the skids as well.)

Is it a matter of products being made here, employing Australian labour, regardless of the ownership of the company?

What about products made by an Australian-owned company, but employing offshore labour and materials? Do products assembled here from imported components qualify?

This is all very confusing and, not surprisingly, it tends to smother patriotic urges at the point of purchase. (Most consumers say they try to support Australian goods—often sounding as though Australian industry should be viewed as a kind of sheltered workshop—but they generally end up buying what they want, and then being chuffed if they find that it also happens to have a map of Australia on the label ... whatever that might imply.)

But the country-of-origin question goes beyond mere patriotism. Given their confusion—or ignorance—about the meaning of foreign brands, many consumers operate according to an informal hierarchy of countries, sometimes allowing more than a hint of racial prejudice to creep in. Food products are particularly prone to judgments based on both geography and ethnicity: on both grounds, New Zealand strikes most Australians as a 'safe bet' (in some cases, even safer than Australia, since New Zealand's reputation for clean air and water, and a more unspoiled agricultural environment, is still strong).

A third extrinsic discriminator is based on perceptions of corporate citizenship. When there are no intrinsic reasons to prefer Brand X to Brand Y, the fact that it sponsors a favourite charity, or a sporting or cultural activity, *might* influence a purchase decision (though plenty of commercial sponsors have failed to receive an adequate return on their investment and some, in any case, sponsor charities out of genuine altruism, with no expectation of a commercial reward).

Where corporations publicly associate themselves with 'good works'— for example, by advertising their intention to donate a share of their profits to a good cause—this can tip the scales in their favour (though consumers may also perceive the moral ambiguity of a position that says: 'I expect to get a commercial advantage from my altruism').

Negative perceptions of corporate citizenship can be rather more potent in their effects on consumers' perceptions of a brand. If a brand is associated with the exploitation of sweat-shop labour in Asia, for instance, that can adversely affect the brand's reputation (though even that might not be enough to weigh against it if the product is attractive, the price is right and the brand is fashionable: extrinsic factors only operate if intrinsic ones are weak or non-existent). If a company is found guilty of environmental pollution or unhygienic practices, these can count against it when the brand itself is not strong enough to withstand such an assault on its reputation.

Of course, the way a company responds to a crisis can enhance or harm its reputation for corporate citizenship. When Arnott's had to deal with a criminal threat to poison its products, it was so prompt, so transparent and so thorough in its response that an already strong brand image was further enhanced.

In the end, most judgments about corporate citizenship are made on the basis of the way a company deals with its own customers. Good products and good service—as well as good employee relations—are generally taken to be the sign of good ethics.

Hugh Mackay

Marketers, beware! There's a new wave coming and it's called 'transparency'

In spite of all these reservations and all this wariness, consumers still *want* to trust their favourite brands; they love being swept away by an irrational purchase decision; they enjoy the pace, colour and buzz of the marketplace. Brands with something worthwhile to say will continue to attract attention, and those who properly understand the physical and emotional needs of their customers—provided they have a unique benefit to offer them—will be rewarded by the loyalty of grateful consumers.

But the mood of the market is changing and the message coming from the new breed of consumer is brutally simple: Tell me who you are: don't hide behind a phoney identity! Convince me! Woo me! Explain the deal ... precisely, honestly and *transparently*. Don't take me for granted: I'm in charge here!

Consumers know there are always plenty of other options if they are offended, disappointed, bored or unimpressed by one particular product or service. Their brand loyalty, like their loyalty to an employer, a partner or a political party, has become conditional. They are more sceptical than ever about 'paying for the name'. There's a new wave on the way in marketing and retailing, and the marketers who catch it will be the ones who understand the need for transparency: consumers want *the inside story* when they are buying branded products, in precisely the same way as they do when they are being ratepayers, patients, clients, members of resident action groups, supporters of a sporting team or voters. The sea of consumerism is no longer calm.

CHAPTER SEVENTEEN

Quality of Life

Life is Getting Better ... and Worse

Turning Point: How can a country that seems to have so much going for it be regarded by so many of its citizens as being 'at risk'? While Australians praise Australia as the best country in the world, they are nervous about the many signs that life here is actually getting worse. Some blame the media for exaggerating our awareness of trouble, but many people acknowledge that we have often made life worse for ourselves by not knowing when to stop—for example, in trade unionism, in parenting, and even in car ownership. There is also some anxiety about politicians' tendency to think of us as an economy rather than a society.

What are we hoping for? The courage to face up to the threats to our quality of life, and intelligent leaders who can temper economic management with a sharp social conscience.

Australians are torn between two conflicting propositions, both of which seem to be true. Roughly summarised, the paradox sounds like this:[1]

> Progress is exciting and, in so many ways, life in Australia seems to be getting better. Women are taken far more seriously than they used to be; men are discovering the joys of fatherhood; technology has done brilliant things; children have educational opportunities most of their parents never had. In spite of all our difficulties, you would be better off here than anywhere else. Yet, *at the same time*, we seem to be under more pressure, we are experiencing more stress, job prospects are uncertain ... and I'm feeling depressed.

Sometimes the same paradox is expressed in almost contrary terms:

> Australia seems to be in big trouble. We can't get unemployment under control; we're selling off more and more of our industries to foreign investors; tax reform will be as big a mess as superannuation; the hospital system is in crisis; discipline in the schools has vanished; loyalty is a thing of the past; everything is subject to the bottom line; we seem divided over too many issues, from Aboriginal reconciliation and immigration to the republic. Yet, *at the same time*, my own life seems pretty good; I can't complain; we have paid off our house; the future looks quite rosy as long as we keep our jobs ... and you wouldn't want to raise your kids anywhere else.

A 1998 survey of public opinion, directed by Richard Eckersley for the CSIRO, asked people whether the overall quality of life was getting better, worse, or staying the same, taking into account social, economic and environmental conditions and trends. Eckersley reported that 52 per cent of Australian adults believe life is getting worse—with half of those saying it is getting *much* worse. Only 13 per cent said it was getting better.[1]

Yet Eckersley's research has also uncovered the better/worse paradox: he notes that, at a personal level, 'most people in the developed world are satisfied with life and optimistic about their future. However, from a broader social perspective, most no longer appear to believe life is getting better despite being richer'.

The same thought was expressed in 1997 by one of Australia's most highly respected pollsters, ANOP's Rod Cameron: 'Never before have so many felt so unhinged in such good times.'

This paradox can't easily be resolved. Yes, there is an epidemic of depression, even among young people; yes, there is widespread personal pessimism, and there is never a shortage of people ready to complain about the state of the nation. At the same time, plenty of Australians report that life has never seemed better or more satisfying, and that Australia's own future is bright. It is true that some people who believe that they themselves are doing well, still think the country is going to the dogs; others have concluded that if the country's doing so well, they must have missed the bus.

If you were forced to make a generalisation based on the available evidence, you'd say that Australians, when pushed, will decide that life in Australia is getting generally worse—violence, greed, drugs, family breakdown, unemployment, environmental pollution, adversarial politics, fragmenting neighbourhoods—but that *my life* is okay (and might even be getting better).

Yet even this is too neat. The paradox is more subtle, and more pervasive, than that. Many people want to say, quite reasonably, that their own personal lives are getting better *and* worse. (I'm a better parent than I used to be, but I'm under more stress at work.) Others will want to say that, on the national level, life is getting better *and* worse. (We are tackling the environment, but technology is complicating our lives; the Federal Budget is handsomely in the black, but foreign debt is still too high; company profits are up, but morale is down because too many people are working too hard, and too many others have been retrenched.)

There is no way of unravelling the strands of this paradox, nor should we expect to unravel them. They are a symptom of our present uncertainties, and a signpost to a future in which we are destined to be less bothered by paradox. The truth is not simple: our attitudes are a bundle of contradictions and inconsistencies. If it were not so, that would be a sign that we were out of touch with our present, turbulent, contradictory reality.

Ultimately, we must catch the growing wave of uncertainty and ambiguity, and learn to ride it. But that doesn't mean that every contradiction is inevitable, nor that economic and social turbulence produces unavoidable casualties. For people suffering personal hardship and an all-too-apparent decline in their personal living standards, talk of 'a paradox' simply seems cruel. They would rather talk about inequity and injustice: 'We keep hearing about growth and prosperity. Obviously, some people are doing very nicely, thank you. Unfortunately, we're not among them.'

Do the media give us a false impression?

When all else fails, blame the media! This is a time-honoured practice in Australia. Your kids are spending too long in front of television? Blame television! Their table manners are appalling? Blame the media! Children can't spell any more? Blame the media! Moral standards are in decline? Blame the media! There's been *another* shooting? It's the copycat effect: blame the media! (World War III? Blame the media!)

So when it comes to negative perceptions of the quality of life in Australia, the media automatically come in for a large slice of the blame. Although some people freely acknowledge that their own experience has led them into feelings of disenchantment and despair, there is a commonly held view that the mass media tend to exaggerate the dark side— sometimes by their selective reporting ('they love the doom and gloom'), and sometimes by their excessive repetition of stories that create an impression that crime, in particular, is more widespread than it really is or that disasters are virtually on our doorstep.

My mother said she didn't want to live until the year 2000, and she hasn't. I can understand what she meant: every time you pick up the paper ... it's horrible. The media's the killer. It beats up and beats up.

Violence and crime are getting worse. When you get a five-year-old smashing windows and stealing cars, like they showed on the TV, it shows how bad things have got.

While media consumers complain of a 'constant negative bombardment', they are not only referring to domestic news. The steady diet of 'bad news' about Australia is increasingly set in a global context and the implications of that are both positive and negative. Some people are reassured about the quality of life in Australia by seeing TV coverage of hardship in other parts of the world; others are disturbed by the sense that social and economic deterioration is so pervasive that Australia won't be able to escape the consequences:

Not to be racist, but what about the curry-munchers setting off nukes? Let's face it, the world's going to end in 1999. That's what Nostradamus said. When you think of the ability of the world to blow itself up ...

People who spend three or four hours each day in front of a television set are inevitably influenced by media fare in the conclusions they draw about the state of the world. Similarly, people who rely heavily on talkback radio for their sense of connection with the wider community are inclined to accept 'today's stories' as a legitimate agenda and an accurate reflection of the way the world is. The electronic neighbourhood seems real enough.

So people who might well be living in personally tranquil circumstances can find themselves agitated by other people's tragedies, or even by the sense that their own experience can't be typical. In a small, local community, the sharing of another's troubles can be borne as part of the responsibility of being a neighbour. In a vast electronic neighbourhood, spanning the nation and the world, the burden of other people's troubles may become so heavy that it creates a generally downcast spirit.

People with stable marriages are conscious of the increasing instability of the institution of marriage. People with apparently secure jobs remark that *no job* is really secure any more. People who have had no direct experience of crime or violence nevertheless come to believe that crime is on the increase and they might have simply been lucky to escape a mugging, a car theft or a domestic break-in. Trouble is in the air, even for those people who have not experienced it.

But not all people who believe that Australian society is deteriorating will blame the media for that impression. Some regard media stories as the mere tip of an iceberg:

> It's not right that you can't go to a nightclub without getting into trouble for no reason, because of drugs and alcohol and crime. My son and his girlfriend were leaving about one o'clock and this gang just came up and started picking on Janine. Luke tried to stand up for her and they flogged him. They said to her, 'When we're finished with him, you're next, bitch'.

> You come home from work every day and think, 'Oh, my God, I hope my house hasn't been broken into today.' So many people around here have been done over. You walk in and your eyes do a quick flick, just to check ...

> I was walking down my own street at 2.00 a.m. and this 15-year-old kid came up behind me and attacked me. I ended up on the ground. I kicked him off with my stilettos and ran the rest of the way home ... Was he trying to steal your money? ... No, he was trying to rape me, and this is suburbia.

> We had another racist fight in the school grounds today. It used to be just verbal abuse against Greeks and Italians. Now it's violence involving Asians. They're only using knives now—guns will be next.

Whether induced by media coverage or personal experience, there is a widespread and persistent belief that Australian society is breaking down; that we are trapped in some sort of decline (perhaps economic, but more likely social and moral). For all its glittering successes and its undoubted strengths, Australia is regarded by its own citizens as a society *at risk*.

For some people, the threat is seen as coming, rather vaguely, from 'Asia' (perhaps economic, perhaps military) or from the new bogey: globalisation ('Are we simply pawns in someone else's game?'). Others believe the greater threat is from within, arising from our own apathy, our divisiveness—reinforced by our adversarial approach to politics—our self-centredness, or our failure to think creatively about the kind of future we want.

And all this coexists with the belief that this is the best country in the world!

'We're better off here than anywhere else'

However much Australians might complain about life in Australia, and however confused they might be by the mixed signals they are receiving about our quality of life, on one point they are united: you wouldn't want to live anywhere else.

Australians' prejudices on this point are clear. Crime might be an issue, but it's better here than in many parts of the world, especially the USA. Pollution is getting worse, but we're not in the same league as Los Angeles, or parts of Asia and South America. Unemployment? Worse than some places, better than others—but at least you are looked after here by a generous welfare system. Drugs are a growing problem, but still less of a problem here than almost anywhere else. The cost of health care might be rising, but try getting sick in America. There might be a growing split between rich and poor—and we might be creating a class system of our own—but imagine how much worse it must be in India, or even England.

Australians praise our religious and personal freedom, our climate, our stable democracy, our tolerance, our egalitarianism (though the praise, in that case, is growing fainter), our standard of education, our increasing sensitivity to the environment, our sexual equality and, in Sydney and Melbourne, our cosmopolitanism. In all these ways, they see Australia as being superior to most, if not all, other countries of the world—even if they've never ventured beyond our boundaries.

News from Indonesia, Yugoslavia, South Africa—and even from

America—fuels the perception that Australia is well off, by world standards, and that even if we are suffering some unravelling of the fabric of our society, we are still capable of being the envy of the world.

I can't imagine living in a country where you go to a demonstration and you're run down by tanks.

There are a lot of things we take for granted but when you travel, you appreciate them more. This is a good country.

You see some of these things on the TV and you say, 'Thank God our country's like it is.' We are privileged to live in a country where we're not afraid to express our ideas. It's wonderful that we have freedom of the press, freedom of speech, and freedom of the courts to defend ourselves.

Once Australians begin reflecting on such matters in a global context, they generally find something to appreciate about Australia. Often, they end up expressing great contentment with their lot even when, half an hour earlier, they had been complaining about the decline in our quality of life. The point is, of course, that both assertions are valid, and this captures part of the inherent paradox in Australians' current view of life in Australia. It's not simply that we are the best of a bad lot; it is that we are *both* wonderful *and* at risk; we are a society that encourages outbreaks of optimism and pessimism, sometimes almost simultaneously.

'The pendulum always swings too far'

One ingredient in Australians' confusion about the quality-of-life issue is their perception that we seem inclined to 'go overboard' about things, converting virtues into vices by carrying them too far.

It is widely believed, for example, that the decline of public respect for trade unionism during the 1980s and 1990s is directly related to an excess of union zeal in the 1970s. The folklore puts it like this: Having fought so successfully for justice, the unions didn't know when to stop. They kept fighting, and ended up demanding privileges and conditions that now look like injustice—or, at least, like excess. Holiday leave loadings, excessive overtime payments, penalty rates, as well as basic wages and conditions in some industries (such as the waterfront), are all cited as examples of union initiatives that have turned out to disadvantage the workers themselves, by encouraging employers to seek ways of reducing their workforce (and thus their reliance on union labour).

So, from having felt grateful to unions for their historic role in helping to protect working people from the possibility of rapacious exploitation at the hands of ruthless or insensitive employers, many people—including many unionists—now feel some resentment towards the union movement.

Some other examples:

Parents' anxieties about the welfare of their children have been heightened by both direct and indirect experience of adolescent depression, by the obvious hazards of drug abuse, the horrors of anorexia and other eating disorders and, most disturbingly, the chilling statistics of youth suicide. This sometimes leads parents to be overprotective and, out of the finest motives, to find that they have 'trapped' their children in such highly-structured activities that the out-of-school schedule has itself become a source of pressure.

In trying to provide 'the best' for their children, parents come to feel that they have actually created a straitjacket both for themselves and their children. So parents have a new worry: *Do our kids have time to be kids?* In the light of all these opportunities and all this parental concern, have our children's lives become better or worse?

Some women who are combining motherhood with paid employment are rethinking the impact of *feminism* on their lives and wondering whether they went too far, too fast. In some cases, the promise of liberation has turned out, in practice, to feel more like a sophisticated form of enslavement. The women's movement was going to make their lives better, but an excessive or unbalanced application of the principles of feminism has made things worse.

While acknowledging that we might have needed to pay more attention to *people's rights*—especially the rights of women, children, customers and employees—many older Australians now feel that this particular pendulum has swung too far, and that people have become so concerned about their rights that *they have lost sight of their responsibilities*. Taking people's rights seriously should make life better; taking them *too* seriously makes things worse.

The *overcommercialisation of sport* is often cited as an example of a good trend that's turning bad. Even when people acknowledge that professional sport was probably destined to become another form of commercial entertainment, particularly when television rights are involved, they believe that players' attitudes and the 'spirit of the game' have been adversely affected by commercial pressure. The Olympic Games are the archetype, but cricket and football are thought to be going the same way.

The clearest of all the manifestations of this dilemma is the inexorable march of *materialism*. Virtually no-one would like to be reduced to a lower level of prosperity, nor to sacrifice their material comforts, but many people now believe that, when it comes to being consumers, 'we don't know when to stop'. People who claim to yearn for a simpler way of life sometimes acknowledge that materialism has gripped them—and their children—in a way that makes 'downshifting' difficult to imagine:

You hear people saying that they couldn't survive on less than two incomes. What they mean is, they couldn't survive at their present high standard of living. It's no good bleating about the fact that you have to work so hard if you are only doing it because of your own material values. If the kids are suffering [because the parents are overworked], where's the point in it all?

Even in the case of the *motor car*—one of the most potent symbols of the good life, Australian-style—some people believe we've gone too far. Not only have our cars polluted our skies, clogged the streets of our cities, and killed or maimed thousands of our fellow road-users every year, but the car has become an antisocial vehicle by isolating us from each other in our personal capsules and giving us a protected position from which to launch attacks of road rage against each other. The massive incidence of car ownership has also diminished the footpath traffic that helps to bind communities together through casual, incidental contact. Yet the car is an unbelievably convenient, comfortable and flexible form of personal transport. So has it made life better or worse?

Permeating all such discussion is the recurring sense of paradox: life is better, life is worse. I am better off, I am worse off. Australia is richer, Australia is poorer. But underneath it is a clearer message: we are in danger of letting a wonderful country be destroyed by neglect, by apathy, or by our failure to insist on the best—and fairest—future we can possibly create.

'We're a society, not just an economy'

Australians' faith in Australia's future is being dented by the growing belief that, among government and business leaders, 'the bottom line' has become tyrannical. Among employees, it is now virtually taken for granted that where there is tension between the bottom line and the social conscience, the bottom line will win.

A famous international example, described by Jerry Mander in his book *In the Absence of the Sacred*, reveals this tension at its most acute:

In 1986, Union Carbide Corporation's chemical plant in Bhopal, India, accidentally released methyl isocynate into the air, injuring some 200 000 people and killing more than 2000. Soon after the accident the chairman of the board of Union Carbide, Warren M Anderson, was so upset at what had happened that he informed the media that he would spend the rest of his life attempting to correct the problems his company had caused and to make amends. Only one year later, however, Mr Anderson was quoted in *Business Week* as saying that he had 'overreacted', and was now prepared to lead the company in its legal fight *against* paying damages and reparations. What happened? Very simply, Mr Anderson at first reacted as a human being. Later, he realised (and was perhaps pressed to realise) that this reaction was inappropriate for a chairman of the board of a company whose primary obligations are not to the poor of Bhopal, but to shareholders; that is, to its profit picture.[2]

Australian employees would not need to point to such extreme cases to support their growing conviction that here, too, the social conscience of many corporations is stifled by commercial imperatives that, at least in memory, seemed once to have been less compelling than they are today.

As Chapter 10 suggested, *job insecurity* has become a fact of life. Until we adapt to it—or solve it—it will continue to diminish our quality of life, simply by making so many people nervous about their working futures, by threatening traditional concepts of loyalty between employer and employee, and by undermining one of the sources of personal identity upon which we used to rely.

In politics, a similar issue arises: is social policy driven by economic policy or vice versa? In other words, do governments set their economic agendas in the light of their social policy, or are economic policies pre-eminent, and social issues dealt with only as they arise as consequences of economic policy? The choice is presumably never quite that stark, but the prevailing view in the electorate is that governments are *mainly* about economic management and that political leaders see the nation *mainly* as a depersonalised economy.

It's also true that constant political emphasis on 'economic growth' is interpreted by some people as meaning that if the engine that drives prosperity is properly fired up, the social consequences will be positive (including the creation of jobs, but also including the proper provision of social welfare for those at the bottom of the economic heap). The Prime Minister, John Howard, said as much when he articulated his government's priorities in a speech to the World Economic Forum in Melbourne in March 1998. Though he presented his overriding goal as being to deliver an annual growth rate of over four per cent in the coming decade, he emphasised that his economic objectives were not ends in themselves: they were the means of achieving more jobs, higher living standards and an effective social safety net.

That is a message people want to hear. Too often, they receive the impression that the commitment to growth *is* close to being an end in itself and that it might even mean 'growth at any cost'.

Ross Gittins, Economics Editor of *The Sydney Morning Herald*, puts it like this:

> Perhaps the greatest limitation of the economists' model is its unspoken assumption that increased consumption equals increased happiness. . . . But there's growing evidence that we're consuming more and enjoying it less.[3]

Gittins is clear about the limitations of economic theory and economic policy:

> Economists are specialists and they specialise in maximising just one narrow aspect of our lives: the material. They ignore all the other aspects—the ecological, the communal, the social, the spiritual— because it's not their department. . . . So that's why too much economics is bad for our wellbeing. And it's why, if we have any sense, we balance the advice we get from economists against the advice coming from people who specialise in the other aspects of life.

The debate about the GST was, for Gittins, a classic case of economists diligently going about their professional work, largely ignoring the social consequences of their proposals. Writing before the GST vote was taken in the Senate, he said:

> Many economists fought for a GST believing it would make the economy more efficient, but most have fallen silent while John Howard seeks to introduce the GST in a package that favours the rich at the expense of the poor. Not their department.

Ross Gittins' advice is 'for us to resolve to be less influenced by the siren song of the economists'. He implies what many Australians are already feeling: that our future wellbeing—as individuals and as a society—will depend on our insistence that non-economic factors get, at the very least, equal time in the debate on public policy.

One of the most disturbing of all our anxieties is that the economy could be booming while our quality of life was deteriorating. Addressing the 1999 'Australia Unlimited' conference organised by *The Australian*, the Federal Labor leader, Kim Beazley, warned that it was all too possible for Australia 'to scale the heights of national prosperity while leaving large numbers of our fellow citizens behind'.

It is precisely that conundrum that creates confusion in the public mind between the talk of prosperity and the reality of widespread poverty, hardship and uncertainty. If governments can convince us that economic growth is being explicitly and deliberately pursued as a means of enhancing the quality of life for all Australians, especially low- and middle-income earners, then that is a policy we will enthusiastically endorse.

On the other hand, if the famous 'trickle-down effect' turns out to be the myth it now appears to be, our scepticism and disillusionment will only deepen.

The trickle-down effect is where someone stands there and pisses down on you.

CHAPTER EIGHTEEN

Republic

The People Have Their Say

Turning Point: Regardless of its outcome, the November 1999 referendum on the republic will mark a significant turning point. We are declaring *either* that we are so keen to take the symbolic step of appointing our own, non-monarchical head of state that we will even support a model whose details we don't fully endorse, *or* that the issue lacks urgency for us, and we are therefore prepared to wait for a model of republican government that is more to our liking. The outcome of the referendum will also be an important indicator of current attitudes to the Federal parliament, and the faith we have in our politicians, since the proposed model places great power in their hands.

What are we hoping for? If the proposed model is adopted, we'll be hoping for a smooth transition to republican government in which nothing changes but the symbolism of appointing a head of state who is exclusively our own. If the referendum proposal is defeated, we'll be hoping for a more comprehensive, more thoughtful and less sloganistic debate about the whole political system, before the question is again put to the vote (preferably by a prime minister who supports it, next time).

Before the 1996 Federal election, I interviewed the then Leader of the Opposition, John Howard.

I asked him whether he thought Australia would still be sharing a head of state with Great Britain 100 years from now. 'It seems highly improbable,' he said. He was less sure about 25 years hence. 'It's a strange debate,' Mr Howard mused, back then. 'I think, inevitably, perhaps I do feel a bit more open to it. My belief that the present system works hasn't changed, but I detect a maturing in the debate. It's less simplistic.'[1]

There might have been a further maturing of the debate during 1999, but Mr Howard's position had not materially changed from the view he put in 1996: 'If there was a vote tomorrow, I'd vote against a republic, but I accept there are a lot of people who don't agree with me and I've got the Liberal Party into a situation now where we will provide a mechanism for people to talk about it and vote on it.' Which is, indeed, what he subsequently did. To many Australians—especially the republicans—it was a particular irony that a pro-monarchist prime minister should be the first one to put the republic question to the people.

Although he was unwilling to make a prediction about when we might sever our links with the British monarchy, Mr Howard's apparent acceptance of the inevitability of this outcome has been echoed throughout the Australian community. Yes, there are monarchists so committed to the monarchy that they will never concede the need for change, and there are many keen republicans who remain uncomfortable with the specific proposal submitted to the November 1999 referendum.

But in the same way as it has been hard, over the past five years, to find people who thought the republican question was urgent, so it has been hard to find those who believed it would never happen (even if, like John Howard, they would personally prefer no change). Ever since the republican debate was reignited in 1994 by the then Prime Minister, Paul Keating, this sense of inevitability has both helped and hurt the republican cause.

While drawing comfort from the fact that most Australians, whatever their personal preferences, have assumed that we will eventually make the change, the republicans have always known that that very same assumption lay behind the lack-of-urgency argument: 'It's going to happen one day,' has been the response of many stereotypically laconic Aussies, 'so what's the rush? Don't push it.' Converting the republic into a high-priority issue has been one of the republicans' greatest challenges in the lead-up to the referendum, especially since apathy often turns out to be inertia in disguise and is more powerful than it sounds, sticking like glue to the status quo.

This book was written several months before the referendum. The signs, in mid-1999, were pointing to the referendum's likely defeat. Both quantitative polls and diagnostic qualitative research suggested that support for the referendum model was actually waning. But that was before the Yes and No cases had been formally put to the people, and before the voters were forced, by the looming prospect of *having* to vote, to confront all the issues and clarify their attitudes.

This chapter is therefore confined to an exploration of the issues in people's minds, before the heat of referendum battle, and to some reflections on the likely consequences of the referendum's outcome, whichever way it goes.

The forces ranged against the Yes case have been formidable

In a different political climate, republicans might have been blithely confident of victory from the very beginning of 1999. But the circumstances in which they were hatching their plans for the referendum were anything but favourable.

For a start, the problem of apathy would not go away. The republic did not seem to be a subject capable of generating the kind of passion being evoked by Anzac Day (see Chapter 1), or even the prospect of a goods and services tax.

I'm strongly apathetic on this. I know that sounds crazy, but it's true. I really believe it's something we shouldn't get too worked up about.

How are we going to choose the president? ... I don't know, but someone who speaks English would be good.

By mid-1999, there were nine clear points of resistance to the referendum proposal. If the Yes case was to prevail, it was clear that, leaving aside the committed and unswerving monarchists (who were always a lost cause anyway), these were the key points it had to address.

First, the role of the **Prime Minister** himself. In the whole history of Federation, no referendum question has ever been carried without the active support of the prime minister of the day. Unless the majority of voters were simply going to set John Howard's attitude to one side, his lack of support for the proposed model was bound to be a significant hole in the republicans' bucket. The paradox of Mr Howard having called the referendum while opposing the republic has been a further complication. Some voters have seen that as Machiavellian ('he knows it won't get through without his support, so that's why he's done it'); some have praised it as 'incredibly fair and even-handed' to give Australians an opportunity to support something he didn't personally want; others have simply assumed that the lack of a lead from the PM on this issue meant that there was no compelling reason to support it.

A second factor has been **our famous reluctance to say 'yes'** to constitutional amendments. Of the 42 proposals put since Federation, 34 have been rejected. Before the official Yes and No campaigns were launched, it seemed unlikely that a proposal which aroused so little public passion would deviate from the historical norm.

Third, the monarchists have been united, while **the republicans are divided**. The monarchists, though fewer in number, have always been completely clear about their objective: they want to go on treating the British monarchy as if it is also our monarchy.

Although the republicans are equally clear about their central goal—a non-monarchical, Australian head of state who is uniquely ours—they have been far from united on the best way of achieving their goal. As with elections, so with referendums: internal divisions are potentially lethal—and so it has seemed in the lead-up to the republic referendum.

Proponents of the Yes case have tried to turn this question against the No case, representing it as being the one that is divided. And, in one sense, it is: it comprises not only the monarchists but also republicans who are in favour of the direct election of the head of state, and assorted others who are unhappy with specific features of the proposed model. It was always going to be hard for such a disparate group to present their opposition in a united, coherent way.

The fourth factor weighing against the Yes case has been the widespread sense in the community that, given all the other matters demanding our attention, *the republic lacks significance as an issue*. Needless to say, this view outrages those who have embraced the republic as a dramatic symbol of Australia's fully independent national identity. But the resistance has nevertheless been there. Faced with the challenges of globalisation, the fragility of Asia's economic situation, youth unemployment, the implementation of the GST and the prospect of further industrial relations reform—to say nothing of Aboriginal reconciliation—it has seemed to many Australians that the republic could be shelved, as an issue, until a more propitious time. As with the urgency question, so with the significance question: the Yes case has faced a formidable task in convincing reluctant Australians that the symbolism of the switch is sufficiently significant to warrant its promotion up the national agenda.

'It's not the people's preferred model' has been the cry of those representing the fifth point of resistance. Many committed republicans have simply found themselves unable to support a model that fails to give them what they have regarded as the most fundamental of their demands: the right to have the president directly elected by the people. They have strongly opposed what they have seen as an 'elitist' approach in the referendum model, in which parliament would appoint the president (though admittedly in response to popular nomination of candidates).

The direct-electionists have been unfazed by the bitterness of the attacks on them by their fellow republicans. They have always believed that if a republic was ever to get off the ground, it would need to be driven by public support for popular election. They have therefore assumed, from the outset, that the November referendum was doomed.

When such people have been told that direct election of the president would destabilise the present system and might shift the balance of power in politics, they have merely smiled. A change to the system is precisely what they want, because they feel that the present system is less than ideal. Indeed, their basic position has been that they couldn't see much point in making the move to a republic unless it involved some significant overhaul of our political machinery; in their terms, they want 'more democracy, not less'.

Direct-electionists tend to be sceptical about the integrity of politicians, suspicious of their motives in wanting parliament to control the appointment process, and strongly of the opinion that the people can and should be trusted with the task of choosing their own president.

They have remained unmoved by the argument that it's better to get one slice of the loaf than nothing at all. They have suspected that if they were to settle for one slice, that would be all they would ever get: once the referendum question was passed, the prospect of mounting a successful subsequent campaign—for the reform they *really* wanted—struck them as being close to zero. So the fifth hurdle in the path of the Yes vote has been that the proposed model simply didn't offer the possibility of direct election of the president.

The sixth problem for the Yes case was that many republicans, even if they accept the idea of parliamentary appointment of the president, still feel that *the proposed model is flawed or deficient* in significant ways. There have been two major issues. One is the position of the states in a republic. The proposed model makes no reference to the states, and so the question of whether each state would become a republic—or whether the Commonwealth would consist of a bizarre federation of six constitutional monarchies, with vice-regal governors still representing the monarch—has remained unresolved.

That omission has led some people to conclude that the process of creating the referendum model was rushed and incomplete, and should therefore not be supported. In their view, a matter as important as a switch to a republican system of government should not be regarded lightly, nor acted upon hastily. Many of them had been hoping for a more comprehensive and even radical review of our entire system of government, so that a decision about a republic could be a *big* decision, rather than a small one which seemed merely symbolic.

Another major reservation about the model coming from otherwise enthusiastic republicans has concerned the method of dismissal of the president by the prime minister, with ratification required only by the House of Representatives (by definition, the House controlled by the prime minister) within 30 days. The essence of this objection was articulated by Padraic McGuiness in *The Sydney Morning Herald*, in an article in which he noted that this feature of the model would make Australia unique among the world's republics and, in his view, lacked adequate safeguards.

Considering that Australians who are in favour of a republic are generally also in favour of the president's role replicating, exactly, the role of the Governor-General, the question of dismissal has raised difficulties in the minds of many people who might otherwise have endorsed the model. The events of 1975 have lurked in the back of their minds: if a president were attempting to force a government to go to the people to resolve a deadlock, for instance, between the House and the Senate, what would prevent a prime minister from summarily dismissing the president?

As McGuiness put it almost a year before the referendum: 'While many republics trust the parliament to elect a president, few or none trust it to remove a president without due process and difficulty. There is no example of a popularly elected president subject to immediate and legal removal.'[2]

Problem number seven: *feelings of personal affection and loyalty towards Queen Elizabeth II* have inhibited some people from supporting the Yes vote. Some of those are monarchists, but some are half-hearted republicans who have felt that it would be discourteous to the Queen to, as it were, throw her out. (The counter-argument is covered in the second half of the chapter.)

Eighth, *'if it ain't broke, don't fix it'*. For some people, this has always been the crucial point in the whole debate. The view is common among monarchists, but there are many 'agnostics', too, who are favourably disposed to the idea of Australia eventually becoming a republic, but who can't see the need for change 'as long as the present system works'. Some of those people assume that, one day, there'll be a precipitating event—such as the Queen's own decision to abdicate from the Australian monarchy, or her death, or some crisis involving the Governor-General—and we would then need to act. Meanwhile, they are disposed to leave things as they are.

John Howard's decision to open the Olympic Games in Sydney, rather curiously, cancelled out one reason why some people would otherwise have wanted to vote Yes: to relieve us of the embarrassment of having the Queen, or some other member of the British royal family, open the Games. While some people still think it should be a job for a head of state rather than a head of government, the fact that 'Howard grabbed it' settled the question—and postponed, in the minds of some of the 'ain't-broke' brigade, the need to act on the republic.

Underlying these nine issues have been some less distinct reservations: a vague fear of the very idea of a republic, and an associated discomfort with the word 'president'. Some of this uneasiness has been based on awareness of disreputable or unstable republics around the world, some of it on a strong disinclination to be 'more like America', and some based on nothing more than resistance to change: 'Why couldn't they still call the person the Governor-General?'

The forces ranged against the proposal have been formidable. They have included three camps who have had virtually nothing in common with each other but who, taken together, have looked likely to form a majority in at least three of the states—Queensland, Western Australia and Tasmania.

The first and most obvious camp are the monarchists. To their opponents, they have appeared hopelessly conservative, up to their knees in the bog of nostalgia. Yet the pragmatic part of their message—'don't tamper with a system that works'—has clearly struck a responsive chord in many Australian hearts.

The second camp contains a veritable army of apathetic, uninterested people who have consistently claimed that they didn't really care one way or the other. Whilst they have appeared likely to favour the status quo, they have also been the best prospects for conversion to the Yes cause.

Those republicans who will settle for nothing less than direct election of the head of state by the people comprise the third camp. Their position has loomed as the most significant of all the barriers to the Yes vote: it is the one that the overwhelming majority of Australians would embrace if, having rejected the specific model submitted to the 1999 vote, they were ultimately to decide that we should become a republic.

Powerful arguments have also been advanced in favour of the Yes vote

The starkest, most ideologically definitive statement of why *Australia should reject the idea of any hereditary monarchy* appeared in *Open Australia*, the 1999 book by Federal Labor parliamentarian Lindsay Tanner:

> Australians should reject the concept of monarchy in the same way that we reject slavery and burning heretics at the stake. Monarchy is a feudal concept which should have no place in a modern democratic society. It is a direct affront to the notion that all positions of importance in our system of government should be open to all citizens irrespective of race, religion or birth. The fact that many other countries retain monarchies in various forms should not divert us from this fundamental principle. As a mature and stable democracy, Australia has no need of feudal mechanisms of government designed for societies in which disputes over political power were invariably resolved by war and violence.[3]

Tanner nevertheless insists that the elimination of our 'anachronistic connections' with the British monarchy should not be fuelled by 'facile bunyip nationalism or infantile Pom-bashing'. For him, republicanism is about *reshaping our national identity to reflect contemporary reality* and, in putting that view, he has been speaking for the majority of supporters of the Yes case.

Most supporters of the referendum model have not been so concerned with rejection of the philosophical concept of hereditary monarchy; they are more interested in cutting Australia's last remaining ties with Britain as *a symbol of our true independence as a nation*. To them, the declaration of the Australian republic would be the final step in a long process of gradual disengagement from Britain—not to deny our British heritage, nor to denigrate Britain's crucial role in establishing the Australian colonies, but to demonstrate that Australia had achieved full nationhood, in its own right. This is thought not only to have the potential to send a positive message about Australia to the world, but also to energise and inspire Australians themselves with a more distinct sense of their own national identity.

Even among people not harbouring strong anti-monarchist feelings, there has, nevertheless, been a growing feeling that *the British Royal Family has run its course as far as Australia is concerned*. Few Australians believe that the Queen would be interested in, or even particularly well informed about, Australia. Some even wonder whether she herself might be wondering why we have persisted with a monarchy so remote from Australia's region and Australia's concerns. ('She'd always back Britain against us, if it came to the point.')

The widely publicised shenanigans of the rising generation of royals have inclined many Australians to the view that even if they were prepared to persist with the monarchy for the rest of Queen Elizabeth's reign, they would not necessarily be comfortable with the idea of Charles as our next King, with or without Camilla as Queen. Speculation that the time of Charles's coronation might not be far off has led some people to favour a Yes vote, simply to avoid being 'caught out' in an unwelcome transition. The prospect of acquiring a less acceptable monarch than Queen Elizabeth II might therefore drive some voters, who are otherwise not particularly committed republicans, to support the switch to a republic.

That view—that we should not stand idly by while an 'unacceptable' monarch succeeded Queen Elizabeth II—is closely related to another basis for supporting the Yes case: *we should grab the opportunity while it is available*. Even some people who have been half-hearted about the proposed model have nevertheless been persuaded by the now-or-never argument: 'I wouldn't be able to live with myself if I said No, now that we've finally got the chance.'

Though some advocates of a No vote have tried to assure them that there would always be a second chance, they have seen this as an opportunity that should not be allowed to pass, even if the proposed republican structure turned out to need finetuning after a few years of experimenting with it.

'If you go for direct election, you'll end up with a politician.' This threat, repeatedly issued by Yes advocates, has produced a mixed reception. It's true that some people have been utterly persuaded by it, and have therefore been prepared to submerge their intuitive preference for direct election beneath their desire to ensure that any new-style head of state would not be a politician. (This is a somewhat paradoxical position: they want to avoid the election of a politician because of their low esteem for politicians and their feelings of mistrust towards them, yet they are prepared to entrust the appointment of the president to those self-same politicians!)

But this proposition has also generated some backlash. Looking at the recent list of Governors-General, some people have decided that ex-politicians like Paul Hasluck and Bill Hayden were perfectly acceptable as constitutional heads of state and, in any case, not everyone is convinced that popular election would result in the election of a politician. A worse outcome, in the minds of some uneasy voters, would be the election of a popular sporting or media celebrity—though others could see nothing wrong with an admirable figure from any field holding what would be, after all, a largely ceremonial post.

Worst of all, for some opponents of direct election, is the prospect of 'Australia going the way of America' where the money required to campaign for the presidency might limit it to the wealthiest members of the community or the best fundraisers. By comparison with such a development, the prospect of an ex-politician getting the job seems positively benign.

A key point in favour of parliamentary appointment, though, has been the desire of the community to ensure that 'the sort of people who wouldn't want to take part in an election campaign could be appointed to the job'. The present Governor-General, Sir William Deane, is often cited as a case in point. Indeed, for those favouring appointment of the head of state by parliament, the history of generally acceptable governors-general—appointed, in effect, by the prime minister of the day—is seen as instructive.

Either way, the referendum is a turning point

If we say Yes: Support for the referendum proposal will mean that, even though many people are not entirely happy with the proposed model, most Australians believe the time is ripe to assert our identity as a fully independent nation, beholden to no-one. If the Yes vote prevails, it will be on the basis of the powerful *symbolism* of a relatively small step. People will be assuming—and even hoping—that the change will have no impact on their day-to-day lives, though they will be understandably keen to see who the first president will be.

A Yes vote would also mean that, when it comes to the point, people are prepared to put their faith in the parliament to choose their president. Even though a Yes result might be interpreted as something of a repudiation of John Howard's personal opposition to a republic, it would certainly amount to a declaration of support for the supremacy of parliament.

If we say No: Rejection of the referendum question will be open to a wider range of interpretations, if only because its opponents represent such a broad coalition of views. Almost certainly, it would *not* mean that most Australians are opposed to the ultimate switch to a republican form of government, since dyed-in-the-wool monarchists are in a distinct minority. Rather, it would mean that many republicans are as keen as ever to make the change, but not *this* change. Direct-electionists, in particular, would be encouraged to believe that, next time around—and with a supportive prime minister—they could garner strong support for a different model.

A No vote would also mean that many Australians would have taken their lead from the Prime Minister, John Howard. Even if they do not share his monarchist position, they will have decided that if the PM doesn't think there is any need to tinker with the present system, then neither do they. At the same time, a No vote might be symbolic of a lack of sufficient trust in the parliament to give politicians the power to appoint—and the PM the sole power to dismiss—the president.

Nevertheless, if the No vote prevails, it is likely that Australians will be so shocked by their own rejection of the republic that moves to maintain and broaden the debate would quickly gather momentum.

Whichever way we vote, the aftertaste of the referendum will be bittersweet. While many Australians will be cock-a-hoop over the result, many others will be devastated. Those who had set their hearts on change will be either triumphant or despairing. Those who had opposed the change—with equal passion and an equal commitment to doing what's best for the country—will be either massively relieved or deeply disturbed.

If the proposed model is adopted, the disappointment of its opponents will recede as the nomination process gets under way and Australians become engrossed in the selection and appointment of their first republican president. If the proposal is defeated, however, the aftermath will be more difficult and painful. While monarchists will be wanting to claim that this is a victory for the status quo, republicans who opposed this particular model will be keen to propose an alternative model, almost certainly incorporating direct election of the president by the people.

This will be a moment for strong, sensitive, healing leadership. It will be a moment for encouraging Australians on both sides of the question— and those in the middle who don't care much, either way—to put the rancour of the debate behind them and focus on the future. Smugness, on either side, would be damaging.

CHAPTER NINETEEN

Spirituality ... or Sport?

Seeking Heaven on Earth

Turning Point: Given the extent and depth of Australians' doubts and uncertainties, the present time might be considered ripe for a revival of religious faith and practice. But the signs do not seem to be pointing in that direction. Although the decline in church attendance has slowed, fewer than 20 per cent of Australians are regular churchgoers. On the other hand, there appears to be a growing interest in spirituality (loosely defined) and some speculation about the possible links between a decline in religion and a decline in 'moral standards'. While sport is sometimes described as 'Australia's real religion', the sporting urge and the religious urge actually have little in common ... and sport, too, is at a turning point as we come to terms with the true meaning of commercialisation.

What are we hoping for? For some, a clearer set of 'rules' to help us make sense of the confusion; for others, a less rigid 'guiding story' will do. We want the church to be more active in the community (but most of us don't want to be more active in the church, even though we admire sincere 'belief'). And we want sport to be 'pure'!

Australia has never been famous for the depth or breadth of its religious life. We have produced some outstanding theologians, and an abundance of churches (including our own, unique Uniting Church, combining three formerly separate denominations: Congregational, Methodist and Presbyterian). But apart from the role of the Catholic Church in two major splits in the Labor Party—in 1916 over conscription, and in 1955 over fears of communist infiltration of the trade union movement—organised religion has never been an integral, intrinsic force in Australian political, cultural or social life in the way it has been, for instance, in America or Western Europe. God is mentioned in the preamble to our Constitution and our parliamentary sessions begin with prayers to 'Almighty God', but religious faith is generally regarded as an essentially private—and, for most Australians, relatively unimportant—matter.

This doesn't mean that we are a bunch of atheists: there is a very big difference, in the Australian culture, between being 'religious' and believing in God. A 1999 survey, conducted jointly by Edith Cowan University and the National Church Life Survey, found that 74 per cent of Australian adults professed belief in God (though no attempt was made to establish what they meant by 'God'), 53 per cent claimed belief in heaven, but only 32 per cent in hell.[1]

Reflecting the Christian basis of most Australians' religious education, the survey also found that 43 per cent claimed belief in the resurrection of Jesus, 42 per cent in his divinity, and 33 per cent believed in the existence of the devil.

These figures might strain your credulity, given the fact that fewer than 20 per cent of Australians attend church at least monthly (though nearly a quarter attend at Easter). Church attendance in Australia went into free-fall during the Seventies and Eighties, but has stabilised during the Nineties. Among Anglican and Protestant churches, attendance has declined by only two per cent during the period 1991–96, though researchers at the Catholic Church Life Survey estimate a ten per cent decline in attendances at Mass over the same period. (The Catholic Church is the single biggest Christian denomination in Australia, with 4.8 million members, followed by the Anglicans with 3.9 million.)

The picture is patchy, but there are signs of particularly strong growth in attendance at churches closest to the fundamentalist end of the theological spectrum—such as the Salvation Army—and among the so-called 'charismatic' churches—such as the Pentecostal Christian Revival Crusade. But every denomination has its star performers, in terms of church attendances, and 24 per cent of all church congregations are reporting growth, against 18 per cent in decline.

Some of the cultural reasons for the growth of fundamentalism have been discussed in Chapters 3 and 14. Although the growth and decline of particular religious organisations and movements can be subjected to social analysis, it must be acknowledged that the question of religious faith is ultimately both individual and mysterious.

Was religious faith missing from the start?

Professor Horst Priessnitz, a Dutch scholar who has made a comparative study of the cultural histories of Australia and America, has been particularly struck by the utterly different religious climates surrounding the foundation of these two New World nations. Whereas the seeds of American colonial civilisation were sown in the puritanism of the Pilgrim Fathers, European settlement in Australia was, from a religious point of view, inauspicious:

> Australia was founded at the time of the Enlightenment and its character formed by men and women who shared the preoccupations of that period. Eighteenth century science seemed to have established a universe which no longer needed God as an explanation of its development and further progress; at most He was the distant First Cause of a cosmos which got on quite well on its own. If this was the

attitude of the upper classes, it had its counterpart in the hatred among the convicts and their descendants for the British establishment, with which virtually all the religious [institutions] were intimately connected. This led to an a-religious, if not anti-religious spirit spreading through certain strata of Australian society. If Australia is frequently described as the Garden of Eden, it is a garden from which God, not Adam and Eve, has been banished.[2]

Yet Priessnitz, drawing on the historical work of Australians Richard Ely and Bill Lawton, also acknowledges that there has been an extraordinarily vivid sense of 'covenant' in Australia's religious history—the sense of a divine calling among those religious groups who have seen themselves as 'the chosen people of Australia'. Like Manning Clark, he concludes that the Australian Dream has long possessed 'a Puritanical, Protestant element alongside its secular mainstream'.

In contemporary Australia, in spite of the large majority describing themselves as theists, that 'secular mainstream' has remained dominant. In a 1992 Mackay Report on Australians' beliefs, people found it easier to discuss their belief in the family, or the doctrine of the fair go, or the importance of education, than to articulate the nature of their belief in God. 'There must be something out there' or 'we must be here for a reason' was about as far as the participants in that study seemed prepared to go. God, in Australia, seems still to occupy an essentially external, impersonal place in the public imagination, rather in keeping with the Enlightenment view of a First Cause to which Priessnitz referred.

The clear impression to emerge from the 1992 study was that Australians place a high value on religious belief. They admire people of strong religious conviction ('as long as they don't try to ram it down our throats') and, in spite of reservations about the cultural aspects of Islam, Australians will generally concede a grudging respect for the devoted religious practices of Muslims.

Indeed, one of the strongest beliefs expressed in that study was that 'we would be better off if we believed in something'—suggesting, for a start, that the majority's professed belief in God doesn't actually *feel* like a significant belief or doesn't, perhaps, form part of a coherent *set* of beliefs.

Hugh Mackay

Sometimes, this 'belief in the value of belief' seems to be connected with a yearning for a clearer set of *moral* convictions, rather than a spiritual, or specifically religious, quest. Clearly, the church is more strongly associated, in the public mind, with moral instruction (and, indeed, moral stricture) than with mysticism.

People don't seem to know where they stand any more. I think people who have a definite religious belief might have an easier time, because they have a set of rules to live by which have been proved over centuries.

When I used to go to church, I walked out and felt a better man. I think believing is a great thing in life.

Even churchgoers will sometimes admit that they are more comfortable, and more confident, with the church's teachings about morals and values than with the mysteries of faith or doctrine.

In the current wave of interest in 'spirituality', the church is the last place many people would think of: their sights are set on New Age awareness centres, or Buddhist retreats, or psychic fairs, or crystals, or aroma-therapy ... a far cry from the traditional liturgical uplift obtained from the singing of hymns, the recital of creeds, participation in corporate prayer or other rituals of the mainstream churches.

And yet, in spite of their reluctance to attend church services and the vagueness of their religious convictions, a common theme in discussion of religion is that 'society would be much worse off without the church' and even that 'part of the problem with society today is that not enough people go to church'.

I'm not religious myself, but I wish the church could become a focal point for society again.

I love seeing those little groups of people standing outside churches on Sunday mornings. It's nice to know that kind of thing still goes on.

It might be 'nice to know it still goes on' but the vast majority of Australians seem massively indifferent to the idea of joining in. It is as if they want the church to be more active in society, but they don't see themselves becoming more active in the church.

Sometimes they will defend their non-churchgoing by reference to the hypocrisy of Christians who 'profess to believe one thing but do another', sometimes to the fact that the church has been 'discredited' through media reports of child sexual abuse by priests or its material wealth, sometimes to their conviction that 'you don't have to go to church to believe in God'.

It's very appealing to think you could get a ready-made set of beliefs, but there are so many bigots and hypocrites in the church that I don't think I could stand it.

Many church attenders offer their own criticisms of the church, including a sense that the institution has lost its sense of direction, is out of touch with the community, and is preoccupied with its own agenda. Nevertheless, the idea persists that the church has something important to offer a bewildered and restless society.

You hardly know what to believe these days—even the church keeps changing its mind. But at least there are certain basic teachings which you can stay comfortable with. I think Christians are more interested in honesty and decency and things like that.

I know some blokes who are involved with the Salvation Army and they seem to have the game sewn up. I think they really live the way they claim to live.

Spirituality, mysticism, and the search for meaning

The word 'spirituality' has gained currency in Australia through the Nineties in a way that could conceivably be interpreted as an early sign of a major uprising in religious faith and practice. But the available evidence suggests that 'spirituality' has become a code word for almost anything but religion of a traditional, conventional kind. Indeed, those mainstream churches that have attempted to align themselves with a non-doctrinal embrace of spirituality seem not to have fared well in the current patchy upswing in church attendance.

Writing in *The Sydney Morning Herald*, columnist Padraic McGuinness put a political perspective on it:

> Mainstream Christianity in Australia has always been dominated by the major churches, and increasingly these have moved to the Left in recent years ... There is a lot of talk about spirituality and the search for meaning, which seems a kind of warm inner-glow form of progressiveness requiring self-discipline and no doctrine. But at the same time the congregations in these churches are dwindling, and their political influence in real terms, that is, the authority they have over and through their flocks, has virtually disappeared. However, overall Christianity is far from being in decline.[3]

McGuinness' analysis is closely related to the inarguable proposition that society has moved to the Right—politically and culturally—and that, where the major churches have moved to the Left, this has put them out of touch with the prevailing mood. (Such churches would no doubt defend themselves on theological rather than political grounds and, in any case, some of them are growing, too.)

It is too early to know whether McGuinness' analysis will be borne out in the long term. But there is plenty of anecdotal evidence to suggest that many people are looking to the churches for a tougher, 'straighter' line on religion with a strong doctrinal basis, but also for moral guidance on everything from tax policies to euthanasia. The idea of church leaders as moral teachers is coming back into vogue, in direct response both to the deepening sense of uncertainty and widespread perception of 'community breakdown', and to the perception that we lack a strong moral agenda in national politics. There is increasing attentiveness to prominent clergy, like the Baptists' Tim Costello and the Catholics' Frank

Brennan, who are prepared to fill the vacuum in public discussion about vision, purpose and the moral dimension of life.

Some sceptics will inevitably regard forays by church leaders into political and social debate as a sure sign that the churches have 'lost the religious battle' and are struggling to recapture a sense of relevance through social activism. Tim Costello acknowledges that charge: 'As one who speaks out on public issues, I can assure you it's not easy. In a fragmented culture, it raises a lot of anger.'[4]

Frank Brennan argues that he has never seen himself as a priest who would mainly be about filling churches: 'You can't just view your pilgrimage through life as some isolated activity or the activity of some kind of sect. You have to take the world seriously.'[5]

Tim Costello is certainly right about the fragmented culture. In the field of religion and spirituality—as in every other arena of contemporary Australian life—there is no single trend. Some churches are waxing and others are waning, even within the same denomination. Some clergy have built huge congregations by avoiding social issues and concentrating on matters of personal faith, while others make constant connections between faith and society. Some people treat religious leaders as nothing more than moral advocates, while others see the moral aspects of religion as mere implications of a particular set of spiritual beliefs. Some believe that religion has no place at all in political debate, while others see politics as the primary focus of attention for a 'social gospel'.

But there is no doubt that many people are preferring to look right outside the church—sometimes to ginger groups like the hugely successful Spirituality in the Pub movement set up by questioning, but still active Catholics—for something they would loosely describe as 'a sense of meaning and purpose'. This often has less to do with the formal liturgical practices of organised religion and more to do with a sense of the 'mystical', or a connection with the cosmic 'energy field', or the creation of a particular kind of 'head-space'. 'Put it out to the universe,' say utterly non-religious people, in circumstances where more traditional believers might suggest prayer.

Some members of mainstream churches are coming to the view that conventional, church-based religion might be overdue for a revolution.

Hugh Mackay

When the Reverend Peter Hughes resigned in 1996 as rector of St James' Anglican Church in King Street, Sydney (the second-oldest parish church in Australia), he revealed that he had harboured, for some years, deep misgivings about the role and direction of the institutional church. And the prolific religious writer Don Cupitt, also an Anglican priest, now speaks of a 'sea of faith' movement that is gathering momentum outside the structure of the established church and might, in his view, eventually replace it. The 'home church' movement, small but growing, is a sign that some people still wish to practise their religion in a communal setting, but not to go to a place recognisable as a church.

Some churches are responding to this pressure by reforming and extending their range of activities. Like ecclesiastical versions of the chameleon bars and bistros described in 'The Big Picture', they are adopting different styles at different times of the day, or on different days of the week, in order to address different needs and to appeal to people looking for quite different experiences from the church. A formal liturgical program may coexist with less structured, more mystical retreats and exploratory spiritual exercises. The church choir might be heard on Sunday mornings, and a contemporary *a capella* group in the evenings. Formal sermons are available for those who want to hear them; informal talks and discussions groups are available at other times. Sometimes music is the dominant mode of worship; sometimes silence, and sometimes both, at different times of day, in the same church.

Other churches have established centres to attract and support the work of local creative artists. Others have embarked on programs of support for the lonely, the disadvantaged and the dispossessed.

The message inherent in all such intiatives is that traditional, 'one-product' church programs are inadequate in meeting the needs of an increasingly sceptical society that doesn't regard churchgoing as a natural, or even 'normal', thing to do.

Will our uncertainties propel us towards religious faith?

The contemporary mood of Australians could well turn out to favour a gradual revival of religious faith. Uncertainty, combined with a yearning for meaning and purpose, is the traditional catalyst for journeys of spiritual exploration, and Australia at the turn of the century has no shortage of uncertainty. The 'spirituality' movement might, indeed, presage a renewed interest in religion—though the signs do not yet appear to be pointing in that direction.

As people learn to incorporate uncertainty into their view of the world, some will be troubled by the absence of a core of stable beliefs, religious or otherwise. Perhaps they will seek the comfort of a 'guiding story' that allows them to make sense of an otherwise confusing and perhaps even meaningless existence.

Does faith thrive on doubt, or replace it?

Theologians disagree about whether religious faith spells the end of uncertainty. Some argue that doubt is the very essence of faith: that the whole point of believing something is that it is unknowable in the ordinary sense; that faith is simply a means of moving forward with hope, perhaps even with confidence, but not with absolute certainty. Others insist that once the 'leap of faith' is taken, belief is indistinguishable from knowledge. In both cases, there is support for the intensely postmodern view that *believing is seeing*, rather than the rationalist's insistence that *seeing is believing*.

The varieties of faith are as great as the varieties of everything else in this hybrid and swiftly-evolving society. In the realm of religion, the greatest difference is between those whose faith settles their doubts— the fundamentalists—and those whose faith depends upon, and even thrives on, its own uncertainty—the mystics.

Pope John Paul II, writing on the search for truth, speaks for those

Hugh Mackay

who want a transcendent certainty to relieve the insecurities of the postmodern world:

> The truth comes initially to the human being as a question: *Does life have a meaning?* At first sight, personal existence may seem completely meaningless. It is not necessary to turn to the philosophers of the absurd in order to have doubts about life's meaning ... No-one can avoid this questioning ... Whether we admit it or not, there comes for everyone the moment when personal existence must be anchored to a truth recognised as final, a truth which confers a certitude no longer open to doubt.[6]

For the French intellectual, political activist and mystic Simone Weil, that 'final truth' was as vast as it could possibly be:

> We should identify ourselves with the universe itself. Everything that is less than the universe is subject to suffering.
>
> Even though I die, the universe continues. That does not console me if I am anything other than the universe. If, however, the universe is, as it were, another body to my soul, my death ceases to have any more importance for me than that of a stranger. The same is true of my sufferings.[7]

For many believers, though, absolute certainty is neither the reality nor the goal. The American theologian M Holmes Hartshorne:

> Truth and doubt belong together. As St Augustine observed, serious doubt is always for the sake of truth. The motive behind authentic scepticism is the desire for certainty. We doubt in order that we may not be wrong ... The man who lacks the courage to doubt his beliefs fears to accept his existence.[8]

Albert Einstein:

> The fairest thing we can experience is the mysterious. It is the

fundamental emotion which stands at the cradle of true art and true science. He who knows it not and can no longer wonder, no longer feel amazement, is as good as dead, a snuffed-out candle. It was the experience of mystery—even if mixed with fear—that engendered religion. A knowledge of the existence of something we cannot penetrate ... constitutes the truly religious attitude.[9]

Marion Woodman:

Church rituals were set up, not to do away with the mystery, but to allow people to experience it.[10]

Hans Küng:

Faith in God is not an irrational, blind, daring leap, but a trust that is responsible in the eyes of reason and grounded in reality itself.[11]

So ... what might Australians make of all that?

There is no 'typical' Australian belief in God, nor a distinctively Australian variety of religious faith, any more than there is a 'typical' Australian marriage or a 'typical' voter. Even our two most numerically strong denominations—Catholic and Anglican—contain such theological and cultural diversity within them, it makes little sense even to speak of a typical Australian Catholic or Anglican. The fundamentalists and the mystics coexist uneasily, with most believers being somewhat uncomfortable with either label.

Considering that Australians are so free with their assertions of belief in God, it is perhaps surprising that they aren't more willing to discuss the concept itself. Among the large body of non-churchgoers who profess belief in God, the concept they claim to believe in seems neither well defined, nor of much interest:

I respect God, wherever he is.

The first person you reach out to in a crisis is God.

I believe there is something and I'd like the children to believe there is something. We talk about God, but it's not a big issue.

To each his own. To me, religion isn't a matter of four walls, but how you feel inside.

I think you can lead a perfectly good life without being religious. On the other hand, you could say that there has been a decline in religion in Australia at the same time as there has been so much moral deterioration. Maybe the two things are connected, after all.

To put it mildly, Australians are easygoing about religion. Among non-churchgoers, the prevailing attitude is closer to indifference than scepticism. They are suspicious of extremists, generally benign in their attitude to the church and its influence in the community, though some associate any form of religion with oppression, conformism and bigotry. While they may connect their desire for greater clarity of purpose with a vague desire for stronger religious belief, they seem content to stick with a relatively unformed idea of 'God'. They are rather embarrassed about discussing it.

In many ways, the Prime Minister, John Howard, typified a quite general attitude to religion, even among occasional churchgoers, in the 1996 interview referred to in the previous chapter. Discussing his Methodist upbringing and subsequent religious experience, Mr Howard had this to say:

[As a churchgoer] I'm sort of halfway between twice a year and regular. I go sporadically. I'm not a heart-on-your-sleeve person ... I have a view that the private values of religion are a private source of support: the code it might give you for conduct. I feel uncomfortable with excessive evangelism.

But I'm undoubtedly Christian. I certainly wouldn't regard myself as either an atheist or an agnostic. I think you always have uncertainty and that's why there is a certain reserve or caution when I speak of myself in a religious context. I don't want to pretend I'm something that I'm not.

I regard the religious or spiritual component of somebody's life as being quite important, but I have an abhorrence of people who parade spirituality or religiosity.[12]

Australians' *other* religion

If you really want to hear Australians—especially Australian men—getting excited about ritual, doctrine and tradition; if you really want to see a congregation of Australians standing and singing with passion and commitment; if you really want to understand how intensely Australians can debate a moral issue ... listen to them talking about sport, or go and watch a major sporting contest. (If it's an international event, you'll wonder how anyone could say Australians are unsure of their national identity.)

No wonder it is so often said that Australians' passion about sport is positively religious in its fervour. There are some striking parallels, and not all of them are flattering to religion.

Take football.

Followers of the different codes—Aussie rules, soccer, rugby union ('the game they play in heaven'), rugby league—are about as indifferent to each other as are Christians, Jews and Muslims. There might be occasional, arcane debate about points of similarity or difference, but once people have made their choice of code—or religion—the alternatives don't really exist for them.

Ah, but what about the people who follow the right code, but barrack for the wrong team? (By the way, that word 'barrack' is an Australian original, dating from the time when convicts in Sydney's Hyde Park Barracks would lean over the wall to shout encouragement to the teams playing football in Hyde Park.)

The real passion, and the real hostility, is reserved for those who belong to the same code family, but who dare to support a different team from ours—not unlike the furious conflicts that have sometimes erupted between Catholics and Protestants, or even between Protestants of different theological persuasions. The tensions between High and Low Anglicans, for instance, have something in common with the tension between Carlton and Collingwood supporters: on each side, there's a tendency to think the others are misguided, if not unhinged.

But there's a deeper connection between sport and religion: they are both capable of taking us 'out of ourselves' and providing welcome escape from the uncertainty and insecurity in other areas of our lives. And they both depend on faith—faith that has to be sustained by regular attendance at the ritual; faith that doesn't remotely depend on who's wearing the team jersey (or cassock) this week; faith that survives even the most bitter disappointments.

'If only life was like sport'

The magic of sport is easy to describe: it's a ritualised version of ancient hunting techniques that appeals to something deep inside our primitive psyches. Better yet, it offers us a glimpse of how we might wish our lives could be:

> Everyone knows what the rules are, and offenders are punished on the spot. (*'I wish we had a referee at the check-out at my supermarket, sending off the people who try to take too many things through the eight-items-or-less line.'*)

> There are clear winners and losers. (*'I wish life was like that, but it's never that black-and-white.'*)

> In spite of the high excitement and deep despair wrought by the performance of my team, or my hero, past results are quickly forgotten in the passion of the next contest ... and hope springs

eternal: even if the bad guys win this time, they might lose next week.

Once you know the rules, the plot line is easy to follow, yet the drama is as intense as any soap opera.

A typical game involves a series of intense highs and lows for both players and spectators, and this emotional colour is a welcome enrichment of lives which might otherwise be rather grey. (*'My husband gets more worked up at a football match than any other time—including when he's behind the wheel of a car.'*)

The rituals are a source of comfort—the drinks breaks, the umpire's signals, the players' huddles, the spectators' scuffles. (*'Let's face it, sport is the new religion.'*)

Sport is not above corruption, scandal and intrigue. The loss of 'purity' has become a big issue for sports-lovers, as commercial interests have become more intrusive, and the motivation and loyalty of the players have sometimes seemed to be compromised by money. (Is it drawing too long a bow to suggest that this is symbolic of our diminished trust in most of our social institutions?)

So is sport the true Australian religion? Is all this passionate devotion a form of spirituality?

It's a nice idea but, in the end, it won't work. The essentially competitive, aggressive nature of sport is utterly at odds with the key messages of religion: harmony, cooperation, turning the other cheek, humility, loving-kindness, concern for the other. (Does any of that sound like a grand final?)

The truth is that the spiritual impulse and the sporting impulse coexist in most of us; they both have important messages for us, but they have almost nothing to say to each other. And that, in a way, signifies the tension that has Australian society in its grip at the end of the century. Our sporting impulse encourages us to think about economic growth, or globalisation, or industrial relations reform, in terms of *winning*; our spiritual impulse drives us to think about equity, fairness and justice, and about the impact of our success on the poor, the disadvantaged, the marginalised. In a culture that almost deifies competition, the sporting urge prevails most of the time. But, every now and then, we catch a glimpse of the spiritual impulse as well.

Harnessing the power of both impulses requires constant adjustment. The way we make that adjustment will play a big part in the shaping of our future.

CHAPTER TWENTY

Technology

Why the Luddites had a Point

Turning Point: Technology is moving to new levels of sophistication: the question is whether we will uncritically move with it. We have reached another turning point: should we adopt whatever technology is available, simply because it is there? Should we evaluate it more carefully in terms of its long-term social consequences? Should we be prepared to adapt our working and living styles to match the capacities of the new machines?

What are we hoping for? Technology that serves us without revving us up still further; technology that allows us to do what we want to do, rather than making us do what it 'wants' us to do. And we must hope for sufficient wisdom to deal with the ethical issues rushing towards us from the frontier of genetic engineering.

Neil Postman, American author of *Amusing Ourselves to Death*, recently had this to say:

> The first question [that] needs to be addressed when anyone tells us about a new technology such as interactive television, virtual reality, high-definition TV or the information superhighway [is this]: What is the problem to which this is a solution? The technology writer Nicholas Negroponte envisions a time when we may speak to a doorknob so that it opens. It is certainly possible; but you have to ask what is the real problem that this technology solves ...
>
> Whatever it is, we are entitled to ask about it and even be sceptical about it.[1]

Postman's question is echoed in the minds of a growing number of Australians. Quite apart from the out-and-out technophobes, many of those who are embracing new technology with unrestrained vigour are quite unsure about the social impact, and the true benefits, of what they are doing. And they are particularly nervous about the long-term effects of some of the technology now flooding into their children's lives.

Nevertheless, when it comes to technology, Australians are voracious. We led the world in the rate of adoption of microwave ovens and VCRs. We currently own more than six million mobile phones—that's one mobile for every three of us, including babies. (I've even seen a man talking on his mobile while sitting in a dodgem car at a fair.) According to the Australian Mobile Telecommunications Association, we are the fourth highest per-capita consumers of mobile phones in the world; Sweden is the highest.

One-third of Australian adults (4.2 million people) used the Internet at home, work or some other location during 1998, and 18 per cent of households are now connected to the Net.

Back in 1981, a study called *Computers, Technology & the Future* suggested that Australians were generally rather pessimistic about the likely impact of computer-based technology on their lives. To quote from that report:

A recurring theme ... is that society will become depersonalised, that people and groups will be alienated from each other, and that life will become emotionally colder. These fears depend upon the idea of machines coming to dominate people in a way not thought to have occurred previously ... People feel that the future holds technological innovations which are in some way more complex and more persuasive than we have previously seen. It is this prospect which is frightening and which leads to the idea of a diminution of the significance of human beings themselves.[2]

Seventeen years years later, our *Mind & Mood* (1998) report found that 'technology continues to polarise the Australian community. There are those who are constantly astonished by the latest manifestation of the information revolution, [yet] at the same time, technology stimulates fear, mistrust and anxiety'. That report, and an earlier study, *Living With Technology* (1993), suggested that people are most enthusiastic about technology that allows them to do what they are already doing—like telephoning or typing—but to do it more conveniently or more efficiently. They are most resistant to technology which forces them to change the way they are doing something—like banking.

The story of adaptation to technology is as old as humankind itself. We invent something, we use it, we become accustomed to it, and gradually our attitudes towards it become more positive. (People who have used telephone banking, for instance, generally swear by it, even if they were initially resistant to it.)

People used to run and hide when they saw a car on the road. You can't stop the march of progress.

You can't stop the march of progress, indeed, but, as Neil Postman suggests, you can be more sceptical, more questioning and more cautious about it than Australians generally have been in the past. They speak of their own tendency to 'go overboard' about new gadgets and to develop a kind of 'machine mind-set' that can easily turn them into victims of the technology they have embraced with such verve. Postman suggests that 'we live in a world in which the idea of human progress ... has been replaced by the idea of technological progress in which the aim is not to reduce ignorance, superstition and suffering but to accommodate ourselves to the requirements of new technology'.[3]

I was vacuuming the carpet the other day and I was going backwards and forwards over a particular spot, over and over, trying to pick up a bit of cotton. The vacuum cleaner just wouldn't get it. Finally I realised it would be quicker and easier to bend down and pick it up, but I had been persisting with the vacuum cleaner.

My husband wants me to make my shopping lists on the computer. I tell him I can have it done before he's even turned the thing on.

There are a lot of things I do on my computer that I wouldn't have bothered doing if I didn't have the computer ... and a lot of calls I make on the mobile phone that I wouldn't make if I didn't have the mobile.

Australians recognise their own unstoppability, but there are pockets of thoughtful resistance:

Will we go too far? Will Jurassic Park become a reality?

Tomatoes are being genetically engineered so they have a longer life and don't rot. Animals are fed growth promotants and when we eat them, it affects us. You wonder where the whole thing is leading.

I have just come back from living in Japan. Over there, I didn't know one family with a computer. Here, I don't know one family without one. In Japan, you see piles of paper in lots of offices—no computers. And they use cash—no EFTPOS. Australia has gone too far. We have gone computer mad.

We're raising some moral questions, at last

The moral issue most commonly raised about technology is this: *is it depersonalising our society?* Sometimes, this is a question about the effects of replacing people with machines in a growing range of situations—Melbourne tram conductors, ATMs, automated phone message systems. But sometimes it is a more intensely personal issue: does the time we and our children spend in front of a computer screen rob us of time we could be spending together?

This is not the misty-eyed question it might appear to be. People are not hankering after the mythical days when they all spent jolly hours together, singing around the piano, playing Scrabble, Monopoly and cards with their kids, and not a care in the world. We know that, in our lifetime, there has always been technology on tap to distract us from ourselves and each other, radio and television being the most obvious examples.

Still, it is a question that specifically arises in the family context: are our kids becoming more isolated from us because of the range and appeal of the things they can now do with their computers, especially if they are connected to the Internet?

But it's a broader question, as well. What about the impact of new technology on our interactions at work? Is e-mail reducing our tendency to talk to each other? Are we confusing 'telephone tag' with a relationship?

Paul Burton, in *Information Technology and Society*, reminds us that when we allow ourselves to become too gung-ho about new technology, an attitude of 'technological determinism' can remove any real consideration of human values from the process of technological development.[4]

In five years' time, society will be worse off, because technology dehumanises people. There's now even an electronic egg you can wear: you program it if you want a sexual relationship, friendship, or whatever, and it beeps when there's another one programmed the same way within five metres, or something. Things could really get out of hand on a Friday night.

Many executives now fear a serious breakdown of face-to-face communication in the workplace because of an overreliance on e-mail, and a drop in productivity because of the amount of time being spent sending and retrieving e-mail.

I think the ultimate was reached when a colleague e-mailed his secretary and asked her to make him a cup of coffee. And her desk was only a few feet from his office.

Such things don't disturb everyone. Plenty of Australians are happy to be along for the technology-driven ride of their lives:

Technology is bloody marvellous, as far as I'm concerned. It has virtually changed my life. I'm talking about things like the mobile phone and my computer linked to the Internet. It's a revolution, and we're in the middle of it.

Yet even the most devoted advocates of the new technology will sometimes reflect on its impact on their personal relationships. Wives complain about the time their husbands spend in front of the screen (the reverse complaint is far less common); friends complain that they have been reduced to swapping messages on their answering machines; parents complain that they long to hear the sound of their children's voices, when all they are getting is e-mail messages (while other parents, admittedly, express gratitude to e-mail: 'at least they're keeping in touch'); inveterate mobile phone users sometimes wonder whether they are actually seeing less of their friends 'because it is so easy to keep in touch with that damn phone'.

On the subject of depersonalisation, a number of practical worries nag the minds of parents. Will our children's social skills suffer? What are the long-term health consequences of spending all that time in front of a computer screen? Will they become addicted to the idea of instant action, instant solutions, and an instant answer to even the hint of boredom?

When mine have been playing with the computer for hours, it makes them really scratchy. They want instant food, for a start, because that's usually the only reason they've torn themselves away from the screen. It certainly doesn't do anything for their manners.

It's clear from these concerns that we must constantly remind ourselves—and we must remind our children—about the difference between machines and people. For a start, we should delete the term 'user-friendly' from our vocabulary! Machines may be easy or difficult to use, but they are neither friendly nor unfriendly. Machines may be quick, accurate and convenient, but they do not possess such qualities as courage, integrity, fidelity or moral sensitivity. Machines are not patient, generous or tolerant. Those are qualities which people possess, and those are the very qualities which are fundamental to the whole process of human communication.

Meanwhile, technology offers its seductive charms to younger and younger children. A computer game called JumpStart Baby, released in the USA in 1998, is designed for use by babies as young as nine months: they control a teddy bear who is playing hide-and-seek. 'Lapware' is the trade name for this kind of material, because the baby is supposed to sit on its parent's lap while playing. (Will inflatable plastic parents with sheepskin laps be next?) The London *Times* reported in 1998 that games designed for children aged between 18 months and three years are one of the fastest growing sectors of the US market. Many children now sing the words, 'Load from hard drive, load from hard drive ...' to a tune you used to know as 'Frère Jacques'.

Moral question number two: *Does technology increase unemployment?*

For most Australians, this question has a ready-made answer: 'Of course it does; you hear examples every day of people being retrenched because technology has done away with their jobs ... look at the banks.'

Occasionally, other voices are raised: look at all the new employment being created in high-tech industries; industry is constantly being restructured because of new technology—this is just another phase in a continuous process. While the theory of that proposition appeals to some people, the short-term impression is that Australians are generally unconvinced by it.

Old joke: 'The computer company was so successful, they had to move to smaller premises.' That about sums up the dominant attitude of Australians. For the foreseeable future, they imagine that computer-based technology will throw more and more people out of work, and that the alternative jobs that might become available are unlikely to be comparable—in status, or in earnings—with the jobs lost: 'The growth is all in part-time work in service industries.'

In fact, this question runs deeper than merely being a question about jobs, important though that is. It is really a question about 'winners and losers' as a result of new technology; a question about how to weigh the pros and cons—for employment, certainly, but also in relation to the broader question of the community's quality-of-life. When people complain that new technology costs jobs, they may be airing a deeper fear: the fear that new technology changes our lives in all kinds of ways that we can't always anticipate—some good, some bad: look at the motor car.

Neil Postman doesn't oppose new technology; he simply argues that we should not go into the future with our eyes closed. We need to speculate thoroughly about the possible negative consequences of new technology *before* we decide to embrace it. He urges us to ask: Which people and what institutions might be most seriously harmed by a particular technological solution?

This question gave rise to the Luddite movement in England from 1811 to 1818. The Luddites were skilled manual workers in the garment industry. They knew what advantages mechanisation would bring to most people, but they also saw how it would ruin their own ways of life and especially harm their children, who were being employed as virtual slave labourers. So they resisted technological change by destroying industrial machinery.

The word Luddite has come to mean a person who resists

technological change, and it is usually used as an insult. Why this is so is a bit puzzling, since new technologies always produce winners and losers, and there is nothing irrational about user resistance. Bill Gates knows this and he is no fool: his propaganda continuously implies that computer technology can bring harm to no-one. That is the way of winners. They want losers to be grateful and enthusiastic and especially to be unaware that they are losers.[5]

The third moral issue on the agenda concerns *the privacy of electronically stored information* and the related question of trustworthiness of data obtained electronically, especially via the Internet.

Particularly in the banking market, and in areas where government departments store information about us, people are becoming increasingly aware of the possibility of all kinds of sharing and transferring of this data. Sometimes their fears are based on deliberate decisions to spread data around; sometimes they fear less legal access to private and sensitive information.

Hackers can break into any system. It's easier to get hold of electronic data than stuff that has been written down and locked in a filing cabinet somewhere.

They didn't have to worry about that ID card business, after all. I'm sure government departments can get hold of any information they want about any of us.

You wonder how far the information goes. I'm building a house in Melbourne, and I got sent some furniture information from a crowd in Adelaide.

Tales of allegedly 'private' e-mail that has fallen into the wrong hands fuel people's vague sense of anxiety that 'nothing is really secure' once information is put into a vast electronic network.

John Gray, Professor of European Thought at the London School of Economics, sees this as a major emerging moral issue:

New technologies, even as they make it easier for people to communicate with one another, make it harder to achieve or protect privacy. We've entered an age in which anonymity has become virtually impossible.[6]

The privacy issue is becoming increasingly complex and sophisticated. New computer chips are now capable of identifying the user (through so-called 'data strings in your browser') and a growing number of websites now demand that 'visitors' to the site be identified. Commercial pressures on Internet procedures are likely to accelerate this trend, so that Internet traffic through websites can be monitored and, where appropriate, pursued. (Needless to say, new technologies are being developed to help web-users protect their privacy: new 'scrambling' techniques promise anonymity for e-mail senders, a development hardly likely to please those who receive unwanted e-mail, especially when it contains sexual abuse or other forms of harassment.)

But the other side of privacy is anonymity, and electronic information networks raise questions about this as well: how can I be sure the information I'm getting is really coming from where they say it is coming from? How do I evaluate the accuracy or authority of data that just 'floats' in cyberspace? How do I know that this 23-year-old Swedish woman I'm 'chatting' to on the Net isn't, in fact, a 12-year-old in Manhattan? (Answer: I don't know. Next question: Does it matter, since we're never going to meet?)

America's infamous Drudge Report—source of many of the salacious bits of information about President Bill Clinton and Monica Lewinsky that first reached the public—operates according to a rather different set of journalistic principles from the conventional print, TV and radio media: the mere fact of being on the Net gives the Drudge Report a certain latitude. Indeed, Matt Drudge describes himself as a service provider rather than a reporter and he envisages a new order of news and current affairs technology: 'an era vibrating with the din of small voices ... I envision a future where there will be 300 million reporters.' (Though it is true that Drudge receives thousands of e-mails each day from the 'little people', most of his biggest stories are thought to have come from insiders and lobbyists who have used 'the protective anonymity of e-mail and Drudge's lack of scruple to get their stories out.')[7]

Discussing the impossibility of monitoring the veracity—and morality—of everything that flickers through cyberspace, the Australian Broadcasting Corporation's head of multimedia, Colin Griffith, has said that 'with the Internet, you are only two or three links away from the dark corners of humanity. That is part of the risk that comes with Internet culture'. And the chairman of the Australian Securities and Investments Commission, Alan Cameron, has said that 'taking advice from someone over the Internet is the same as taking advice from someone on a street corner'.[8] (He should know: the ASIC ran an Internet scam of its own on April Fool's Day 1999, and attracted $4 million from 233 investors who responded to an offer to triple their money in 15 months. They sent money to a company that had a website and an impressive sounding history—allegedly founded by three Swiss business leaders to insure against millennium bug problems—but which didn't actually exist.)

Another moral question that lurks in the back of some Australians' minds—though it is receding as we continue to adapt to the world of electronic data, is this: *Has the system taught us to depend on credit?*

Reflecting on their personal histories, many Australians believe that it was the introduction of the credit card—and the electronic developments that have flowed from card technology—that effectively blurred the distinction between money and credit. While acknowledging the enormous convenience of credit cards, they sometimes worry that they have adapted so well to the system that they have actually become dependent on the credit it so painlessly extends to them.

Even though EFTPOS is praised for being 'morally superior' to credit cards (because you can't spend it if you don't have it), there is a concern, even here, that 'invisible' money is much easier to part with than the real thing.

I know it's up to us to be careful with these things ... but it's so easy.

You can even have EFTPOS put through the poker machines at the Diggers. You put the card in and a voice says, 'Hi, Jeff, how are you?' and away you go. You just withdraw money to feed the machine. You don't even have to leave the machine. You could wipe yourself out that way.

Australians are also asking themselves this question: *Is this just the latest form of 'mindless consumerism'?* Again, that's related to a deeper question: will the gap between rich and poor turn into another gap between information-rich and information-poor? (That's already happening. Internet access is highly correlated with household income: the higher the income, the more likely the access.)

All this money spent on technology and yet there is still such poverty.

The computer has revolutionised kids' presents. Now all they want is new video games, or to upgrade the software—and it's all so expensive compared with the things they used to ask for.

The kids soon learn to keep up with the latest. People always want the latest model.

The murmuring of another moral question can barely be heard, but it's a question that is bound to gather momentum: *What is the likely future impact of genetic engineering?*

Most Australians don't easily connect their reservations about computer and telecommunications technology with the news they are hearing from the scientific frontier of genetic engineering. But, as Chapter 6 suggested, there is already a groundswell of concern about the consequences of tampering with the genetic structure of food, and a dim awareness that developments in artificial methods of human conception are the leading edge of yet another revolution.

It's too early to say how Australians will react to the growing sophistication of genetic engineering. In a *Sydney Morning Herald* account of the 11th World Congress on IVF (in vitro fertilisation), journalist Deborah Smith described germline engineering—cheating nature to create 'designer' babies—as the last scientific taboo. She quoted Professor Roger Short, one of Australia's leading reproductive specialists, as saying that there are enormous ethical objections to carrying out germline gene repair.[9]

It's safe to say that 'germline gene repair' is not yet in the vocabulary, or even in the imagination, of most of us. But we know there is an ethical minefield out there, waiting for our understanding to catch up with the experimental work being done.

Genetic engineering has already raised a number of ethical issues, including this unexpected question for the fathers of IVF babies: are you simply passing on a genetic deficiency, in the form of a low sperm count, to a son created by artifical insemination? (The most likely response, according to Dr David Cram of the Monash IVF clinic: Most fathers would still choose to go ahead with the treatment because they will assume that if genetic science can give them children now, it will be able to treat their sons' infertility in 20 years' time.[10])

Cloning Dolly the sheep, or creating green mice by adding the genes of green-glowing jellyfish to the freeze-dried sperm of mice—these are funny, fascinating news stories that intrigue us without connecting with our daily lives. But when it comes to the kind of babies we will conceive in the future—who will conceive them and why, whether marriage will become even less relevant to parenthood, and whether we would want to start specifying not just the sex but other characteristics of our future offspring—we may finally realise that because something *can* be done doesn't necessarily imply that it *should* be done.

When that debate gets under way, we might even extend it to embrace some of the non-reproductive technology that is rushing towards us through cyberspace, promising to transform our lives, one way or the other—or both ways.

Run faster, work harder ... react!

Never mind the future; what about now? What is likely to be the effect on us of our exposure to existing technology, especially when its primary characteristic is its speed?

Already, many people report that they are running harder than ever, just to keep up with the demands of the technology. (But they keep running.)

First, it was the fax, which seemed to generate a sense of such urgency that people felt obliged to reply quickly. Then it was the mobile phone, allowing 24-hour accessibility if you are prepared to keep it switched on. (And people are.) Now e-mail has stepped up the pressure even more, and opened the floodgates for people to 'broadcast' messages which might once have been sent to only one or two people. (So now people in offices all over the country are complaining that they spend an hour or more, each day, sifting through their ever-expanding e-mail in search of messages to which they really should respond.)

The machines that promised to serve us have certainly done that: they are quick, convenient, accurate, efficient—and irresistible. But by those very characteristics, they have mastered us as well.

Is this a turning point? Will we decide to keep the machines in their place? Or will we rush on, determined to keep up with them? Is there a limit to our adaptability to electronic technology? How will we know when we've reached it?

John Gray, of the London School of Economics, offers this analysis of our headlong rush into new technology:

> The dream that technology serves is a dream of complete control. It's a dream with ancient sources in Western traditions. It's the dream that we can cease to be mortal, earth-bound creatures subject to fate and chance. It's a product not so much of science as of magic. The project of using technology to remake the world according to our will captures the fantasy by which we have been ruled during much of the 20th century. It is a fantasy of progress without instability.[11]

From a more personal point of view, Pulitzer Prize-winning novelist Richard Ford sounds a warning:

People who know a lot about technology would like to console us with their faith that it's neutral, that tools won't change human nature. But how do they know? And what if they're wrong? Or right? What is human nature anyway, and why do we think it's so well settled in us that we can't louse it up by taking it for granted?

Put simply, the pace of life feels morally dangerous to me. And what I wish for is not to stop or even to slow it, but to be able to experience my lived days as valuable days. We all just want to keep our heads above the waves, find some place to stand. If anything, that's our human nature.

I don't have e-mail. I'm not on the Internet. I don't have a cell-phone or call waiting or even a beeper. And I'm not proud of it, since my fear, I guess, is that if someone can't find me using any or all of these means, they will conclude that, for technical reasons, I don't exist any more.[12]

CHAPTER TWENTY-ONE

Unravelling

Reweaving the Social Fabric

Turning Point: The structure of Australian society is undergoing a fundamental shift. Households are shrinking, and people living alone will comprise the most common household type by 2006. At the same time, there is a growing belief that we are losing our sense of community and, with it, our shared values.

What are we hoping for? Revitalised communities; a restored sense of mutual obligation; strategies to reduce our feelings of alienation and vulnerability.

Here's a simple question: what is the most common household type in Australia right now? Mum, dad and a couple of kids? Mum, dad and one child? A couple without children? A person living alone?

A 1999 study by the accounting firm KPMG confirms that our long-established trend towards smaller households is gathering momentum. The classic nuclear family—mum and dad living with one or more children—currently accounts for only 19 per cent of Australian households. The front-runner, at 31 per cent of all households, is couples.

But here's the most significant finding from the KPMG study: *single-person households*, already 24 per cent of the total, are growing so rapidly that the researchers predict that this will have become the most common household type by the year 2006.[1]

Significant—but hardly surprising. These figures go hand-in-hand with our soaring divorce rate and plummeting marriage and birthrates. For instance, 1998 had the lowest birthrate on record, and the average number of babies per woman is down to 1.8 (from 2.6 just 25 years ago). The Australian Bureau of Statistics recently estimated that if our birthrate remained at its present low level *and* if we had no net population gains through migration, our population numbers would soon plateau, and then begin to decline by the middle of the 21st century. The growth in childless, two-person households is one signpost to that trend. (In fact, the two provisos—low birthrate and zero gain through migration—make this a rather hollow prediction. The ABS's own population projections put Australia's population in 2051 at 26 million, and even that figure is based on a steadily declining *rate* of population growth.)

The rise in single-person households, similarly, is a reflection of some recent ABS estimates. As we saw in Chapter 13, the Bureau's projections from current marriage rates, also at an all-time low, suggest that among the rising generation of young adults, about 42 per cent of men and 44 per cent of women will never marry, though many will cohabit with one or more partners.

What are we supposed to make of all this? Superficially, it might look as if those who are nervous about overpopulation can relax somewhat, given the collapsing birthrate. In fact, there is a growing body of opinion that Australia is already overpopulated: that very point was made by New

Hugh Mackay

South Wales Premier, Bob Carr, when he opened the 1997 conference of Australians for an Ecologically Sustainable Population.

By contrast, those who believe that the place is underpopulated had better start echoing Victorian Premier Jeff Kennett's call for an urgent lift in both the birthrate and the migrant intake.

An aside: Here, yet again, is an example of the ambiguity which faces people when they try to form an opinion about such matters. In the absence of a properly researched and articulated population policy, most Australians will be confused by hearing the uncoordinated views of assorted political, scientific and industrial organisations and individuals, some with vested interests. Faced with inconsistency and contradiction among those who might be expected to know, the lay person will most probably suspend judgment and, for the time being, simply let nature take its course, demographically and environmentally.

We pay a high price for cutting ourselves off from the herd

Economically, the trend towards smaller households seems to be good short-term news for the building industry, since, on present indications, we will need a steadily increasing number of dwellings to accommodate the same number of people. It's also presumably good news for cafes, restaurants and fast-food providers: young people who choose to live alone or in 'couple' households where both partners have paid work, will continue to drive the trend towards eating out or dialling in. (In many such households, cooking a meal has already become something of a novelty—a form of entertainment you turn on for friends, perhaps, or a trick you perform when your parents visit.)

Socially, it's a bit more complex. If you were to judge by these changes in our living arrangements, you might be tempted to think that we are in the process of evolving from herd animals into isolates. According to our 20th-century view of society as being based on the unit of the nuclear family, you might even wonder whether the traditional social fabric is unravelling.

There's already been a great deal of hand-wringing over our transition from the extended family of the village to the nuclear family of the cities and towns spawned by the Industrial Revolution. Urban and suburban life has separated people from their work (and, in most cases from the land that ultimately sustains them), increased the mobility of the population and, in the process, disrupted the networks of family and friends that were once such a stable source of personal identity and emotional security.

Now even the nuclear family seems to be imploding. Does this mean that the herd has lost its pull? Are we truly becoming a society of loosely-connected individuals, drifting in and out of transient social networks—in the neighbourhood, at clubs, at work—but no longer needing the security of stable, intimate relationships to define and sustain us?

Hardly. Loneliness is still a problem for most people who experience it. Isolation can be liberating for a while, but it can also be a stage on the way to alienation. Demographic trends need to be interpreted in the light of some other statistics that tell us, for example, about suicide among the young, and the record rate of consumption of tranquillisers and anti-depressants.

New technology—from chat-rooms on the Internet to the possibility of conceptions being achieved, at will and on a large scale, by uniting sperm and ova in a vitreous dish rather than a passionate embrace—fuels the idea that the individual is indeed the social unit and that being fully human no longer requires a personal commitment to anyone else. But few people actually believe that: the overwhelming view of contemporary Australians of all ages is that, regardless of the demographic realities, people are generally better off living in 'families' (though that term is itself becoming open to an increasingly broad and flexible array of interpretations).

So how should we reconcile our persistent belief that we are herd animals who belong in families with the growing trend away from life in the herd? Are we making choices we don't really believe in, or are we in a transitional stage on the way to the formation of new kinds of herds?

Perhaps one of the great social revolutions of the 21st century will be the emergence of the *surrogate extended family*. In some cases, this will take the form of non-kin households, already growing apace, where groups of friends band together to create a domestic 'herd' of their own. In other cases, groups of single- and two-person households will form cooperative alliances to share home maintenance, shopping, cooking—ultimately, perhaps, even child rearing.

It's hard to escape the feeling that we're caught up in a vast social experiment, the results of which won't be known for another generation or two. Most of us will adapt, of course, and many people will enjoy living alone. In the meantime there'll be casualties, young and old, staring at lonely walls, confusing disconnection with rejection, desperately waiting for the phone to ring.

Already, our *Mind & Mood* studies reveal an emerging pattern of disquiet about the long-term implications of the present trend.

Community and Morality: two sides of one coin

Over the past ten years, two of the most common concerns aired by Australians in our social research program are these:

> We don't seem to have the same sense of belonging to a *community* as we once had. The neighbourhood doesn't seem to work as well as it once did. (Sometimes this is expressed in comments like, 'We don't know our neighbours' or 'We don't feel at home in our own suburb'.)

> We don't seem to have the same sense of *morality* as we used to. It seems harder to identify the shared values which we would regard as characteristically Australian. (Sometimes, this concern is expressed in terms of a 'moral decline' but, more typically, as a feeling of moral uncertainty or ambiguity: 'The rules aren't as clear as they used to be.')

Those two concerns are really only one.

Our values are acquired from the experience of living in community with others. Morality is the *expression* of community. An ethical system would simply have no relevance to a life lived in isolation. It is through the process of forming and nurturing relationships with each other—starting with those painful childhood lessons about how we must cooperate with each other in order to satisfy our own needs—that we gradually evolve our understanding of what works and what doesn't work. These evolve into our notions of 'right and wrong'. Morality can't easily be separated from the idea of harmonious coexistence. (To put it at its most pragmatic: you behave differently towards someone you meet today if you know you are going to meet them again tomorrow.)

In other words, morality is a social construction. At its core is the idea of *mutual obligation*. The foundation of morality is our willingness to take the rights, needs and welfare of others into account, on the assumption that they will do the same for us.

One obvious implication of this is that we must first understand and appreciate what those needs might be. We require some insight into the circumstances of others, and some sense of connectedness with them, before we are likely to feel any obligation to respond to their needs or to enhance their welfare. The acceptance of moral responsibility tends to increase in direct proportion to our feelings of being 'connected' (which is why people usually find it easier to vandalise the property of strangers than friends).

If we don't feel as if we belong to a community, we are unlikely to feel any sense of moral responsibility towards those who live there. (And if people in a particular street, suburb, town or workplace don't feel some sense of responsibility towards each other, in what sense can those places be described as 'communities'?)

We are social creatures and we thrive—socially, intellectually, culturally and morally—on our *personal* connections with each other. We are at our best when we are fully integrated with the herd; we are at our worst when we are isolated, anonymous and alienated.

We might as well acknowledge that the savage lurks within even the most civilised breast. When we loosen our social connections, we increase the risk that the savage will break the leash. (It's no surprise to find that 'flaming'—the sending of inflammatory, abusive, defamatory and insulting messages to other people via the anonymity of cyberspace—has become a major problem among some Internet users.) The great enemy of moral sensitivity is anonymity—just look at the way people address each other from the insulated safety of their motor cars.

When Australians talk about life in contemporary Australia, 'community breakdown' is a recurring theme. In many parts of urban, suburban, regional and rural Australia, our sense of community is under threat.

Upheavals in our patterns of *marriage and divorce*—with implications for the dynamics of family life—have fractured many neighbourhoods. Of the one million children who live with only one of their natural parents, about 45 per cent visit the non-custodial parent regularly, often spending their weekends in a different neighbourhood from the one where they live during the week.

The emergence of *the working mother* as a mainstream cultural phenomenon has changed the way we live and produced a generation of women who are unable to devote as much time as their mothers did to maintaining the life of the neighbourhood.

The *falling birthrate* and the dramatic rise in one- and two-person households, referred to at the beginning of this chapter, break the traditional nexus between 'family life' and the life of the neighbourhood.

Upheavals in *the labour market* have further fragmented our sense of being a community: radical and inequitable redistribution of work over the past 20 years has led to a correspondingly inequitable redistribution of household income. (With a large pool of long-term unemployment and welfare dependency, we may already be witnessing the emergence of an Australian version of the underclass.) As Chapter 5 suggested, the gap between the haves and have-nots has created divisions in Australian society that are too big and ugly to ignore, and sometimes those divisions occur within one street or suburb.

New technology poses a further threat to our sense of community. The smarter electronic communications technology becomes, the more we will be tempted to spend time with machines rather than each other, and the more we will be inclined to confuse data transfer with human communication. The consequence of that would be a further erosion of our sense of being part of a human community and, in turn, our sense of moral responsibility towards those with whom we share our neighbourhoods, as opposed to those we 'meet' on-line.

The *mobility* of the Australian population creates an inherent instability in local communities. Australians move house, on average, once every six years.

In some communities, the arrival of *new ethnic groups* has altered the cultural milieu in a way that long-term residents initially find uncomfortable. Although this is often an evolutionary process towards a harmonious integration of different ethnic groups, its short-term impact frequently causes some disruption to the sense of community.

Perceptions of a rising *crime rate*, generally assumed to be worse than the actual situation, inhibit many people (especially older people, and parents with young children) from moving freely around the neighbourhood. The 'domestic fortress' mentality feeds off its own fears, and reinforces the belief that 'the community is not safe any more'.

The classic response to 'community breakdown':

over-regulation

Once we begin to detect, or even to imagine, a decline in the health and cohesiveness of the community, the overwhelming temptation is to rush in with a contrived and regulated 'morality'. Chapter 9 referred to the current spate of so-called 'educative laws' which take matters previously thought to be the province of private consciences and individual moral choice, and put them squarely into the domain of the law.

Everything from the anti-vilification laws to the council regulations that compel people to keep their dogs on a leash can be read as symptoms of our belief that the community isn't working as it should, and that we can no longer trust each other to behave with an appropriate sense of mutual obligation. Once we have lost trust in each other—and in the institutions, like schools and churches, that have been traditionally concerned with upholding our values—it's a short step to deciding that matters previously left to the normal processes of social pressure on individuals must now be taken over by the various authorities of the state. We must take the short-cut to 'good behaviour': we must ban; we must regulate; we must legislate; we must *control*!

You can see where the motivation for all this comes from: if people think the social fabric is unravelling, their natural response is to want to re-weave it. If it isn't going to happen spontaneously, they reason, we'd better *make* it happen.

So we accept ever-stricter bans on smoking, compulsory wearing of crash helmets for children riding bikes (previously thought to be the responsibility of their parents), tougher media censorship ... even amendments to the Family Law Act that define the role and responsibilities—the meaning—of 'parent'.

The hardline, proregulation mentality is perfectly understandable as a response to insecurity and uncertainty, and it's been a recurring pattern in human history. In 1831, for example, the Roman Catholic Church, responding to the threat posed by 19th-century liberalism, invented the doctrine of papal infallibility to shore up its authority. The contemporary surge in support for black-and-white religious fundamentalism is a comparable response: 'Relieve me of my uncertainty!' Even the dramatic increase in the number of Australians professing to believe in astrology could be interpreted as further evidence of our obsession with the need to regain a sense of *control* over our destinies.

While that response might be easy to understand, it points to a dangerous vulnerability. It means that we are not only running the risk of unduly limiting our freedoms, but we might also be stifling the very consciences we are trying to quicken.

After all, the essence of morality lies in the freedom to make moral choices—including the choice to act badly. If we impose too many regulations on ourselves, we will ultimately limit the sense of choice and, in the process, discourage people from thinking that moral choices need to be made: 'There's no regulation prohibiting this, so it must be all right.' Or, 'I mustn't do this, *because* there's a law against it', without acknowledging the need for moral judgment. 'I'd rather you didn't smoke here, because it's affecting the comfort of other people' becomes 'You can't smoke here, because it's prohibited'.

If we continue down the path of increasing regulation, we may well succeed in imposing order on our society in ways currently thought to be desirable, but we will also have to recognise that obedience is a very different thing from sensitivity.

The real challenge is not to find ways of making it *look as if* we have reconnected with each other. The challenge is to understand what's gone wrong and address the underlying cause, not the symptoms.

If we wish to recapture some of the values which we believe underpin an effective system of morality—accepting responsibility for others' wellbeing, paying attention to others' needs, being willing to contribute to the common good—we are unlikely to achieve this by preaching about ethics, or vaguely hoping that the divorce rate might come down, or wishing that people would stop spending so much time in front of their computers, or start going to church.

We are unlikely to succeed in rehabilitating our moral systems, or in generating a more powerful sense of shared values, until we find ways of reviving the feeling that we each belong to a community. The relationship between morality and community may be somewhat chicken-and-egg but history suggests that we are more likely to succeed if we start with the community. People first need to reconnect—face-to-face, one-to-one—if their communities are to be regenerated; once that starts to happen, the rest will follow in time. ('I don't even know my neighbour's name' might be a common complaint, but it is hardly an indictment of my neighbour!)

For many Australians, the word that best captures this idea of a restored and functioning community is the word 'village'. Intuitively, we seem to recognise that 'village life' is our natural habitat. The question is, can we create villages where we are, or will we have to go somewhere else? And that's the subject of the following chapter.

CHAPTER TWENTY-TWO

Village

It's Not Where You Live, But How You Live

Turning Point: Our affection for the word 'village' is a sign of our yearning to live in more connected, interdependent communities. Romantic dreams of rural village life can blind us to the possibility of establishing a village style in suburban settings. The turning point comes when we realise that 'village life' is about a way of life, not a geographical location.

What are we hoping for? Closer connections with the neighbourhood; the security of feeling 'safe' (both physically and emotionally); ways of compensating for our shrinking households.

Considering how few Australians have ever actually lived in a village, it's surprising how often, and how fondly, we dream of village life. Indeed, 'village' seems destined to become a millennial buzzword, implying a richer, more connected, yet somehow simpler and more satisfying life.

This might strike you as nothing more than a lingering symptom of the nostalgic and unrealistic notion, explored in Chapter 4, that our hearts are really in the bush. Or perhaps it's a fragment of folk memory, still lingering from the time when we were, indeed, village-dwellers in the classic sense: when we lived close to the land; when home and work were in the same place; when networks of family and friends were stable, not just over a few years, but over several generations.

The truth is that we have long been a predominantly suburban culture. Our values are essentially middle-class, suburban values, and what's wrong with that? To pretend we are some other kind of society would be to rob us of an important truth about ourselves: that we have managed to create a diverse and harmonious society by crowding into cities on the coastal fringe of a fairly inhospitable continent.

So when we talk so romantically about the joys of village life, we need to be clear about what, precisely, we have in mind. One of the hazards of 'village talk' is that we might delude ourselves into thinking that the only satisfactory way to make the village dream come true would be to move to an actual rural village in an actual rural setting. Unhappily, such places are getting harder and harder to find (or, more correctly, they are easy to find but, when it comes to the point, fewer and fewer people want to live in them).

Yet the fantasy persists—a little hamlet, out in the mulga, or somewhere 'up the coast' (ABC television's *Sea Change* has a lot to answer for!): a place where we could grow our own fresh food, organically, in a huge vegetable patch; where the kids could attend a quaint little village school with an eccentric but lovable old teacher; where the neighbours would be friendly and free with advice about everything from snake repellents to pump repairs; where we could finally indulge our dream of becoming a blacksmith, wood-turner or weaver, or perhaps a bestselling poet.

The dream sometimes focuses on the idea of a simpler life in a close-knit local community, where everyone knows (almost) everything about everyone else, and where local pub-talk follows a reassuringly familiar agenda, dominated by the vagaries of the weather and commodity prices, the insensitivity of politicians and the ignorance of city folk . . . all peppered with little gems of homespun wisdom. This, above all, would be a place where people make their own fun; where the kids would build billycarts instead of playing video games; where the local church fair and the village ball would outdo a BBC period costume drama for charm and *character*.

Of course, we're not going to do it. The only people moving in significant numbers from city to country are the poor and unemployed, in search of cheaper housing, or the rich who are creating glamorous weekend retreats where authentic village life is the last thing on their minds. More generally, the inexorable march of migration is from country to city.

And yet, the more urbanised we become, the more we indulge in the rural fantasy—overlooking the fact that that quaint village school is either underresourced or long-since closed, necessitating an hour's drive to school each day or the wrench of having to wave the children off to boarding school. Those backyard vegetables would not survive the first grasshopper plague or drought (or both), the clean air is polluted by dust and chemical agents, and social problems are at least as great in the bush as in the city. Idyllic remoteness also means that the occasional yearning for cultural input will involve a journey to a major centre to take pot luck with whatever touring production happens to be on offer.

Sorry to sound brutal. Your dream, perhaps, was of something more emotionally lush; rustic, yet *chic*? Perhaps you were hoping to satisfy your urge to be part of a community without sacrificing the comforts of the city. If so, you just might be able to make your village dream come true, after all.

Welcome to the 'burbs

There are people all around Australia, especially in the more densely populated inner suburbs, who have found that it is possible to create a suburban neighbourhood that works just like a village. Some of them live in tiny houses that back onto lanes where the life of the street is played out. You can see their folding tables and chairs set up in the lane on summer nights, as neighbours share a drink and a reflection on the day.

Some live in cul-de-sacs (despised, suddenly, by urban planners, but prized by the people who live in them), where the kids play cricket in the street and the parents sit on fences, watching and chatting. Some live in brilliantly designed medium-density housing developments, where common spaces encourage informal contact without robbing the residents of their privacy.

And some live in utterly conventional suburban streets—not a park, nor a lane, nor a dead-end in sight—designed in the Forties or Fifties for a very different way of life from ours (when mothers at home were the glue that held the community together). They might have to work quite hard at keeping in touch with their neighbours, but they've found it can be done.

The dream of village life is powerful, valid and potentially energising, as long as we don't interpret it too literally. It springs from our herd instinct: a deep-seated desire to belong to social networks that nurture us and help us define ourselves. Incidental, unplanned encounters with neighbours feed our sense of being part of a functioning community and, in the process, feed our moral sense as well ... since, as we have seen in the previous chapter, morality is what we learn from the experience of rubbing along with the other people in a community.

Change the environment, and watch

the attitudes change

The smartest urban planners understand all this, and are redesigning suburban environments—housing estates, parks, plazas and shopping centres—to make them more inviting places for walking, talking and playing together. The revival of coffee shops, and the proliferation of all kinds of places to eat, create more opportunities to graze with the herd— and that's one step towards reconnection.

There's even some imaginative office renovation going on, where existing spaces are being reconfigured to encourage the kind of interaction—eating, chatting, child-minding—that converts a disparate collection of workers into a corporate neighbourhood. 'Vertical village' is, inevitably, the preferred label.

But we still need to do more:

> We need to gradually shift *the balance between private space and public space*, bearing in mind that most people in two-income households haven't got time to maintain their traditional house-and-garden, anyway, and many low-income Australians would be happy with smaller houses at lower prices, especially in areas that provided the compensation of more community infrastructure.

> We need to stimulate and support *the creative arts*, because artistic expression—both doing it and viewing it—has a clarifying and unifying effect on us, giving us a feeling of being connected to each other. (Creative artists are also valuable, because they are often sending us messages from our future which can alert us to what might become of us if we proceed the way we are going.)

> We need to encourage people to establish personal connections with other people in the neighbourhood by offering more *communal activities*—drama groups, yoga and exercise classes, dancing, art classes, book clubs, bands and orchestras, choirs, bushwalking clubs, clean-up campaigns—which reassure people that 'the village' exists and that they can belong to it. (Many adults ruefully admit that they have never sung or played a note, read a serious book, written a poem, painted a picture or acted in a play since the day they left school ... and those who return to such activities in later life generally report feelings of pleasure and satisfaction.)

Many communities—some inner-city, some stock-standard suburban, some rural—have found ways of bringing people together. When you hear a community band playing at a local fete, or hear a local choir put on a concert, or feel the energy of a local drama group, or watch an informal jogging or touch-football group in action, or see the enthusiasm of older people for the activities of the University of the Third Age, you realise that, in many places, that elusive 'community spirit' has already been captured.

When you look at the success of resident action groups in marshalling the support of local communities in a common cause, you realise it can be done. When you see the way people band together in time of disaster— a hailstorm, a bushfire, a cyclone, the death of a child—you realise that it only needed a catalyst for the connections to be made.

We nodded and smiled at each other for three years. Then the hailstorm hit our street, and we were out helping each other and talking like old friends. Now we say hello whenever we meet.

When you hear about the volunteers who are giving up nights and weekends, year after year, to lead local Scout or Guide groups, or to train sporting teams or choirs or drama groups, or to supervise after-school play groups, or to clean up local bushland, you realise that the life of the community is far from dead.

When you see suburban parks on Sunday afternoons teeming with people of all ages and varieties, interacting with each other and with their bats and balls, bikes, kites and dogs, you realise that many people have already caught the wave.

We have long since abandoned the extended family as a standard living arrangement. Now, as Chapter 21 has shown, it seems that we are no longer going to maintain traditional, nuclear family-sized 'herds' on the same scale as we did for most of the 20th century. Growing numbers of us are choosing to satisfy the herd instinct in some other way. The more we strive to compensate ourselves for the loss of emotional connections by acquiring more material objects, the more we deny that herd instinct. And the more we deny it, the more restless and even neurotic we are likely to become. Cocooning ourselves in velvet-lined comfort won't help much.

As households shrink and more people choose to live alone or in couples, the demand for activities that 'connect' will steadily increase. The winner, in that process, is likely to be the life of the local community—and the life of the community is the key to its moral sensitivity.

At the heart of the dream of village life lies the concept of *security*—both physical ('I'm safe here') and emotional ('I belong here'). It's this feeling of security that unlocks our disposition towards mutual obligation: once we feel connected—'part of the place'—we are more likely to accept moral responsibility for the wellbeing of others. All over the suburbs, you can still see people 'popping next-door' to do some baby-sitting, or to take a meal to a sick neighbour, or to borrow the stereotypical cup of sugar. These are the signs of village life.

The challenge is not to teach people 'values': the challenge is to put them back in touch with each other. We are still, inherently, village people and the dream of village life is both natural and legitimate. The trick is to recognise that it's a dream about *how* to live, not where to live.

CHAPTER TWENTY-THREE

Women and Men

Are We There Yet, Mum?

Turning Point: We are at a critical stage in the gender revolution, where both sides are open to reappraisal and further change. The impact of the women's movement in Australia has been profound and far-reaching, revolutionising our views of marriage, parenting, work, politics ... and equality. While older men are still less attuned to feminism than their wives (or ex-wives) might wish, younger Australians show signs of having integrated the ideals of women's lib into their thinking. Retreating from the Superwoman madness, women have embraced 'choice' as the central theme of contemporary feminism.

What are we hoping for? A cessation of hostilities in the gender war, based on male recognition of the fully-fledged personhood of women, and female recognition of the major cultural adjustments men have had to make; a new spirit of cooperation, based on sensible accommodation of each other's different styles and different goals.

Whom shall we believe? Germaine Greer, telling women in her 1999 book, *The Whole Woman*, that it's time to get angry again; time to launch a new offensive in the war on men?[1]

Or Richard Morin and Megan Rosenfield? (*Richard who? Megan who?*)

After reviewing research done on more than 4000 American men and women, *Washington Post* journalists Morin and Rosenfeld have come to roughly the opposite conclusion from Greer's:

> Men and women have declared a cease-fire in the war that raged between the sexes through much of the last half of this century. In its place, they face common new enemies—the stress, lack of time and financial pressure of modern life ...
>
> After nearly a generation of sharing the workplace and renegotiating domestic duties, most men and women agree that increased gender equity has enriched both sexes. But both also believe that the strains of this relatively new world have made building successful marriages, raising children and leading satisfying lives ever more difficult.[2]

Since neither Greer nor the *Washington Post* have based their conclusions on the distinctive Australian experience of the women's movement, we'd better not embrace either view uncritically. (We certainly shouldn't assume that Greer is closely in touch with the experience and attitudes of women who choose to have children, or those who willingly adopt a nurturing role. Her assertion that women who act as providers are 'offering meals nobody really wants', among many similarly dismissive statements, makes you wonder when she last visited a family home where crockery was not being thrown.)

When you listen to Australian women and men talking about the state of play, it certainly sounds more like a cease-fire than the beginning of a fresh skirmish. From women's point of view, the revolution is slow, but it is looking like a long-term success; its momentum is unstoppable, but it is no longer carrying women inexorably in only one direction.

Christine Wallace, Greer's unauthorised biographer, argues that Australian women have generally been more successful with the 'don't get angry, get even' approach and she points out that although the rising generation of young Australian women still face 'formidable barriers', they are entering a public realm 'where it is realistic to aspire to prime ministership, managing directorships and even the helm of spaceships'.[3]

Indeed it is. In the three years from 1995–8, the proportion of women in Federal Parliament jumped from 14 to 21 per cent (more than double the international average). In the same period, women's representation on corporate boards rose from a miserable 4 per cent to a fast-improving 10 per cent. In the ten years to 1998, women as a percentage of all academics rose from 27 to 34 per cent. At school, 77 per cent of girls are completing Year 12, compared with 66 per cent of boys.[4]

But Greer claims that it's this 'get even' approach that has got women into trouble: in confusing liberation with equality, they have sacrificed their distinctive femaleness. And, by continuing to shoulder most of the housework and child-rearing as well, such women are slowly killing themselves. (Perhaps she hasn't heard that only 40 per cent of Australian pre-schoolers are now cared for by a parent at home, that the birthrate is at its lowest ever, or that the domestic cleaning industry is booming. But she has a point, nevertheless: women are doing 70 per cent of the unpaid housework still remaining to be done.)

When Greer writes that 'on every side, we see women troubled, exhausted, lonely, guilty, mocked by the headlined success of the few', she could be quoting from any number of Australian research reports from the Eighties and early Nineties. But, at the turn of the century, that is a very small part of a rapidly-changing story.

More recent research suggests that, in fact, the current mood of Australian women has anticipated her argument: they are thoughtfully reappraising the impact on their lives of the early thrust of feminism. Many of them would agree with Greer that simply chasing the same goals as men, while simultaneously trying to pursue their traditional and distinctive goals as homemakers and mothers, would ultimately bring them undone. This is something they have long since worked out for themselves and, in response, they are already transforming the meanings of 'liberation'.

But their typical response has not been to mount a new assault on men; their approach has been to pause, decide what they really want for themselves—and their marriages and their children, if they have them—and approach the question from a different angle. Having painfully worked out how to negotiate with the men in their lives, at home and at work, they are not about to sacrifice all that with another burst of fire from both barrels, Greer-style.

Some of them are deciding that they will, indeed, press on with careers and compete directly with men, if that's what it takes (but as a path to self-fulfilment, not as an act of aggression). These are the revved-up career women who have reached a clear decision about their priorities. The job comes first. They are well qualified, highly motivated and oblivious to the alleged 'glass ceiling' that other women complain about.

If they are retrenched or sidetracked, they are quicker than men at getting back on their feet. A 1999 survey of 500 executives by career consultants Davidson and Associates found that women had better networking and organisational skills than men (possibly because of their experience at juggling careers and families), and they used them to good effect when retrenched. The survey showed that men who were retrenched took an average of 5.9 months to find a new job; women took just 3.6 months.[5]

New South Wales Ombudsman, Irene Moss, commenting on the results of the survey, speculated that senior professional women 'don't give up as easily as men because they've had so many hard knocks getting to that position'.

But other women are ordering their priorities differently. Some of them have looked at the executive suite and decided it's not for them: they are not in the market for stress and overload, and they can look at the demands on many senior men with a clear eye and say, 'no thanks'. (And, as Chapter 10 suggests, their attitude is infectious: a growing number of men are reaching the same conclusion.)

In the ten years to 1997, the proportion of working women with part-time work increased from 37 to 45 per cent, and working mothers, in particular, overwhelmingly report that they prefer part-time work to full time. (Indeed, recent research shows that 60 per cent of working women would prefer to work shorter hours than they presently work.)[6]

And then there are the previously reviled, but newly-respected, stay-at-home women, who have chosen to spend part of their lives as full-time mothers and housekeepers. Ten years ago, they were made to feel defensive and embarrassed; today, they are widely seen as women doing what women have a perfect right to do: exercising choice about how they will live.

The brave new word in the lexicon of Australian feminism is 'choice' and it's a word with a mission. That mission is 'a balanced life'.

My theory [about men] is you don't live with them, you just go out with them.

My marriage lasted five years and after that I vowed I'd never have another joint bank account. I never want to be dependent on a male again. That's why I'm going to university.

I feel no guilt about being at home with the children. I have no desire to go back to work. I believe passionately that when I'm with them, I'm doing something really worthwhile. I'm using this time to mould them.

The 'all-at-once' trap

In the first flush of the women's movement—from about 1970 on—it seemed as if there was really only one acceptable symbol of liberation: paid work. So women who were in the workforce stayed put; those who had left it, gradually found their way back in; those who couldn't, or didn't want to, found they were being called upon to defend their stay-at-home status, as if they had somehow let the sisterhood down.

But how to cope, if you were trying to combine marriage, motherhood, housekeeping and paid employment, and you haven't had time to train your partner to clean and cook? Enter Superwoman—the crazy ideal of the late Seventies and early Eighties: a woman who was supposed to be proving that you could have it all.

Fine, said her mother (or her mother-in-law); but why are you trying to have it all *at once*? Couldn't you balance things a bit: part-time work, perhaps, or a few years off while the children are young? No, said Superwoman, this is a matter of principle.

What principle, her mother wanted to know, perplexed by the idea of a principle that might be more important than the health of a marriage or the welfare of the children.

This is what liberation is about, Superwoman said. Looks more like slavery to me, said her mother.

But this is the Nineties, and Superwoman has fled the scene. She was resistant to her mother's advice, but she couldn't ignore the messages coming from her own body: fatigue, loss of appetite, diminished sense of humour, loss of sexual energy.

Almost as bad were the signals coming from her daughter: as she moved through her teens, daughter of Superwoman made no secret of the fact that she wasn't going to lead such a lopsided life. She bought her mother's argument that women should be allowed to 'have it all', but she, like her grandmother, thought the *all-at-once* strategy was impractical.

So Superwoman started to see herself through the eyes of her mother and her daughter, but also through her own drowsy eyelids, as Super-victim. She'd criticised her mother for being a doormat; now she felt like one herself. Still, she consoled herself with the thought that this was nothing less than a revolution and revolutions have always needed revolutionaries; revolutions always call for sacrifice; revolutions always demand bloodshed (symbolic, if not actual).

But now: phase two. By the end of the Eighties, many women were already deciding things had gone too far. Even those who had successfully enlisted their husbands' help with housework and parenting were still feeling the strain, on their relationships as well as their energy levels. And so began the big rethink.

Obviously, something had to go, if women were to experience anything approaching true fulfilment. Sometimes, it was the husband (hence the soaring divorce rate, and the fact that most divorces are now initiated by women). Sometimes it was the job, or part of it. Sometimes it was the tidy house, or the home-cooked meals, or the social life. Gradually, the adjustments are being made and the prospect of that elusive 'balanced life' seems a bit more realistic.

But women will work this out for themselves, case by case, and they won't be falling for anyone else's view of what it means to be liberated.

They've been there.

There's still a lot of resentment about

Who's surprised that even after 30 years of the gender revolution, many men—especially in the over-40 age group—still harbour some resentment towards women as a result of sustained negotiations over power-sharing? Given another generation, these matters won't be an issue, but they are an issue for the men who have had to make the initial adjustment to a new way of thinking about male and female roles and responsibilities.

Nor is it a real shock to discover that men are, on average, still only doing about 30 per cent of the unpaid housework. This is not supposed to be a book of predictions, but here's one: men will never, on average, do half the housework. What will happen is that as the pressure increases on them to do more, they'll become the world's greatest supporters of the idea that unpaid domestic work should be outsourced. Nothing will drive the growth of the domestic services industry like men's realisation that there is an economically viable alternative to doing it yourself: pay someone else to do it.

Men came to the last quarter of the 20th century out of a long tradition of a particular division of labour, arising from the heritage of the hunter-gatherer, in which they typically did completely different things from women; the complementarity of male and female roles and responsibilities was an inherent feature of early village life. Even when the agrarian revolution arrived, man-the-hunter became man-the-farmer, rather than man-the-knitter-of-socks and changer-of-nappies.

In contemporary suburban life, however, the dynamics of the hunter-gatherer village culture are a fast-fading memory. Pushing a super-market trolley, however demanding and competitive an activity it may be, is a long way from the ancient business of felling your dinner with a spear or hooking it on a line. And now, even the last vestige of the hunter-gatherer culture—the idea that the man would earn the money to pay for the contents of the supermarket trolley—has given way to the idea that men and women can both be breadwinners.

Goodbye, hunter.

Resentment? Inevitably, even among the vast majority of men who think the gender revolution was long overdue, that women had a valid point to make and that, incidentally, being a more active father is a very satisfying thing (though changing nappies actually isn't all that satisfying—a point often made by women, as well).

There's another, less obvious source of resentment. It comes from women who, having recovered their equilibrium, are retrospectively annoyed by the expectations imposed on them during the Seventies and Eighties.

When I was working full time, I could have killed the bra-burners who'd made women go so far, and who'd put such expectations on us to go so far.

This is the stage I was really looking forward to—being at home with a baby. I never wanted to work full time when I had kids, but that was the thing you did. I was just hanging out for the time we could afford for me to stop. Now I wonder if this is what I've been waiting for, all these years ...

I wish I hadn't put off having kids for so long. I hadn't any idea what joy they bring into your life.

So ... how's the revolution going?

For a young woman raised in a family and a school that believe in equality between men and women, it's a huge shock to find that the whole world doesn't necessarily see things that way. Stories abound of young women, freshly launched into adult life, finding that even when older men say they're in favour of equality, it doesn't always feel as if they mean it:

I sat through a whole meeting at work, and the boss didn't make eye contact with me. Not once. He looks at all the guys, but it's as if I'm not there. It mightn't even be a conscious thing, but you end up feeling like a non-person.

You're very sheltered at school. People take you seriously, and there's no hassle from the boys ... well, not much. But at uni! I was shocked. Some of the lecturers look straight through you. Some of them act as if they think women shouldn't even be there. And some of them obviously think you're fair game. What century are they living in?

The mothers of these women are saddened, but not shocked by such tales. That's why they had a revolution, after all, but they imagined, back in the Seventies, that the revolution would have been well and truly over by the end of the century.

Almost, but not quite.

There's work to be done, even now, in the baby-boom generation. The women are still coming to terms with the fact that some men are never really going to 'get it', but they are also prepared to take another look at their own goals and aspirations. They know what men wanted all along—no change—but now they're getting clearer about what *they* really want. They want more control over their lives, less pressure to be 'liberated' according to someone else's lights, and more time to enjoy the undoubted gains they've made. And some of them are even prepared to admit that men might have suffered a little more than they needed to. They're concerned about whether their sons are getting a worse deal than their daughters.

Indeed, it is the mothers of sons who often held back from a total embrace of Seventies-style feminism. They have wanted their sons to be sensitive to the feminist perspective, but not to have their masculinity swamped by it; they have generally held to the view that, say what you like, males and females are ... well, just *different*.

As for the men, they are relieved to hear some reappraisal of feminist thought, partly because they are no longer being typecast as the enemy, and partly because many of them had a sneaking feeling, all along, that their wives (or ex-wives) were somewhat confused about what they *really* wanted: 'If she had seemed happier, I'd have been more convinced. But she was just wearing herself out.'

Plenty of women are still wearing themselves out, because they know the revolution isn't over. They know, for example, that women in many workplaces are still being paid less than men for doing the same work; they know that women are still under-represented at the most senior levels of business, government and the professions (though the numbers are steadily growing); they know that sexual harassment is still an issue for many women; they know that when they go to buy a car—or get it serviced— they will probably be treated like idiots. And they know that women in the spotlight, like politicians, still find that their clothes are the subject of media interest, and they are still being described as 'mother of three'.

When they hear their own daughters decrying feminism, but reaping the benefits of the revolution, the pioneers might silently curse, weep, or just roll their eyes. Perhaps they console themselves by recalling that Molly Jong-Fast, daughter of the outrageous and iconoclastic Erica Jong, recently delivered herself of this opinion: 'My generation has to become responsible and accountable. I don't want to hear any more whining. That's not getting us anywhere.' Followed by: 'My generation isn't interested in being called feminist. Feminists these days are associated with lesbians and polyester.'

Between the Baby Boomers and their children, there's a generation of post-boomers (rather ridiculously dubbed Generation X, as though they might be too mysterious to be understood) where the signs of the revolution's impact are particularly encouraging. Here, it is virtually taken for granted that men need to be more sensitive than their fathers were to the needs and aspirations of women, and that women will have quite independent expectations of themselves and their futures. You will also encounter the idea, fully-formed, that men and women should cooperate in earning money, running the household and raising the children.

The Post-boomers seem to accept, largely without demur, that the world has changed in the time since their own parents were getting married and having children. Inevitably, there are some recalcitrant chauvinists among the males and some uncompromising feminists among the females, but the impression to emerge from this mid-twenties to late-thirties age group is that both sexes have benefited from a more carefully negotiated approach to relationships between them.

What's acceptable and what's not has really changed since my father's day, As males, we have to be very aware ...

I'd rather be a female than a male, in this time. We're very fortunate because we can have the best of both worlds. And if you're assertive enough, you can get men to do things around the house.

But let's not get carried away; social change is never all-embracing:

My life hasn't changed much since I got married. Me and the mates go to the casino every Thursday night and to the pub till late every Friday night. I go on a fishing trip for two weeks every year with the boys, too. I think I'm lucky. I've got a very good wife. A lot of guys couldn't go to the pub or the casino. My wife wouldn't stop me. I take her out for a romantic dinner every two months.

Lay down your arms ... but keep sentries posted

Because it has probably been the single most significant cultural revolution of the 20th century, the women's movement was never going to proceed smoothly. Nor could it conceivably have proceeded any more quickly than it has. Considering its ramifications, its speed has been impressive. Having transformed our attitudes to marriage, to parenting, to work, to politics, and to notions as fundamental as 'personhood' and 'equality', it's not time for feminism to rest, but it is perhaps time for that cease-fire. Women are quite capable of working out what they want, and men have learned to accept that much, at least.

CHAPTER TWENTY-FOUR

Xenophobia and Politics

Why Hanson was Good for Us

Turning Point: The rise of Pauline Hanson's One Nation party is a sign of deep disquiet in the body politic. Support for Hanson was based partly on classic xenophobia (fear of foreigners), partly on frustration with the major parties' perceived unresponsiveness to the concerns of ordinary Australians, partly on the fact that Hanson is a woman. But the residual effect of One Nation seems to have been to force us to reconsider our view of multiculturalism and to decide that we like it, warts and all.

What are we hoping for? More responsive politicians; more pride in our multicultural achievements; more open debate, without rancour or violence.

Who was this woman called Pauline Hanson? (I don't mean by the 'was' to imply she no longer exists, but only to suggest that she might have served her purpose; her moment, for most of us, has passed.) Where did she spring from? How did she manage to capture our imagination in 1996 and hold it so vividly for almost three years? Why did almost one million Australians vote for her One Nation Party in the 1998 Federal election?

Was she, as so many of her detractors wanted to say, a mere creature of the media—as if the media were so powerful they could tell us what to feel? Was she, as others darkly insisted, a creature not of the media, but of some sinister operatives with a nasty political agenda, hidden from our view in a filthy laboratory somewhere, cultivating seditious policies like some vile bacteria? (Did we really need to postulate any backroom boys when those out front were as disturbing as David Oldfield?) Or was she, as her staunchest supporters still claim, the voice of the people, the true leader of those who felt overlooked and undervalued by the so-called political elites, an amateur taking on the professionals and beating them at their own game?

Rivers of ink have flowed in analysis of the rise of Hanson and her party. We know all we could possibly wish to know about her fish shop, her Asian employee, her divorce, her estranged son, her maiden speech, her red hair that turned blonde, her clothes, her breathlessness as a public speaker ... yet none of it explains the thrust, or the trajectory, of the spectacular political rocket named Hanson.

We could read her party's manifesto, listen to her political advisers, hear her and her colleagues talking about revolutionising the tax system or launching a rural bank, sense the oft-denied racist slant in her views on immigration, cringe at the lack of understanding—let alone compassion—in her approach to Aboriginal or welfare issues ... and none of it would explain the strength and range of our reactions to the Hanson phenomenon. Other people, at other times, have said all that, and their views might have jangled and rattled briefly in the rowdy marketplace of ideas, but which of them ever seemed even remotely messianic to their supporters, or worryingly demagogic to the rest of us?

We needed her more than she needed us

The awkward, unpalatable, uncomfortable truth is that we—all of us—created Pauline Hanson because we needed her. It wasn't her timing that was impeccable; it was ours. It wasn't her manipulation of us, but our manipulation of her, that drove her to such heady prominence. And it wasn't just electoral defeat that brought her back to earth: it was a discernible shift in our view of ourselves; a coming to our senses; a recognition that, in the same way as a torrid love affair can sometimes clarify and deepen a person's commitment to a marriage, we didn't want to run the risk of undermining the fragile edifice of our culture, for all its shortcomings and weaknesses, in the pursuit of reckless and unworkable dreams.

On reflection, the rise and fall of Pauline Hanson's One Nation Party has probably been good for us. (It hasn't been good for our reputation around the world, of course: a nation famous for its tolerance and hospitality both to tourists and immigrants can hardly afford to be cast as a mob of ethnic isolationists, hostile to those we once wooed and welcomed.)

At first, it didn't look as if things would turn out so well. The early hubbub of interest in the rhetoric of Hanson, and the vitriolic abuse hurled at those who dared to oppose her (and, later, at those who dared to support her), suggested that a dark force had been unleashed in the Australian community that might run amok. It looked, for a while, as if prejudice, intolerance and a taste for black-and-white simplicities might become dangerously fashionable.

This was easy to understand, even if it was hard to admire. A society suffering from the effects of 25 years of relentless change—cultural, social, economic, technological—was bound to seek refuge, sooner or later, in the comfort of easy-sounding answers. The same insecurities that drive people into fundamentalist religion or into the call for increasingly tough rules and regulations also propel them into the arms of political extremists and, in the process, nurture some of their darkest phobias—most particularly, xenophobia, which is manifested in racial vilification, ethnic prejudice and, at its ugliest, in the desire for so-called 'ethnic cleansing'.

Hugh Mackay

'I don't agree with everything she says, but ...'

It is doubtful whether the huge minority of voters who were attracted to One Nation (perhaps as many as one-third of the electorate at one point) were ever buying the whole policy package. One of the most common remarks heard in support of Hanson was this: 'I don't agree with everything she says, but ...'. The 'but' might have signalled support for her views on the immigration rate from South-East Asia, outrage at the reported banning of Christmas carols from a primary school's end-of-year celebrations, uneasiness about the 'generous' treatment of Aborigines, or a hand-on-heart endorsement of the appealing idea that we are all 'Austrayans'. It was as if there were hundreds of thousands of voters each connected to One Nation by a thin thread of support for one thing Pauline Hanson had said: if you had assembled them all in one place, you might have found little *general* agreement about anything.

But those who had faith in the basic decency and good sense of the Australian people seem ultimately to have been proved right. The outbreak of racism provoked by Hanson, whether intentionally or unintentionally, was ugly and uncivilised. It has undoubtedly set back the cause of racial tolerance in Australia and, for some Asian immigrants, made life more miserable than it otherwise would have been. We have been reminded that civilisation is a fragile thing. Nevertheless, the fabric of our society has not seriously frayed and whatever damage we have sustained seems reparable.

It is one of the many paradoxes of a civilised society that even people with hate in their hearts have the right to be heard. And, in the light of Hansonism, who is to say that we would have been better off if we had continued to suppress racism and other destructive prejudices? At least One Nation has brought them out into the open where, knowing such sentiments have currency, we can examine them honestly. (This is no doubt part of the explanation for the success of Paul Sheehan's book, *Among the Barbarians*, published in 1998.)

So that's one reason why we needed Hanson: we were overdue for an outbreak of honesty about the divisions in our society on subjects ranging from native title to immigration and foreign investment. We needed to clear the air; to appreciate the range of opinions in our midst; to test the limits to our view of ourselves as a culturally diverse, open, tolerant and harmonious society.

The irony is that, had any of the leaders of the major political parties been prepared to encourage that kind of debate, we would not have had to invest Pauline Hanson with such magical powers. She was neither intellectually nor politically up to the task of being a national leader, but that didn't matter: we needed a trigger, and she served the purpose. We needed someone to force us to deal with our doubts, and we chose her.

A powerful combination: a woman *and* a political outcast

But why Pauline Hanson? Apart from her obvious appeal to those suffering from various forms of cultural or economic xenophobia, two factors favoured Hanson: she was a woman, and she had been dramatically expelled from the Liberal Party, on the eve of the 1996 election. Both of these attributes positioned her as a figure outside traditional, mainstream politics and, in an electorate growing ever more cynical about the political process, this gave her instant appeal.

More than 50 years after our first female Federal parliamentarian, Dame Enid Lyons, entered the House of Representatives in 1943, Australians are still yearning for a woman to *dominate* the political theatre. That is not simply part of a feminist push to see more women rising to positions of greater influence in business, politics and elsewhere; it is also the expression of a particular strain of dissatisfaction with the way politics is conducted in Australia. Parliament is widely regarded as a kind of boys' club; women who stray into this domain are generally assumed to have chosen—or been forced—to play the game the men's way. Adversarial politics, like adversarial law, is strongly associated with masculine stereotypes: aggressive competition, a reflexive resort to conflict, and a take-no-prisoners approach to the crushing of the opposition.

In the same way as Australians welcome the idea of some feminisation of the workplace culture under the influence of women in senior positions, so they look to women to gradually transform the parliamentary culture into something less abrasive, less ego-driven, and more constructive.

The fact that there are now more women in Federal Parliament than ever before—and more than 120 female parliamentarians in total—is not enough: the electorate wants a *symbolic* woman who will stand for the culture shift they dream of. (Beware: not everyone who dreams of a softening of the parliamentary culture actually wants their dream to come true. Many voters relish the outbursts of larrikinism for which some Australian politicians are famous; a political stoush is as riveting as any other kind. People complain of violence on television, too, but many of them eschew the softer options.)

There is the usual set of contradictions involved in this dream of the mother figure who sweeps into politics and changes the culture overnight. What voters seem to want is a woman who is tough without seeming to be; a woman with a strong voice but a 'softer side'; a woman who can somehow dish it out to the blokes without appearing to have been drawn into their way of doing things; a woman who won't even want to join the male club, yet will wield power and influence over the men who do. (In May 1999, the Democrats' Meg Lees came close to the embodiment of this ideal in her dealings with the government on its proposed tax legislation involving the GST.)

The dream is of a woman with a particular *edge*; someone who can take the fight up to the men without compromising certain stereotypical feminine virtues. (Everyone's list of the virtues is different, but 'good manners' often crops up: women are widely considered less likely to hurl abuse, less likely to interrupt, more likely to listen . . .)

So the electorate has seized on a number of women who looked as if they might meet enough of these criteria to do the symbolic job: Bronwyn Bishop (once touted as 'the next Liberal prime minister'), Carmen Lawrence and Cheryl Kernot (as Democrat leader) have all been contenders at various times, with Meg Lees the mid-1999 favourite and Natasha Stott Despoja currently in warm-up mode.

(This obsessive quest for a star female must be profoundly irritating to people like Mark Latham, Lindsay Tanner and Brendan Nelson who, from their different perspectives, are all bursting to do politics in a new way.)

Pauline Hanson had roughly the right idea when she said that she felt like the nation's mother and regarded us, the voters, as her children—but it was such an embarrassingly ham-fisted expression of the concept that it did her about as much good as the 1997 leaking of a melodramatic videotape that was only meant to be played posthumously ('If you're watching this, I have been killed ...'). In any case, Hanson was never a serious contender for the title of Symbolic Mother of Parliament, partly because her personal popularity, as opposed to her prominence, was never strong enough to sustain her in such a role.

But her gender, combined with her inarticulate style, certainly helped to position her as a non-professional politician and to distance her from the men's club. Being attacked by politicians and journalists, even female ones, only seemed to heighten her appeal to her supporters by making her appear vulnerable and in even greater need of their support.

Hanson's widely reported appeal to the older rural male may well have been based on the impression she created of being the kind of woman who was comfortable with a culture of male chauvinism. The hair, the make-up, the nails, the clothes, the voice, and the tendency to defer to the chaps when the going got tough (as it did when she was trying to answer journalists' questions about the practical details of her proposed rural bank) all suggested that the mythical helpless female was alive and well. You could hear the murmurs of male approval all over the country.

A wake-up call to the major parties

Hanson's strongest appeal, apart from specific bits of her rhetoric that struck responsive chords with certain minorities, lay in her reinforcement of many voters' disillusionment with the major parties. Those voters needed Hanson's One Nation as a kind of drainpipe for their discontents. No amount of complaint about the behaviour of politicians, no amount of bleating about the gulf between political discourse and the concerns of ordinary Australians, and no amount of 'swinging' seemed to convince the major parties that they had lost contact with their constituency. But they had, and it took One Nation to frighten them into realising it.

The significance of One Nation's support, while obvious in quantitative and qualitative opinion research for two years, had evidently not registered in the minds of the major parties until they had to face the unambiguous result of the state election in Queensland in 1998. Suddenly, they grasped the idea that this was no mere gnat buzzing noisily but harmlessly around the body politic; One Nation had to be taken seriously. Until then, they had assumed that nature would take its course and voters, having been briefly distracted by their flirtation with Hanson, would return to the fold on polling day.

So one of the most notable—and possibly enduring—effects of Pauline Hanson on Australian politics has been to jolt the mainstream parties out of their self-indulgent practice of talking to each other, rather than to us. They have recognised that they will have to listen more attentively to the concerns of voters, and they will have to explain their policies more clearly. So far, the declarations of their intention to do both these things seem more compelling than the evidence that they are actually doing them, but the die is cast—thanks to Hanson.

The Prime Minister, John Howard, came out of the Hanson affair rather badly, perhaps unfairly so. For many voters, Hanson's challenge to the major parties primarily took the form of a call for leadership. Though Howard had strongly supported her expulsion from the Liberal Party for her expression of racist views, the voters wanted more: they saw some of Hanson's outrageous remarks as a test of the PM's mettle, especially when it became obvious that Australia's standing in Asia was being adversely affected by reports of widespread support for Hanson's views. As he appeared to prevaricate and sidestep the issue—refusing even to commit himself on the subject of the allocation of preferences to One Nation in his own electorate until the last minute—Howard looked more and more like a man who was not, after all, distressed by Hanson's line. 'He's not opposing her because he agrees with her,' people began to mutter. Howard's repeated assurances that he understood the concerns of her supporters sounded, to those expecting an unambiguous renunciation, too sympathetic by half.

In retrospect, Howard's refusal to tackle Hanson head-on looks more sensible. It was almost certainly a correct strategy, after all, to let One

Nation run its course, draw its poison, and lose its momentum. And if the Coalition, in response, has moved further to the Right then that will at least help to clarify its philosophical differences from the Labor Party (assuming that Labor, in turn, can work out what it proposes to do next).

The Kennett Factor: Hanson's nemesis?

Not every state was sending the same signal to the major parties. The consistent message of election results, Newspoll research and other assessments of the mood of the Victorian electorate suggests that One Nation will continue to perform worse there than elsewhere. In the 1998 Federal election, One Nation secured 3.7 per cent of the primary vote in Victoria, compared with a national average of 8.3 per cent.

Why?

The answer lay partly in the fact that Victoria is our least decentralised state, so the proportion of rural voters—the backbone of One Nation's support—is far lower than in, say, Queensland. (Seventy-three per cent of Victorians live in metropolitan Melbourne, whereas only 45 per cent of Queenslanders live in Brisbane.)

But an equally important explanation lay in the leadership style and personal influence of the Victorian Premier, Jeff Kennett. As Chapter 12 suggested, Kennett had emerged, during the Hanson era, as Australia's most highly regarded politician. He was credited with having developed a clear vision for Victoria and whether voters approved of the details of that particular vision or not, they generally approved of the fact that Kennett *had* one.

In Victoria, therefore, it was widely perceived that there was *not* a vacuum at the top, whereas many Australians believe that Hanson rose to such prominence precisely because there did seem to be a vacuum at the top of Federal politics in the place where strong, visionary leadership should have been. One Nation's wake-up call was not heard in Victoria with anything like the clarity evident in other states, simply because, in voters' minds, the Kennett Government was already wide awake.

The third factor driving One Nation's vote down in Victoria is also a product of the Kennett style of leadership. From the beginning, Jeff Kennett has understood the ethnic diversity of his state (and, especially, of Melbourne) and has embraced it as a strength. He has celebrated ethnic multiculturalism when other politicians have often seemed anxious to evade it as an issue.

In Kennett's case, more than lip-service has been involved. He has seized every opportunity to praise the contribution of immigrant groups to Victoria's economic, social and cultural wellbeing, and he has not been afraid to speak up on behalf of specific ethnic groups in his constituency— for example, the Greeks—nor even to take sides in the Macedonian dispute.

Given such overt support for ethnic diversity in its Premier, Victoria has generally failed to heed the siren song of One Nation.

The unintended consequence of Hansonism:

she's reinforced our commitment to diversity

Here's the best thing of all about Hanson: in response to the unedifying political ructions, the arguments around family dinner tables, the tensions in workplaces, the ugly scenes in TV coverage of One Nation rallies, the bullying on both sides, the journalistic lather, and the discomfort created by the intrusion of an unfamiliar and ultimately unwelcome style into our political process, Hanson has forced us all to think hard about the question of multiculturalism. (By the way, we're still a bit uncomfortable with that rather contrived word—see Chapter 4.)

With what result? Generally speaking, we've decided we like being part of this fragile, complex, radical experiment we're undertaking. We like being the only country in the world that seems capable of generating a harmonious society out of wildly disparate elements. We love our emerging hybrid identity. We're proud of our reputation for tolerance and hospitality.

No, we haven't yet got it quite right and, yes, we're worried about some signs of imported violence, corruption, and ethnic tensions that have no relevance to Australia's heritage and no place in Australia's culture. We're not entirely comfortable with the idea of old suburbs changing their character under the influence of new arrivals.

But we seem to be on a winner, nevertheless. Diversity can mean strength and enrichment, after all. There's a discernible buzz, an energy, about being cosmopolitan. We will occasionally mock each other's peculiarities and hoot unkindly at our differences, but that's a whole lot better than shooting each other.

One Nation is not dead. Though its level of representation in parliaments around the country would make you doubt it, One Nation actually garnered more support in the 1998 Federal election than the Democrats, and about the same as the National Party. Almost one million Australians gave Hanson's party their primary vote and although this didn't result in a single seat being won in the House of Representatives, the party has acquired one Senate seat and will continue to create electoral beachheads in some states.

In the New South Wales State election of March 1999, for example, One Nation attracted about 8 per cent of the primary vote, outpolling the combined primary votes of the Democrats and the Greens. David Oldfield, Hanson's right-hand man, was elected to the Legislative Council. One Nation again served as an electoral drainpipe: many people who were angry with the Coalition for staging such a woeful campaign (and for having so treacherously knifed both their leaders so close to an election) embraced One Nation as a broadly conservative alternative to voting Labor. In spite of the embarrassing internal ructions in its Queensland branch, with two MPs resigning from the Party in evident despair, many rural New South Wales voters continued to support One Nation as a way of expressing their discontent with the regional performance of the major parties.

Reflecting on the New South Wales election result, *The Sydney Morning Herald*'s ace political commentator, Alan Ramsey, wrote this:

Those who ignore the growth of regionalism and localism are the same people who keep dismissing One Nation, after each election, as an electoral aberration. One Nation has now completed three elections (in Queensland, NSW and federally) and posted winning candidates in each one.[1]

Nevertheless, the hysteria has subsided. The passion is largely spent. The sting has gone out of it. Some enthusiasts still dream of a return to White Australia or a spontaneous uprising in support of some version of Fortress Australia—just as some men are still secretly in love with Pauline herself. But the first flush has faded. One Nation has been relegated to the status of an also-ran: one of the minor parties, destined to remain on the sidelines, occasionally being courted for a crucial vote in one parliament or another, and pondering, from time to time, the pros and cons of coalition—if anyone will have them.

Already, the fervour that saw some supporters seriously expecting Pauline Hanson to become our next prime minister is starting to look more silly than dangerous.

Our xenophobia—one of the human foibles that will always be there, prowling around in our collective unconscious—is back on the leash.

CHAPTER TWENTY-FIVE

'Young and free'

Give Us Time

Turning Point: We criticise ourselves—and are criticised by others—for our rather brash, immature style in politics, business, sport and the arts. But perhaps we are still in a kind of societal adolescence, with more energy than focus; perhaps our destiny is not yet clear to us. We will eventually achieve a new level of maturity in our national affairs, but we need time. This turning point is still some way off. As the national anthem constantly reminds us, we're still young.

What are we hoping for? Some encouraging signs that we are on the way to a greater maturity; more dignity and courtesy in our national leaders in all fields.

Australians all, let us rejoice
For we are young and free.
We've golden soil and wealth for toil,
Our home is girt by sea.
Our land abounds in nature's gifts
Of beauty rich and rare.
In hist'ry's page, let ev'ry stage
Advance Australia fair.
In joyful strains then let us sing:
Advance Australia fair!

'Australians all, let us rejoice ...' for at least we have an anthem that celebrates peace and harmony, rather than revolution or civil war; one that doesn't urge destruction of the infidel; one that hymns honest toil rather than bloodshed.

Unfortunately, the poetry leaves something to be desired. In hist'ry's page, you'd be hard pressed to find doggerel to match this lot. The national cringe-meter runs off the top of the scale every time we sing of a home 'girt by sea'. (Even the indulgent *Oxford English Dictionary* notes that the use of 'girt' as a verb is now rare. Its origins are obscure, but it's probably a corruption of 'gird' as in a girdle.)

And you'd be flat out finding much golden soil hereabouts. Red, certainly, in the centre, and black in some of our lush farming regions. Most of it is a rather greyish brown, but that clearly lacks the poetic potential of 'golden'. Perhaps the lyricist was thinking of golden *sand*, which would have been closer to the mark, but would presumably have created rhyming difficulties if he was determined to get 'toil' in there. (He could have gone for 'work' instead, but then he would've been back to square one, playing with rhymes like murk, lurk, shirk, berk or even Bourke ... all with their rightful place in our culture, but not, perhaps, in our anthem.)

There have been moves, from time to time, to renovate the words and even to replace the anthem entirely, perhaps with 'Waltzing Matilda'. 'Matilda' is undoubtedly our best-loved national song but in spite of New

South Wales Premier Bob Carr's attempt, back in 1996, to crank up support for it as a replacement for 'Advance Australia Fair', there's never been any real interest in elevating it to the sort of status where we'd have to stand to sing it. In any case, a song about an unemployed, suicidal sheep-stealer might not lend itself to state occasions.

'And he sang as he watched and waited till his billy boiled' captures our historical tendency towards procrastination, but as anthem material, it makes 'girt by sea' sound positively majestic. And if people are prepared to stand and sing 'girt by sea' with a straight face, that is all the proof you need that they don't feel too strongly about it. On this point, as on few others, change is *not* in the air. We voted for 'Advance Australia Fair' in 1977 and we're stuck with it, words and all.

How young *are* we?

The best part of the anthem is the second line: 'For we are young and free'. It's bold, clear and devoid of clichés. The question is: is it true?

Freedom is certainly one of the things we most admire about this society: freedom of speech, freedom of assembly (most of the time, in most places), freedom of religion, freedom of the press, freedom of movement. It's only when you visit a country where any of those things are restricted that you realise what precious and extraordinary freedoms they are.

We also relish the freedom of our space: the freedom of the beach, the bush, the mountains, the sky. We celebrate those freedoms with our mobility: our big sixes and V8s haul us all over the countryside—and you occasionally even see a 4WD that's been let out of the city. Our temperate climate encourages us to make the most of the open air.

At the turn of the century it's probably fair to observe that we seem intent on giving too many of our freedoms away, all in the name of 'control'. (See Chapter 3.) But even though we're rapidly becoming an over-regulated society, we're still, by world standards, a remarkably free one.

But what about 'young'?

(We constantly hear about our ageing population, and it's true that by the year 2051, 25 per cent of the population will be over 65 years of age.

That's just a demographic accident, though, and nothing to do with our age as a society.)

Our Federation is not yet 100 years old. The legal status of 'Australian citizen' was only created in 1949. (Until then, we were all British subjects.) It's only a little over 200 years since European civilisation was established here.

So we *are* young.

In terms of comparable societies, we're about the same age as the West Coast of America, but 170 years younger than the East Coast. Canada shook off its colonial yoke about 35 years before we did—though, like us, they retained the British monarchy as their own. New Zealand's history of British settlement was more turbulent and complex than ours—mainly because the Maoris were warlike in a way the Australian Aborigines were not—and they date the foundation of their nation from 1840, when the Treaty of Waitangi was signed.

France might date its 'modern' status from the establishment of the republic in 1793, but its culture goes back, continuously, for at least 1500 years before that. And Britain? Where should we start ... Magna Carta, 1215? The Battle of Hastings, 1066? What's a few hundred years, either way?

When the captain of the Sri Lankan cricket team, Arjunga Ranatunga, was stung by Shane Warne's criticism of him in a newspaper column, he struck back in a way that made our youthfulness sound like our greatest liability: '[Warne's comment] shows more about Shane Warne and the Australian culture. We come from 2500 years of culture and we all know where they come from.'[1]

(The irony in the remark was presumably unintentional: you might have hoped that 2500 years of culture would have produced a wiser, more mature response to Warne's admittedly gratuitous insult. But cricket's a funny game ...)

Is our adolescence nearly over?

Can you talk about the maturity of a society in a way that's analogous to the maturity of an individual? Does it make any sense to say of Australia, as so many commentators have, that we are still in a kind of societal adolescence?

I think it does make a rough kind of sense (and, by the way, I don't think it amounts to self-criticism). It's not an absolutely valid analogy, of course, but it offers a useful perspective. In *Reinventing Australia*, I said this:

> It is unrealistic to expect Australia to act as if it is a mature society. It is unrealistic to expect our national parliament to behave as it might if it had hundreds of years of unique tradition. It is unrealistic to expect Australians to have a fully mature world view when we are only now beginning to come to terms with the nature of our own national identity.[2]

Listen to East Coast Americans talking about California, and there's certainly an assumption that the East has something to show for its extra 170 years of civilisation. A more mellow style, the New Englanders might say of themselves; less brash, less to prove, less obviously in a hurry; more settled, more established.

When Australians watch British or American politicians on television programs like the ABC's *Lateline*, a typical response is that they seem more dignified, somehow, than our politicians; more refined, more civilised. The British, who gave us our adversarial style of parliamentary democracy, seem to treat their political opponents with more grace and courtesy than we do. Even the Americans, whom we expect to be more direct and abrasive, seem to have more—what's the word?—maturity in their public dealings with each other.

The British might well have given us the Westminster system, broadly speaking, but they didn't give us the centuries of history and tradition that go with their version. (On this theory, though, the New South Wales parliament, being the oldest, should be the most civilised in Australia ... Hmm.)

British and American business executives, working in Australia, comment on the brashness, sometimes more charitably described as 'directness', of our management and negotiating style. 'Australian

Hugh Mackay

boardrooms are like boys' schools,' said one senior visiting American in 1999, 'they are unbelievably rude to each other. Their style is so ... immature.' (That word again.)

You have only to switch on a telecast of Question Time in the House of Representatives to know what he meant. We *are* incredibly rude to each other and no matter how much MPs declare their intention of trying to do better, they seem incapable of lifting their parliamentary standards to the levels of personal dignity and maturity that we might expect of the nation's pre-eminent parliamentary chamber.

We often say of ourselves that the Australian style—in politics, in business, in sport and even in the arts—is abrasive and combative. If such a gross generalisation is true, it also seems fair to suggest that this is a stage on the way to something else.

As Chapter 24 pointed out, voters are hoping that the increasing presence of women in our parliaments will gradually change the style of debate and negotiation. In business, similarly, many women—and even some men—say they are waiting for the day when the boardrooms and executive suites of corporate Australia have enough women in them to make an impact on the style and substance of management decisions, and on corporate culture generally.

How did we manage to earn this reputation for a certain brashness, gaucherie and immaturity in our style? One theory is that in Europe and the USA, students generally move away from home to attend university, whereas Australian students typically live at home (and, indeed, stay at home until their mid-20s): perhaps this slows the rate of maturation, the theory runs, and that is reflected in the culture of business and the professions.

Another, more widespread theory is that it's all the fault of our convict ancestors and the rough, anti-authoritarian character of our early culture, though some people maintain that that's really a Sydney problem: Melbourne and Adelaide, they will say, have always been more refined places. ('They're just up themselves,' Sydneysiders would say in response, rather confirming their critics' point.) On the other hand, the former Prime Minister, Paul Keating, once famously remarked that 'if you're not living in Sydney, you're just camping'.

Yet another theory blames our isolation. On this theory, our increasing contact with the rest of the world will inevitably accelerate our progress towards greater maturity and refinement. Still others think that there's a larrikin streak in us that has been positively encouraged by the 'bush' ethos—a bit like the Western cowboy ethos of parts of the American West.

You can acquire instant diversity, but

not instant patina

All this speculation might be missing a very simple point: *we haven't yet had long enough to develop mellow, mature institutions and styles, because our culture is still too young.*

One hundred years? Two hundred years? That's as nothing, compared with most countries whose cultures we admire and whose emigrants have so often remarked, when they arrive here, on the 'rawness' of Australia. ('Where is the *life*?' the Europeans want to know.) Italians love it here, but they are hardly likely to praise us for the depth of our culture. And why would they? They might date 'the modern Italy' from the establishment of the republic in 1946, or from 1860, when Garibaldi and his red-shirts installed Victor Emanuel as King of a unified Italy, previously 20 separate countries. But people from every region of Italy will identify with far longer histories than those, going back to the Renaissance, for instance, or even to Ancient Rome. (La Scala, by the way, was opened ten years before the First Fleet landed at Farm Cove.)[3]

Give us time!

We have created something wonderfully robust, diverse and vibrant, but we need more time—perhaps another 100 years, perhaps another 200—to become the kind of society we aspire to be. This is the time for setting our goals and directions, but there's no short-cut to depth and maturity. We are still, in cultural terms, in our adolescence.

The adolescent is characterised by having more energy than focus ... and so are we. We're dying to make our way in the world; dying to 'prove ourselves'. Yet we're still deeply unsure of our identity, and we don't yet have a clear vision of who or what we want to be.

The adolescent is torn between feeling dependent on parents and impatient to be free of them ... and so are we. The vast majority of older Australians don't really want to cut their ties with the British monarchy, and a substantial minority of younger Australians are still uneasy about the move to a republic.

The adolescent is typically in a tumult of turbulent emotions and conflicting goals ... and so are we. In Australia at the turn of the century, we're doing nothing less than redefining the character of our society, so no wonder we feel unstable, uncertain and unconvinced. (Logan Pearsall Smith put it rather well in *Afterthoughts*: 'Don't laugh at a youth for his affectations; he's only trying on one face after another, till he finds his own.')

Give us time!

The adolescent analogy is rough, and probably overworked. Many other countries in the world are also undergoing social, economic and cultural upheavals, and some of them—like Japan—have ancient cultures. Renewal is always painful, however old you are.

But we're still being formed, and that's the difference between us and many of the countries with which we have to deal, and to which we compare ourselves. This is not simply one of many cycles of renewal for Australia: this is Australia preparing itself for maturity; Australia approaching a turning point that feels like a moment of great significance; a leap; a shift; a reorientation.

Meanwhile, what's wrong with being young? Why not relish the chance to shape our future; to create this Australia in our own image? Soon enough, the place will be old, staid, mature and *set*. When that day comes, reform will be really difficult, change will be really painful, and it will be clear that we were the lucky ones.

CHAPTER TWENTY-SIX

Zeitgeist—the spirit of the times

Unless I'm misreading the signs, Australians are in retreat—and that might be no bad thing. I suspect this is one of those strategic withdrawals that gives us some breathing space; some time to think about whether we actually want to go where we appear to be heading.

You can find the evidence of retreat in the way we're keeping our distance from politics (for instance, in our remarkably low level of involvement in the last Federal election campaign of the 20th century); in the swing away from current affairs programs on radio and television; in the growing pre-occupation with personal and local issues; in the surge of interest in spiritual and mystical experience. (Its shadow can be found in the current epidemic of depression.)

You can also find it in the contradictions and confusions that characterise our outlook on life at the turn of the century. We are searching for a new sense of purpose, yearning for a vision, but while we're waiting, the focus turns inexorably inward.

This spirit of disengagement is a perfectly understandable response to the economic and cultural upheavals of the past 20 years. Many of us are still licking our wounds as a result of a soaring divorce rate, a major recession and a hostile labour market. Some of us are disturbed by the realisation that, as a nation, some old and comfortable alignments have lost their meaning.

We have been adapting to the changes, of course. Given time, we usually do. We learn to live with faster food, slower traffic, and the mystery of why lightning-speed computer transactions can't reduce the time for a cheque to be cleared. Occasionally, we pause and wonder where the roller-coaster is taking us—and, especially, our children—but most of the time we simply hang on and hope for the best.

Our reactions to all this have been well documented by psychologists, anthropologists, statisticians, medical researchers, criminologists and theologians. Their tentative verdict seems to be that, emotionally, we're not in great shape. Insecurity is frequently identified as our bête noir.

But is that really such a bad thing?

If young Australians are learning that life is inherently insecure, then that's a far more realistic lesson than the one their parents learned from the boom years of the Fifties and Sixties. If it is causing them to think differently about marriage and work—once regarded as the twin pillars of personal identity—then they are preparing themselves appropriately for a world that is already unrecognisably different from the one in which their parents grew up.

We tend to think of insecurity as corrosive and ultimately destructive. But in what age did our forebears not live with the unpredictability of disease, war and tempest, or even the great uncertainty of not knowing what lay beyond the skies, or beyond death?

For the time being, it might be a good idea to let our insecurities work for us: to pause and examine this great restlessness inside us; to acknowledge that nothing in life is certain; to ponder, and perhaps even to measure, that uncomfortable gap between what we say we believe in— what our values are—and how we actually lead our lives. (Perhaps that's part of our problem: we know what to do, but we're not doing it.)

It's tempting to characterise Australia as simply being caught in a downdraught of cynicism and disappointment, and both those emotions are in plentiful supply. But something more constructive is going on as well. What about the powerful updraughts? What about the unrestrained optimism that many Australians feel about some aspects of our future—sometimes coexisting, improbably, with pessimism about others? What about our rising levels of education, the explosion of young writing, the new designers taking every field by storm, from cinema to fashion?

Could we be in a phase of disengagement from the tedious posturing and jousting of politicians, from the endless stream of the world's bad news, and even from the harsh truth about the state of our physical environment, because we need to clear the decks for something we haven't yet defined?

Was John Howard sensing this mood when he suggested in 1997 that most people simply wanted the native title debate 'off the agenda'? It sounded heartless at the time, but perhaps it was just another sign of our desire to retreat, to disengage, to regroup. Perhaps we needed a break from 'issues': we didn't mean to dismiss native title as unimportant, but we wanted to resolve it even more than we wanted to debate it. The reform agenda was too crowded.

Times of uncertainty—especially when linked with a half-formed sense of expectancy—have, in the past, been fertile breeding grounds for religious revivals (though, as we have seen on this journey through the social landscape, that seems unlikely in our case). Is there going to be a mass movement of some other kind, in which we will define ourselves by some new-found sense of purpose?

Perhaps this is a kind of interregnum in which we are preparing, even without knowing it, to confront questions we've been avoiding for too long. We might finally be coming to terms with some of the more demanding meanings of diversity, egalitarianism and even the famous Aussie 'fair go'. We might be starting to realise just how vital our social connections are. We might be on the brink of a new level of assertiveness about the role we are prepared to let machines play in our lives. Are we, perhaps, catching a glimpse of the future we want? And the futures we don't want?

If our uneasiness leads us to think more deeply about reconciliation, or unemployment, or the chasm between wealth and poverty, or even about the need for more attention to be paid to 'the care of the soul'—our own and each other's—then this little retreat could be a turning point. It might even teach us that insecurity can be a spur to creativity.

NOTES

THE BIG PICTURE

1. Results of post-budget Newspoll survey, published in *The Australian*, 18 May 1999.
2. Richard Eckersley, 'Redefining Progress', *Family Matters*, Australian Institute of Family Studies, No. 51, Spring/Summer 1998.
3. Marion Downey, 'Hard times send many to GP with depression', *The Sydney Morning Herald*, 21 April 1999.
4. Michael Pusey, 'The impact of economic restructuring on women and families: preliminary findings from the Middle Australia Project', *Australian Quarterly*, July–August 1998.
5. Donald Horne, *The Lucky Country: Australia in the Sixties*, Penguin Books, Ringwood, 1964.
6. Walter Truett Anderson, *Reality Isn't What It Used To Be*, Harper & Row, San Francisco, 1990.
7. Paul Kelly, *The End of Certainty*, Allen & Unwin, Sydney, 1992.
8. Martin Haywood, quoted in 'Perfect Moments?', *Seriously*, Strategic Insight, Auckland, March 1999.
9. Howard Russell, 'Perfect Moments?', ibid.
10. Jane de Teliga, 'Hemlines are old hat in a confused fashion world', *The Sydney Morning Herald*, 13 May 1999.
11. B Headey & A Wearing, *Understanding Happiness: A Theory of Subjective Wellbeing*, Longman Cheshire, Melbourne, 1992.
12. Ronald Inglehart, *Culture Shift in Advanced Industrial Society*, Princeton University Press, Princeton NJ, 1990.
13. Raymond Duch & Michael Taylor, 'Postmaterialism and the Economic Condition', *American Journal of Political Science*, No. 38, 1993.
14. Paul V Warwick, 'Disputed cause, disputed effect: the postmaterialist thesis re-examined', *Public Opinion Quarterly*, Vol. 62, No. 4, Winter 1998.
15. Germaine Greer, *The Whole Woman*, Doubleday, London, 1999.

Chapter 2: BABY BOOMERS

1. Hugh Mackay, *Attitudes to Self-Medication*, Mackay Research Pty Limited, November 1992.
2. Phil Ruthven, quoted in Mark Abernethy, 'Boom, Baby, Boom', *The Bulletin*, 26 January 1999.
3. Findings from Mastercard's Australian Ideals survey, quoted in 'Many of us will retire flat broke', *The Sydney Morning Herald*, 12 April 1999.
4. Phil Ruthven, quoted in David Elias, 'The baby boomers: a generation falls to

earth and learns the cold, hard facts of life', *The Sunday Age*, 11 April 1999.

5. Kevin Bailey, quoted in David Elias, ibid.
6. Mark Abernethy, op. cit.

Chapter 3: CONTROL

1. Dierdre Macken, 'Deconstructing the Decade', *The Sydney Morning Herald: Spectrum*, 27 December 1997.
2. Deborah Snow, 'At war over drugs', *The Sydney Morning Herald*, 10 May 1999.
3. Bryony Jackson, quoted in Lisa Clausen, 'Just an ordinary street', *Time*, 12 April 1999.
4. Paola Totaro & Philip Cornford, 'The drugs we use', *The Sydney Morning Herald*, 15 May 1999.
5. 'Ted Noffs warns on young drug users', 20 May 1967, quoted in *Chronicle of the 20th Century*, Penguin Books/Chronicle Australia, Ringwood, 1990.

Chapter 4: DIVERSITY

1. David Day, *Claiming a Continent*, Angus & Robertson, Sydney, 1997.
2. Hugh Mackay, *Multiculturalism*, Mackay Research Pty Limited, September 1995.
3. Quoted in Lauren Martin, 'Howard warms to the melting pot', *The Sydney Morning Herald*, 6 May 1999.
4. Michelle Gunn, 'Tale of our cities', *The Weekend Australian*, 18–19 April 1999.
5. Paul Sheehan, *Among the Barbarians: The Dividing of Australia*, Random House, Sydney, 1998.

Chapter 5: EGALITARIANISM

1. Hans Baekgaard, quoted in Stephen Long, 'For richer, for poorer', *The Australian Financial Review: Weekend*, 9–10 January 1999.
2. Dusseldorp Skills Forum report, *Deepening Divide*, quoted in Nicole Brady, 'Divide deepens as young people lose out in the race for jobs', *The Age*, 17 April 1999.
3. Michael Ignatieff, *The Needs of Strangers*, The Hogarth Press, London, 1990.
4. Hans-Peter Martin & Harald Schumann, *The Global Trap*, Zed Books, London, 1997.

Chapter 6: FOOD

1. Gawen Rudder, 'A bowl of marbles', *City Ethics*, The St James Ethics Centre, Issue 36, Winter 1999.
2. Rosemary Stanton, letter to the Editor, *The Sydney Morning Herald*, 22 May 1999.
3. Dangar Research Group & John Bevins Pty Limited, *Food in Focus*, The Murdoch Magazines Food Monitor, April 1999.

4. Annette Shun Wah & Greg Aitken, *Banquet: Ten Courses to Harmony*, Doubleday, Melbourne, 1999.
5. Hans Eysenck outlined his research in an interview with Michele Field, 'Personality Engineering', *The Independent Monthly*, February 1990.
6. Quoted in Padraic P. McGuinness, 'Smoking facts hidden by a cloud of exaggeration', *The Sydney Morning Herald*, 28 May 1999.

Chapter 7: GREY POWER
1. Peter G Peterson, 'The coming age wave', *The Australian Financial Review*, 5 March 1999.
2. Hugh Mackay, *Generations*, Macmillan, Sydney, 1997.

Chapter 8: HEROES
1. James Froude, *Oceana*, London, 1905, quoted in Stephen Murray-Smith, *The Dictionary of Australian Quotations*, Heinemann, Melbourne, 1984.
2. Mark Taylor, quoted in *The Sydney Morning Herald*, 26 January 1999.

Chapter 9: INFORMATION
1. Paul Burton, *Information Technology and Society: Implications for the information professions*, Bookcraft, London, 1992.
2. George Miller, *The Psychology of Communication*, Penguin, Harmondsworth, 1970.
3. Bill Gates, quoted in John Seabrook, 'The e-mail from Bill', *The New Yorker*, 10 January 1994.
4. Neil Postman, *Amusing Ourselves To Death*, Heinemann, London, 1986.
5. George Gilder, *Life After Television*, W W Norton, New York, 1992.
6. Stan Davis & Jim Botkin, *The Monster Under the Bed*, Simon & Schuster, New York, 1994.
7. James Q Wilson, *The Moral Sense*, Free Press, New York, 1993.
8. Thomas Moore, *Soul Mates*, HarperCollins, New York, 1994.

Chapter 10: JOB INSECURITY
1. David Fryer & Anthony H Winefield, 'Employment stress and unemployment distress as two varieties of labour market induced psychological strain: an explanatory framework', *The Australian Journal of Social Research*, Vol. 5, No. 1, July 1998.

Chapter 11: KOORIS
1. Martin Krygier, 'A Good Society', *Eureka Street*, Vol. 9, No. 1, January–February 1999.
2. Colin Tatz, *Genocide in Australia*, Research Discussion Paper No. 8,

Australian Institute of Aboriginal and Torres Strait Islander Studies, 1999.
3. Robert Manne, 'Hope for the stolen generation', *The Sydney Morning Herald*, 3 May 1999.

Chapter 12: LEADERSHIP

1. Dick Morris, *Behind the Oval Office*, Random House, New York, 1997.
2. Carl Jung, quoted in William McGuire and R F C Hull, *C.G. Jung Speaking: Interviews and Encounters*, Picador, London, 1980.
3. Walter Truett Anderson, op. cit.
4. Franklin Delano Roosevelt, Second Inaugural Address, January 1937.

Chapter 14: NOSTALGIA

1. Keith Naughton & Bill Vlasic, 'The Nostalgia Boom', *Business Week*, 23 March 1998.

Chapter 15: OPTIONS

1. Walter Truett Anderson, op. cit.
2. Anthony Giddens, *Beyond Left and Right*, Polity Press, Cambridge, 1994.
3. John Shelby Spong, *Rescuing the Bible from Fundamentalism*, HarperSanFrancisco, San Francisco, 1992.
4. Marghanita Laski, *Everyday Ecstasy*, Thames and Hudson, London, 1980.
5. Darren Gray, 'Half of students binge drink', *The Age*, 11 March 1999.
6. Lisa Clausen, 'Just an ordinary street', *Time*, op. cit.
7. Thomas Moore, *Care of the Soul*, Piatkus, London, 1992.
8. Thomas Moore, ibid.
9. Charlene Spretnak, *States of Grace*, HarperSanFrancisco, San Francisco, 1993.
10. William Shakespeare, *Hamlet, Prince of Denmark*, Act I, Scene III.
11. Allan Bloom, *The Closing of the American Mind*, Simon & Schuster, New York, 1987.
12. Christopher Honnery, quoted in Diana Bagnall, 'The Y Factor', *The Bulletin*, 16 March 1999.

Chapter 17: QUALITY OF LIFE

1. Richard Eckersley, 'Redefining Progress', *Family Matters*, op. cit. See also Richard Eckersley (ed.), *Measuring Progress*, CSIRO Publishing, Melbourne, 1998.
2. Jerry Mander, *In the Absence of the Sacred*, Sierra Club Books, San Francisco, 1992.
3. Ross Gittins, 'Guilt pangs of a serious economist', *The Sydney Morning Herald*, 5 May 1999.

Chapter 18: REPUBLIC

1. John Howard, in Hugh Mackay, 'Howard on Howard', *The Weekend Australian*, 10–11 February 1996.
2. Padraic P. McGuinness, 'When a president's post is not safe', *The Sydney Morning Herald*, 20 January 1999.
3. Lindsay Tanner, *Open Australia*, Pluto Press, Sydney, 1999.

Chapter 19: SPIRITUALITY ... OR SPORT?

1. Chris McGillion, 'God all mighty, devil left behind', *The Sydney Morning Herald*, 30 March 1999.
2. Horst Priessnitz, 'Dreams in Austerica: A preliminary comparison of the Australian and the American dream', *Anglia*, Max Niemeyer Verlag Tübingen, Vol. 113, No. 1, 1995.
3. Padraic P. McGuinness, 'Our Right is only rising', *The Sydney Morning Herald*, 8 May 1999.
4. Tim Costello, quoted in Chris McGillion, 'Church asked to show the way', *The Sydney Morning Herald*, 27 April 1999.
5. Frank Brennan, quoted in Chris McGillion, ibid.
6. Pope John Paul II, 'Journeying in search of truth', *Fides et Ratio*, Encyclical Letter, 1998.
7. Simone Weil, *Gravity & Grace*, Routledge, London, 1963.
8. M Holmes Hartshorne, *The Faith to Doubt*, Prentice-Hall, Englewood Cliffs NJ, 1963.
9. Albert Einstein, *The World As I See It*, quoted in Lucinda Vardey (ed.), *God in All Worlds*, Millennium Books, Sydney, 1995.
10. Marion Woodman, *The Pregnant Virgin*, quoted in Lucinda Vardey (ed.), ibid.
11. Hans Küng, *Theology for the Third Millennium*, quoted in Lucinda Vardey (ed.), ibid.
12. John Howard, in Hugh Mackay, 'Howard on Howard', *The Weekend Australian*, op. cit.

Chapter 20: TECHNOLOGY

1. Neil Postman, 'Keep tabs on technology', *Lapis*, New York Open Centre, reprinted in *The Age*, 30 January 1999.
2. Hugh Mackay, *Computers, Technology & the Future*, The Centre for Communication Studies, September 1981.
3. Neil Postman, op. cit.
4. Paul Burton, op. cit.
5. Neil Postman, op. cit.
6. John Gray, 'The myth of progress', *The New Statesman*, reprinted in *The Age*, 8 May 1999.

7. John Sutherland, 'The fight for eyeballs', *London Review of Books*, 1 October 1998.
8. Alan Cameron, quoted in Annette Sampson, 'Make a Net killing—for someone else', *The Sydney Morning Herald*, 4 May 1999.
9. Deborah Smith, 'Sperm countdown', *The Sydney Morning Herald*, 20 May 1999.
10. David Cram, quoted in Deborah Smith, ibid.
11. John Gray, op. cit.
12. Richard Ford, 'A waste of time', *The New York Times*, reprinted in *The Sydney Morning Herald: Spectrum*, 23 January 1999.

Chapter 21: UNRAVELLING
1. Results of KPMG research quoted in Lyall Johnson, 'Singles soon to overtake couples', *The Age*, 28 April 1999.

Chapter 23: WOMEN AND MEN
1. Germaine Greer, op. cit.
2. Richard Morin and Megan Rosenfeld, 'With more equity, more sweat', *The Washington Post*, 22 March 1998 (first of a five-part series on 'The Gender Revolution').
3. Christine Wallace, 'Hear me roar', *The Australian's Review of Books*, April 1999.
4. Megan Walker, 'State of Play: Women', compilation of statistics in *Good Weekend*, 6 March 1999.
5. Research findings by Davidson and Associates, quoted in Trudy Harris, 'Women back on the job faster than men', *The Australian*, 27 April 1999.
6. Megan Walker, op. cit.

Chapter 24: XENOPHOBIA AND POLITICS
1. Alan Ramsey, 'Major parties' boasts just don't add up', *The Sydney Morning Herald*, 3 April 1999.

Chapter 25: 'YOUNG AND FREE'
1. Quoted in Martin Blake, 'Arjuna returns Warne's serve', *The Sun-Herald*, 16 May 1999.
2. Hugh Mackay, *Reinventing Australia*, Angus & Robertson, Sydney, 1993.
3. David Dale, *The 100 Things Everyone Needs to Know About Italy*, Pan, Sydney, 1998.

ACKNOWLEDGMENTS

Five of the chapters in this book began life as speeches, though they appear here in a different and more extended form. Chapter 5 (Egalitarianism) is based on my 1997 Mitchell Oration, 'The Pleasing Myth of Egalitarian Australia', delivered in honour of Dame Roma Mitchell. Chapter 9 (Information) is based on my 1996 Annual Lecture for The St James Ethics Centre. Chapter 10 (Job Insecurity) is based on my keynote lecture, 'Do I Want to Work for You?', delivered to the 1998 Annual Conference of the Australian Human Resources Institute. (I suggested they change the name of their organisation.) Chapter 11 (Kooris) is based on my address on 'Reconciliation and Traditional Australian Values', delivered to the Australian Reconciliation Convention in 1997. Chapter 13 (Marriage and the Family) is based on a public lecture delivered in 1998 for the 50th anniversary of Relationships Australia (formerly the Marriage Guidance Council of Australia: I suggested they shouldn't have changed the name). Seven chapters contain parts of newspaper columns that have appeared in *The Sydney Morning Herald*, *The Age* and *The West Australian* during 1998–9 or in *The Weekend Australian* during 1994–8. An earlier version of the nightmare/dream scenarios in 'The Big Picture' appeared as '2010: Australian Odyssey' in *Driver's World*, published by the Toyota Corporation in 1996.

The title of a book is important as a signpost not only for the reader, but also for the writer. A word or phrase that encapsulates the central themes of the book provides a focus for the writing process. This book had several working titles, but none seemed absolutely right until my friends Meredith Ryan and Jorie Manefield led me, via T. S. Eliot, to *Turning Point*. I thank them for their interest and encouragement.

I am grateful to my family for giving me 'leave of absence' during the final weeks of writing, and to my secretary, Stephanie Wells, for all her support.

I also wish to record my deep appreciation of the contribution to *The Mackay Report* made by my three research associates, Elizabeth Turnock, Prue Parkhill and Margie Beaumont. Elizabeth Turnock has worked continuously on the project since 1981.

The Mackay Report is funded by the annual subscriptions of a number of government and commercial organisations. While they obtain a direct benefit from their exclusive access to our regular reports, their support has helped to create a unique body of information about Australian society. Six companies warrant special mention for having agreed to support the project at its inception in 1979, and for having maintained their support continuously throughout the ensuing 21 years: Ammirati Puris Lintas, Clemenger, The Seven Network, Telstra, Unilever Australia, Westpac.

Finally, I must again express my thanks to all those members of the public who give up their time so generously to take part in our research. Their willing participation makes this kind of work possible; their frankness and openness give it its integrity.

INDEX

Hugh Mackay

men 269, 275–8, 279
  see also women's movement
Generation X 278–9
genetic engineering 247–8
germline engineering 248
Giddens, Anthony 168
Gilder, George 104
Gittins, Ross 204–5
globalisation xvi, 10
Golden Age of Leisure 53, 54–5, 62
Goods and Services Tax 204–5, 208
grandmothers 83–7
'grass roots' politics 183
Gray, Professor John 244–5, 249
Great Depression 77, 78–9
Greenpeace 92
Greer, Germaine 270–1, 272
Grey Power x, 75–87
Griffith, Colin 246
guiding story
  connecting leader and people 139–41
  for postmodern world 168
  for religious faith 220, 228
gun laws 27
Gunn, Michelle 43
Gunner, Peter 128–9

hanging loose 117, 151, 167, 168, 179, 180
Hanson, Pauline 140, 280–1
  why her? 284–7
Harding, Professor Anne 21
hardship and character building 78
have-a-go society 8
Hayden, Bill 125–6, 216
Hayward, Martin xxv
health
  Aboriginal xxii, 121, 123
  Baby Boomers 21
  in 'dying towns' 58
  natural remedies 16–17
  see also stress
herbal healing 16–17
heroes
  the hero within 93–6
  heroic organisations 92–3
  ingredients of 89–91
  media exposure 91–2
  mock-heroism 94
  for national festival 1, 5–6, 7
  the new order 96
  unsung 92–3, 95–6
  women's movement 85
Hickson, Jill 114–15
high-income households 52, 55, 56
Hillary, Edmund 91

Hitler, Adolf 140
Hollows, Fred 91
Holmes Hartshorne, M. 229
home church movement 227
home security systems 27–8
homogeneity myth 37–9, 44, 47–8
homosexuality xxiii
Honnery, Christopher 180
Horne, Donald xvi
households
  below the poverty line ix
  high-income 52, 55, 56
  and mobility of population 258
  moving house in retirement 81
  single-person household 251, 252
  trend to smaller 251, 252, 253, 257
housing
  loan market 188
  nostalgia 162
  trends xxv
Howard, John
  on Aborigines 129, 135, 302
  on drugs 27, 30
  economic objectives ix, 52, 136, 137, 204, 205
  gun laws 27
  on multiculturalism 41
  and Pauline Hanson 287–8
  personal beliefs 178, 180, 231–2
  power of polls 135–7
  on republic 126, 136–7, 207, 209, 217, 218
Hughes, Billy 89
Hughes, Reverend Peter 227
human resources 119–20

illicit drugs *see* drugs
impulse buying 182
in vitro fertilisation 248
income
  and class diversity 42–3
  inequitable distribution 43, 55–6, 59, 257
  and information access 247
info-greed 103–4
Information Age 98
'information club' 99
information revolution xi, xxxi
  children coping 97, 154
  and communication 101–3
  culture of information 104
  information rich and poor 247
  'more is better' danger 103–6
  opinions about everything 99–100
  and social isolation 106
  technology 99–101, 102, 104
  using what we learn 98

insecurity
  of jobs 108–20
  and lack of control 24
  media exposure of 27, 28
  over-regulation response 259–60
  political use of 26–7, 28
  time to take stock 300–2
inspiration
  by heroes 89–91, 95
  by leader 138
instant gratification generation 12, 147
Internet xi, 237, 245–6, 247
  flaming 257
  for shopping xxiv
involvement xix

Jackson, Bryony 31
job insecurity xi
  attitudes to work 113–19
  anticipation of redundancy 111–12
  employment stress 112–13
  'human resource' factor 119–20
  and quality of life 203
John Paul II, Pope 228–9
Johnson, Dick 7

Keating, Paul 207, 297
Kennedy, John F. 140
Kennett, Jeff xii, 139, 253, 288–9
Kernot, Cheryl 285
Kingsford Smith, Sir Charles 89, 96
kooris *see* Aborigines
Krygier, Martin 122
Küng, Hans 230

Landy, John 91
language
  colloquial speech 169
  framework for reality 169–71
  inclusive language 169–70
Laski, Marghanita 172, 173
Latham, Mark 285–6
law and order issues
  and moral nostalgia 165
  political manipulation 26–7
  see also control
Lawrence, Carmen 285
Lawton, Bill 222
leadership
  humility 142
  pitfall of arrogance 141–2
  power of polls 122–3, 134–7
  visionary leaders 133–4, 135–6
  what we want 137–9, 142
leadership vacuum xxxiii, 132, 133–4, 139

choices about realities 168–71, 174, 175
deconstruction 172–4
hanging loose 117, 151, 167, 168, 179, 180
heroes 92
personal beliefs xix, 178, 180
personal relationships 177–8
spirituality 176–7
poverty ix, x, xi
poverty trap xi, 58–9
Priessnitz, Professor Horst 221–2
privacy of information 244–6
prohibition and control 31, 32, 33, 34
public opinion research industry 99
Pusey, Michael xiv

quality of life 192–205
the Australian paradox 192–4, 198, 202, 205
commercial imperative 202–5
dangers of 'going too far' 199–202
role of media 195–8
still better off here xv, xxiii, 198–9

racism 36, 128
Ramsey, Alan 290–1
realities
constructing 168–71, 174, 175
deconstructing 172–4, 177
new understanding of xx
reconnecting with the community xxxiii–xxxiv, 255–61
Red Cross 92
referendum see republic issue
reform fatigue 159–60
relationships xi, xiii
de facto 145, 150, 152
in postmodern world 177–8
quality of 148–9
see also divorce; marriage
religious beliefs
Baby Boomer substitute 15–17
belief in the value of belief 222–3, 224, 225, 227
Catholic/Protestant tensions 46
'chameleon' churches 227
church attendance 219, 220–1, 224
diversity in 43–4
fundamentalism xiv, 221, 228, 260, 282
historically 221–2
home church movement 227
and moral standards 219, 223, 225–6

private affair 220, 221, 222, 230–1
'typical' Australian belief 230–2
Republic Day 6
republic issue xvii
'ain't broke' brigade 207, 212–13, 218
apathy about 208–9, 213–14, 218
arguments against Yes 208–14
arguments for Yes 214–17
inevitability x, 207–8, 217
problems with model 210–12, 217
referendum choices 206–7, 217–18
significance of issue xv, 210, 211–12
republicans 209–11, 214, 218
retailing xvii, xxiv–xxv
retirement
Baby Boomers 12, 13, 14–15, 19–21, 75, 76
complaints about 82–3
pleasures of 80–1
retro style 67, 162–4
revelation experiences 172–3
rising generation
and Anzac Day 3, 8
attitude to work 117–19
boredom 79
concept of struggle 3
de facto relationships 145, 150, 152
despair 177, 179–80
and divorce 150, 152
expectations of change 117
fashion xiii, xxviii–xxix
hanging loose 117, 151, 167, 168, 179, 180
lack of commitment xiii, xxviii, 117, 149, 179
lifestyle xxviii
market for nostalgia 163–4
marriage views 118, 149, 150, 151–2
picture of 150–1
postmaterialism xxvii–xxviii, xxix
rural unemployed 57–8
sense of identity 3
spirituality xxix
street kids 151
suicide ix, xi, 10, 151, 179
unemployed ix, 55, 108, 139
value system xiii, xxix, 77
and working mothers 150, 274, 278
youth cult 82

ritual 176–7
Roosevelt, Franklin D. 140–1
Rowe, Normie 30
Rudder, Gawen 65, 66, 67, 74
rural areas
medical services 58
myth of the bush xiv, 44–5
unemployment ix, 56–7
Russell, Howard xxv
Ruthven, Phil 19–20

sacrifice
Anzac Day 3, 7, 8, 10, 11
of heroes 89, 93–4
scepticism 181, 183–6
security
of information 244–6
personal xii, 82, 268
seniors
advice from 78–81, 83
complaints 82
grandmothering 83–7
lucky generation 77
marriage as an institution 146–7, 148
special treatment 82–3
Sheehan, Paul 45
shopping xvii, xxiv–xxv
single-person household 251, 252
Snow, Deborah 29–30
social capital xxxiv
social fabric see community
society
adolescence of 295–9
at risk 195–8
Australian 'mainstream' 42, 45, 47
breakdown 26
British tradition 41
classless 49, 50
cult of youth 82
diversity of xxiv, 35–48
economic divisions 52–3
freedom of 124–5, 294
homogeneity myth 37–9, 44, 47–8
impact of technology 240–2, 254
quality of life 192–205
sense of inequality 53
spirit of disengagement 300–2
status distinctions 59–60
traditional Australian values 121
tribalism 36–7, 47
see also postmodern society
Spigelman, Jim 9
'spin doctors' xxxiii
spirituality xxix, 176–7, 219, 223, 224–5, 228